Rudolf Sachs
Commercial Correspondence

Faßbender '84

Rudolf Sachs

Commercial Correspondence

Einführung in die moderne
englische Handelskorrespondenz

Max Hueber Verlag

5. Auflage
5. 4. | Die letzten Ziffern
1985 84 83 | bezeichnen Zahl und Jahr des Druckes.
Alle Drucke dieser Auflage können nebeneinander benutzt werden.
© 1967 Max Hueber Verlag München
Gesamtherstellung: Reclam, Ditzingen · Printed in Germany
ISBN 3-19-002103-1

Vorwort

Dieses Buch gibt eine Einführung in die englische Handelskorrespondenz, die den Benutzer mit der modernen englischen und amerikanischen Geschäftssprache, der wichtigsten kaufmännischen Fachterminologie und der Technik des Außenhandels vertraut machen soll. Es ist vor allem als Lehrbuch für Wirtschaftsoberschulen, Handelsschulen, Sprachenschulen, Dolmetscher-Institute usw. gedacht, eignet sich aber ebensogut für das Selbststudium und als Arbeitshilfe für den praktisch tätigen Fremdsprachenkorrespondenten.

Besonderes Augenmerk wurde einem klaren und übersichtlichen Aufbau gewidmet. Das Buch besteht aus 4 Teilen:

Teil I behandelt die äußere Form des englischen Geschäftsbriefes, wobei sowohl die englische wie die amerikanische Praxis berücksichtigt wurden.

Teil II – der eigentliche Kern des Buches – besteht aus 11 Korrespondenzkapiteln.

Teil III umfaßt ein fremdsprachliches Glossar der wichtigsten kaufmännischen Fachbegriffe mit Mustern von Exportdokumenten und einer graphischen Darstellung des Zahlungsvorgangs beim Dokumenten-Akkreditiv.

Zu Teil IV gehören zwei Wortlisten mit dem im Buch vorkommenden Spezialwortschatz: Ein fortlaufendes Wörterverzeichnis für die Teile I und II und ein alphabetisches Wörterverzeichnis unter Einschluß des im Glossar verwendeten Fachvokabulars.

Der Korrespondenzteil bietet eine sehr gründliche Behandlung der wichtigsten Themen der kaufmännischen Korrespondenz. 10 Kapitel befassen sich mit dem Abschluß und der Abwicklung von Handelsgeschäften, das 11. Kapitel mit Bewerbungsschreiben, die vom individuellen Standpunkt aus gesehen ebenfalls zu den wichtigsten Geschäftsbriefen gehören. (Spezielle Gebiete, wie die Korrespondenz der Banken, Versicherungsunternehmen, Spediteure usw., sind hier nicht berücksichtigt; diese sollen zu einem späteren Zeitpunkt in einem eigenen Band zusammengefaßt werden.)

Jedes einzelne Korrespondenzkapitel gliedert sich wiederum in 4 Teile: 1. Eine englische Einleitung, 2. englische und amerikanische Musterbriefe und -dokumente, 3. Ausdrücke und Satzbeispiele (englisch-deutsch), und 4. Übungen.

Die Einleitungen in englischer Sprache sollen Inhalt und Funktion der jeweiligen Briefart erklären, das Verständnis für kaufmännische Zusammenhänge fördern und gleichzeitig den einschlägigen Fachwortschatz vermitteln. Besonderes Gewicht wurde dabei auf den Außenhandel gelegt.

Die Musterbriefe, die sowohl Binnenhandels- wie Außenhandelsvorgängen entnommen sind, dienen als Beispiele für den modernen englischen und amerikanischen Geschäftsstil. Sie sind in einfachem und klarem Englisch abgefaßt und frei von veralteten kaufmännischen Floskeln. Eine Anzahl von Mustern in Maschinenschrift auf Briefblatt-Vordruck zeigt die bei englischen und amerikanischen Briefen übliche Form und Anordnung. Auf Briefreihen wurde bewußt verzichtet, um möglichst viele der verschiedensten Korrespondenzthemen unterbringen zu können.

Das Buch enthält auch zahlreiche Originalformulare, durch die auf die große Bedeutung der Vordrucke in der kaufmännischen Praxis hingewiesen wird.

Die Musterbriefe werden durch sorgfältig ausgewählte englische Ausdrücke und Briefwendungen (mit deutscher Übersetzung) ergänzt, die dem Korrespondenten eine größere Gewandtheit im Gebrauch der fremden Sprache geben sollen.

Die Übungen bestehen aus deutschen Brieftexten, die ins Englische übersetzt werden sollen, und aus Geschäftsvorgängen, nach denen englische Briefe selbständig zu entwerfen sind. Dies entspricht den in der Praxis üblichen Verfahren bei der Bearbeitung fremdsprachiger Korrespondenz. Auch in anderer Hinsicht entsprechen die Übungen den Anforderungen der kaufmännischen Praxis: Sie beschränken sich auf Außenhandelsvorgänge, bei denen auch tatsächlich englische Briefe geschrieben werden.

Der Verfasser dankt allen, die ihm Briefe und Vordrucke zur Verfügung gestellt oder für ihn besorgt haben, ganz besonders aber Mrs. Roland Cartwright, London; Chilton Books, Philadelphia, Pa.; Alois Dallmayr, München und Bremen; The Financial Times, London; G. Hunter (London) Limited, Greys, Essex; Import Motors Ltd., Grand Rapids, Mich.; Körting Radio Werke GmbH, Grassau (Chiemgau); F. Ludwig Kübler, Stoffe, München; National Registrier Kassen GmbH, Augsburg; Peoria Tractor & Equipment Co., Peoria, Ill.; Süd-Chemie AG, München; Steinbock GmbH, Moosburg/Obb.; Volkswagen of America, Inc., Englewood Cliffs, N.J.; Vulkanisier-Maschinenbau Karl Zängl, München; Mr. L. T. Wadsworth, Export Manager, Leeds; Mr. Jack Wilcher, Stamford, Conn.

Besonderer Dank gebührt Mr. Gerald Cahoon, M. A., und Studienrätin Veronika Biebl von der Städt. Riemerschmid-Handelsschule, München, die sich der Mühe unterzogen, den englischen bzw. deutschen Teil des Manuskripts durchzusehen, sowie Dr. Margaret D. Senft-Howie für ihre freundliche Mithilfe bei der Korrektur der Fahnen. Herrn Dipl.-Kfm. Ottmar Schneider, Syndikus der Industrie- und Handelskammer für München und Oberbayern, verdankt der Verfasser wertvolle Auskünfte und Anregungen. Der Verfasser möchte sich an dieser Stelle nicht zuletzt auch bei seiner Frau für ihre unermüdliche Mitarbeit bedanken.

Vorschläge zur Verbesserung und Ergänzung dieses Werkes nimmt der Verfasser gern entgegen. Vor allem aber würde es ihn freuen, gute Geschäftsbriefe und nette Anekdoten aus der Praxis zu erhalten, die dann evtl. bei künftigen Auflagen Verwendung finden könnten.

Verfasser und Verlag

Contents

Part One
The Form of the Business Letter

It should be noted that in the English-speaking countries there are no uniform standards for business letters. Certain general rules are observed in all these countries, but there are many variations in details.

I. Essential Parts

The essential parts of the business letter are: 1. heading, 2. date, 3. inside address, 4. salutation, 5. body, 6. complimentary close, 7. signature and 8. reference initials.

1. Heading

The heading may be printed or typed. The printed heading is called a *letterhead*. (This word is also applied to a sheet of paper with a printed heading.)

The letterhead consists of the name and address of the firm and additional information, such as telephone number or numbers, telegraphic address, cable address, code or codes used by the firm, telex number or numbers, names of partners or directors,[1] branch offices, etc. However, it is not customary for British and American firms to indicate their banking accounts on their letterhead stationery. Many letterheads also include an illustration, the firm's trade-mark, the names of its products, or similar advertising matter. (Information about the firm, or advertising matter, may also appear at the bottom of the sheet or in the left margin.)

When a plain sheet of paper is used, the heading has to be typed. The typed heading, which is placed in the right upper corner of the sheet, consists of the writer's address and the date.

27 Wilton Crescent,
London, S.W.1,
16th May, 19...

2. Date

The date is placed below the printed letterhead, or it forms part of the typed heading, as shown above.

---

[1] In British law a partnership carried on under a name which does not consist of the true surnames of all the partners must show the true names of the partners on its business letters, catalogues, circulars, etc. British limited companies founded after 1916 are required to give the names of all directors.

In Great Britain it is usually written in either of the following ways:

12th August, 19..,

August 12th, 19..

The Americans use the latter form, but omit the *st, nd, rd* or *th* after the day of the month. (This shorter form has also become quite popular in Britain.)

May 2, 19..

The following form of the date is typical of American official correspondence, but it is used in American (and British) business letters as well:

16 September 19..

Such forms as *8/10/66, 8-10-66, 8.10.66* often appear in memoranda, printed forms and the like, but in letters they should be avoided.

3. Inside Address

The inside address includes a. addressee's name, b. his title, and c. house number, street, etc.

a. Name

Individuals have a surname and one or more Christian names. Most American names consist of a first name, an abbreviated middle name (*middle initial*), and a last name (*John B. Smith*).

Business firms have their distinctive firm names.

A one-man business (*US:* sole proprietorship) may be run under the name of the present owner or his predecessor, or under an impersonal name. For example: *L. A. Lewis, Manufacturer of Precision Tools; Brown's Delicatessen Store, Proprietor: George L. Smith; The Modern Laundry, Proprietor: Robert D. Jackson.*

Partnership names usually consist of the names of the partners, or of one or more partners with an addition. For example: *Brown, Smith & Johnson; Black, Smith & Co.; Perkins & Co.; Smith & Son; Baker & Sons; Green Bros.* Some partnerships have impersonal names, such as *The Empire Trading Company.*

The names of British limited companies end with the word *Limited* (abbr. *Ltd.*). For example: *Smith & Baker, Ltd.; J. A. Morris, Ltd.; The British Petroleum Company Limited.*

American stock corporations have names ending with *Company* (abbr. *Co.*), *Corporation* (abbr. *Corp.*), or *Incorporated* (abbr. *Inc.*). For example: *International Harvester Company; Union Carbide Corporation; Eaton Yale & Towne, Inc.*

b. Title

It is customary to place an appropriate title before (or after) the addressee's name. The most common titles of courtesy are *Mr., Esq., Mrs., Miss, Messrs.* and *Mmes.*

Mr. is used in addressing a man who has no other title, or whose special title is unknown to the writer.

In Great Britain, *Esq.* is regarded as being more polite than *Mr.*, although the latter form is generally accepted in business correspondence. In the United States, *Esq.* is rarely used; sometimes it is applied to certain public officials and members of the legal profession.

Esq. is always placed after the name. Do not use both *Mr.* and *Esq.* at the same time.

Mr. Henry Smith

or:

Henry Smith, Esq.

Mrs. is used in addressing a married woman, a widow, or a divorcee (unless she resumes the title *Miss* after the divorce). When applied to a married woman, it should be followed by her husband's name.

Mrs. John D. Baker

Miss is used in addressing a girl or an unmarried woman.

Miss Helen Brown

Messrs. (abbr. of *Messieurs*) is the plural of *Mr.* It is applied to two or more men as individuals or as members of a partnership. *Messrs.* should not be used in letters to partnerships having impersonal names or to limited companies, regardless of whether they have personal or impersonal names.

Messrs. Smith & White

but:

Brown & Smith, Ltd.

The General Engineering Company Ltd.

Mmes. (abbr. of *Mesdames*) is used in addressing two or more women as individuals or as members of a partnership. (When a partnership consists of both men and women the proper form is *Messrs.*)

Mmes. Field & Jones

Note: In the United States, partnerships, just like stock corporations, are usually addressed by their names only. *Messrs.* and *Mmes.* have almost disappeared.

Special titles are *Dr., Professor, Reverend* and *Honourable.*

Dr. (abbr. of *Doctor*) is applied to persons holding a doctor's degree.[1] Doctor's de-

---

[1] Lower academic degrees, such as *B.A.* (*Bachelor of Arts*), *M.A.* (*Master of Arts*), *B.S.* (*Bachelor of Science*), *M.S.* (*Master of Science*), *LL.B.* (*Bachelor of Laws*), etc., are usually not mentioned in the inside address.

grees are, for example, *M.D.* (*Doctor of Medicine*), *Ph.D.* (*Doctor of Philosophy*), *D.Sc.* (*Doctor of Science*), *LL.D.* (*Doctor of Laws*) and *D.D.* (*Doctor of Divinity*).

Dr. Henry L. Benson

An alternative to using *Dr.* is placing the abbreviation of the addressee's specific degree after his name.

Henry L. Benson, M.D.

Professor (abbr. *Prof.*) is used in addressing a person who holds (or has held) a professorship.

Professor Ian Morrison

Prof. Ian Morrison

Reverend (abbr. *Rev.*) or *The Reverend* is the title employed in addressing a clergyman. For higher ecclesiastical officials the forms *The Very Reverend, The Right Reverend* and *The Most Reverend* are used.

The Reverend James D. Franklin

Reverend James D. Franklin

Rev. James D. Franklin

Honourable (US: *Honorable*), *The Honourable, The Right Honourable* and *The Most Honourable* are titles applied to persons holding high government positions, members of legislative bodies, judges, mayors and members of the nobility.

The Honourable
Mr. Justice Baker

Honorable James A. Davis

Hon. James A. Davis

Titles designating a person's office or position, for example, *Managing Director, President, Secretary, Sales Manager*, etc., are placed below or after the name.

James C. Lloyd, Esq.,
Secretary,
Elcott Rubber Company Ltd.

Mr. Henry D. Swift, President
Western Supply Company

Sometimes a person is addressed only by the designation of his office or position, as in the examples given below.

The Manager,
District Bank Ltd.

The Secretary,
Watkins & Baker Ltd.

c. House Number, Street, etc.

The house number ist put before the name of the street. The street is followed by the place of destination, the county, state or province and—in foreign mail—the country of destination (in the language of the sender's country). Should the addressee have a post-office box, the P.O.B. number is substituted for the house number and street. Postal regulations in Britain and in the United States require the *Postcode* or the *ZIP Code Number* to be stated after the place of destination or the name of the state, respectively.

When a letter is sent to a person's temporary address, or to a place where he collects his mail, *c/o* (*care of*) is often used.

> Mr. John D. Smith
> c/o American Express Company

The address may also include postal instructions and special directions pertaining to the addressee. In foreign mail, postal instructions concern the postal authorities of both the sender's country and the country of destination; it may therefore be advisable to give them in both languages, or in French, which is the international postal language.

(By) Air Mail	(Mit) Luftpost
Registered (Mail)	Einschreiben
By Express, Special Delivery (*US*)	Durch Eilboten
Poste Restante, To be Called For, General Delivery (*US*)	Postlagernd
Printed Matter	Drucksache
Personal	Persönlich
Confidential, Private and Confidential	Vertraulich
Urgent	Eilt
Hold for Arrival	Bitte nach Ankunft des Empfängers aushändigen
Please Forward, To be Forwarded	Bitte nachsenden
Attention of . . . , Attention: . . .	z. H. (zu Händen) . . .

4. Salutation

Every English letter—regardless of whether it is addressed to a private person, a business firm, or a government office—requires a salutation.

The most common salutations in letters to individuals are *Dear Sir* or *Dear Madam*; *Dear Mr. Baker, Dear Mrs. Smith* or *Dear Miss Brown*.

Dear Sir or *Dear Madam* is a rather formal salutation. When a more personal relationship has been established, it is usually replaced by *Dear Mr. . . ., Dear Mrs. . . .* or

Dear Miss . . . . *Dr., Professor* and certain other titles may be substituted for *Mr., Mrs.,* or *Miss.*

> Dear Dr. White,
>
> Dear Professor Henley,

The Americans usually prefer the salutation *Dear Mr. (Dear Mrs./Dear Miss)* . . . to *Dear Sir* and *Dear Madam.*

In letters to two or more men and to business firms, the salutations *Dear Sirs* and *Gentlemen* are used. The former is preferred in Great Britain, the latter in the United States.

Mesdames—in the United States also *Ladies*—is the proper salutation when writing to two or more women as individuals or members of a partnership. (When a partnership consists of both men and women, the salutation *Dear Sirs* or *Gentlemen* is used.)

In order to avoid the impersonal salutation *Dear Sirs* or *Gentlemen,* letters to companies are often addressed to an official, for example, the secretary or the manager, and begin with *Dear Sir* or *Dear Mr.* . . .

Business letters exchanged between personal friends may begin with such informal salutations as *Dear Brown, My dear Smith,* or *Dear Jack.* When these salutations are employed, however, the inside address is often omitted to give the letter the appearance of a private message.

The very formal salutation *Sir* or *Madam* is hardly ever met with in business. It is used in addressing persons of high rank, in official letters and letters to the editor of a newspaper or periodical.

5. Body

The body of the letter contains the message.

In Great Britain and the United States, great importance is attached to the paragraphing of letters. A separate paragraph should be devoted to each new topic or idea.

Most letters do not exceed one page. If the letter is longer, it is continued on a second sheet (see p. 18).

6. Complimentary Close

The complimentary close should always be consistent with the salutation.

In Great Britain the suitable complimentary close for letters beginning with *Dear Sir* or *Dear Madam, Dear Sirs* or *Mesdames is Yours faithfully.* Letters using the salutation *Dear Mr.* . . ., *Dear Mrs.* . . . or *Dear Miss* . . . are closed with *Yours sincerely.* Other informal closes are *Yours truly* and *Yours very truly.*

In American business letters *Yours sincerely* or *Sincerely yours* is increasingly replacing *Yours very truly* or *Very truly yours.* Correspondents who know each other well also use the following closes: *Sincerely, Yours cordially, Cordially yours* and *Cordially.*

In a business letter starting with *Dear Jack* or a similar salutation, any of the informal closes mentioned above, as well as such forms as *Best regards, Kind regards,* etc., may be employed.

Formal salutations require formal complimentary closes. Formal closes are *Yours respectfully* and *Yours very respectfully* (US also: *Respectfully yours, Very respectfully yours* and *Respectfully*), but *Yours faithfully* and *Yours very truly* (US) are also acceptable for many formal letters. In Great Britain, the antiquated forms *Your obedient servant, Your most obedient servant,* etc., are gradually being replaced by *Yours respectfully* or *Yours faithfully.*

7. Signature

Since many signatures are difficult to read, the name of the undersigned is usually typed below (or above) his signature.

A man's signature thus looks as follows:

John G. Hall

John G. Hall

A married woman usually signs her name in the following manner:

Mary E. Brown

(Mrs. John D. Brown)

A widow may sign herself as shown below:

Grace D. Clifton

(Mrs.) Grace D. Clifton

A divorcee may use her former husband's name, her maiden name (preceded by either *Mrs.* or *Miss*), or her maiden name together with her former husbands' name.

Mary Wilson Smith

(Mrs.) Mary Wilson Smith

A girl or unmarried woman usually puts *Miss* (in parentheses) before her typewritten name:

Mary E. Steward

(Miss) Mary E. Steward

The power to sign on behalf of a business firm is vested in the owner of a one-man business, the (active) partners of a partnership, the officers of a company, and in the employees to whom this power has been delegated.

15

The typical signature on business letters consists of the name of the firm, the handwritten signature, the typewritten name of the undersigned and his title or position.[1]

Smith & Co. Ltd.,

John D. Black

John D. Black,
Sales Manager.

When letterhead stationery is used, the name of the firm may be omitted.

Employees having power to sign sometimes put *For* or *For and on behalf of* before the name of the firm, or *By* before their signatures, but these prefixes are not necessary.

In Great Britain a person holding power of attorney places *per proc., per pro.,* or *p.p. (per procurationem)* before the name of the firm.

per pro. Robinson & Co., Ltd.,

James Simpson

James Simpson,

Manager.

8. Reference Initials

It is customary for the secretary or shorthand-typist to indicate on the letter the initials of the person who dictated the letter and her own initials. These initials, which are called *reference initials* (US also: *identification initials*), may be typed in the bottom left-hand corner, above the inside address, or following the printed words *Our reference* below the letterhead (if there is such an indication).

The dictator's initials are always placed first and separated from those of the transcriber by a stroke or colon.

ADT/ej

ADT:EJ

(Dictator's name: *Alfred D. Thomas;* transcriber's name: *Elizabeth Jones*)

---

[1] In den angelsächsischen Ländern tragen Geschäftsbriefe immer nur eine Unterschrift. Doppelunterschriften sind nicht üblich.

II. Miscellaneous Details

1. Attention Line

An attention line is used to bring a letter addressed to a business firm or other organization to the attention of a particular person or department. It is usually placed below the inside address; sometimes it appears on the same line with the salutation, or below the salutation.

> Attention of Mr. C. R. Jones
>
> Attention: Sales Manager
>
> Attention: Bookkeeping Department

2. Reference

To expedite handling of the mail, many firms state a reference which the addressee is to quote in his reply. The reference may consist of the reference initials, a file number, or both. It may be placed above the inside address, below the date, or in any of the positions indicated for the subject (see below). Letterhead stationery often bears printed indications for the reference, such as *Your reference—Our reference, Your ref.—Our ref., In reply please quote, When replying please refer to.*

3. Subject Line

For the reader's convenience the subject matter of the letter is often indicated in a subject line.

The subject line is usually placed below the salutation; sometimes it appears below the inside address, or on the same line with the salutation. As an introductory word *Subject* or *Re* is often used. The subject is always underlined.

> Dear Sirs,
>
> Contract No. 574
>
> Gentlemen:
>
> Subject: Machine Tool Lubricants

4. Enclosures and Carbon Copies

When an enclosure is sent with the letter, this is indicated at the left-hand margin below the signature. A similar notation is made when a copy of the letter is to be sent to another department, a branch office, representative, etc. In letters where the reference initials also appear in the lower left-hand corner of the sheet, the notations regarding enclosures and carbon copies are placed directly below them.

HRC/CM
Enclosure

HRC/CM
Enc.

HRC/CM
Encl. 2

HRC/CM
2 enclosures
cc: Mr. C. B. Newland

5. Postscript

A postscript is occasionally used to inform the reader of a last-minute development or to emphasize an important point.

The postscript is placed two spaces below the reference initials or enclosure notation; it is usually preceded by the letters *P.S.*

6. Second Sheets

For the second, and subsequent, pages of a letter, so-called *second sheets* are used.

Second sheets have no letterhead at all or bear only the printed name of the firm. They must therefore be provided with a typewritten heading, consisting of the name (or the initials) of the addressee, the page number and the date, so that sheets of the same letter may be easily identified if they should become separated. (Additional sheets should contain at least three lines of text above the complimentary close.)

- 2 -

Messrs. Watson & Co.   15th May, 19..

Mr. John H. White
Page Two
July 27, 19..

III. Envelope

The envelope bears two addresses, the addressee's address (*envelope address*) and the address of the sender (*return address*).

The envelope address contains all the details of the inside address. If a window envelope is used, the inside address also serves as the envelope address.

The return address is placed in the upper left-hand corner of the envelope. The envelopes of business firms, organizations, government agencies—as well as the envelopes of many private persons—are imprinted with the name and address of the sender. The return address is sometimes preceded by the words *Sender, From, Return to* or *After . . . Days Return to.*

IV. Layout and Punctuation

1. Forms of Layout

There are three standard forms of layout: *indented form, block form* and *semi-block* or *modified block form.*

The *indented form* is illustrated by the letter on p. 20. When this form is used, the second and subsequent lines of the inside address and the first line of each paragraph are indented. The signature may be indented or centred below the complimentary close. The date is either centred below the letterhead, or so placed that its end is in line with the right-hand margin. In the case of a typed heading, the second and subsequent lines of the heading are also indented.

The letter on p. 21 is written in *block form.* In the full block form, the date, inside address, salutation, lines of the body, complimentary close and signature begin flush with the left-hand margin.

The *semi-block* or *modified block form* is shown on p. 22. It is similar to the block form, but the date is either centred or placed on the right, and the complimentary close and the signature begin at the vertical centre of the sheet, or to the right of the centre. Should a typed heading be used, it is blocked and placed on the right-hand side of the sheet. (In some of the letters written in semi-block form the first line of each paragraph is indented.)

The indented form, which dates back to the time when letters were handwritten, is still extensively used in Great Britain. In the United States, block form and semi-block form are preferred. The latter form is also used by an increasing number of British writers.

2. Forms of Punctuation

Punctuation in the body of the letter is, of course, the same as in any other form of written composition.[1]

With regard to the other parts of the letter, however, there are three different forms of punctuation: *closed punctuation, open punctuation* and *mixed punctuation.*

---

[1] *Note:* British and American typists leave one space after punctuation marks within a sentence, and two spaces after punctuation marks at the end of a sentence.

ANDERSON & CO. LTD.

International Shippers and Agents

DIRECTORS:
D. A. ANDERSON, M. I. Ex.
C. L. KING
M. S. BARKER
S. L. GORDON

16 GARDEN HILL
LONDON, E. C. 3

TELEPHONE:
ROYAL 6067
TELEX: 26344
TELEGRAMS AND CABLES:
ANDERSON, LONDON, E. C. 3

OUR REF
CLK/DML

YOUR REF

DATE
29th June, 19...

Messrs. Heike & Breuer,
    Lübecker Strasse 337,
      28 Bremen,
        Germany.

Dear Sirs,

    Our mutual business friends, Handelskontor AG in Hamburg, have been kind enough to provide us with your address.

    We are seeking importers of "knocked-down" upholstered furniture, for which we act as export agents to the manufacturers. The range of their products includes armchairs and rocking chairs of contemporary design, craftsman-made, with modern wipe-clean upholstery. They can be easily assembled and are ready for use in a few minutes.

    The saving in freight and transport expenses is considerable. Are you interested? If so, we should be delighted to send you illustrated leaflets and our price list. Perhaps you could indicate the quantities you normally buy, as this would enable us to suggest economical means of packing and transport.

    We are sure that there is a big potential for this furniture in your market and look forward to hearing from you shortly.

Yours faithfully,
Anderson & Co. Ltd.,

C. L. King

C. L. King,
Director.

GORDON & CO., INC.

33 WINTER STREET
NEW HAVEN, CONN. 06501

November 6, 19..

Mrs. J. A. Hudson
133 Laurel Road
Stamford, Conn. 06903

Dear Mrs. Hudson[1]

Now you can enjoy serving perfect, crunchy toast at any time - for
breakfast, for dinner, for tea, for late-evening snacks. It's so easy
to make, and the countless ways you can serve it provide variety and
zest for every meal.

How simple it is to make Toastmaster Toast! Merely put the bread
in the Toastmaster and press down the lever. When the toast is done
just the way you like best, up it pops, ready to serve, and the current
shuts off automatically. That's all there is to making perfect toast -
always crisp and golden outside, hot and tender inside. It's never
hard, never dry, never scorched. And it stays hot till you're ready
to serve it.

For its beauty, as well as its convenience, you will want to see the
Toastmaster on your dining table. The simple, modern design and
the rich chromium finish lend attractiveness to any setting. Know
the inimitable flavor of Toastmaster Toast, and the matchless ease
of making it.

You will find the new Toastmaster at Black & Brown in your city.
Stop in and see it!

Very truly yours

GORDON & CO., INC.

Walter F. Markers
Walter F. Markers
WFM/DT

---

[1] John C. McCloskey, *Handbook of Business Correspondence*, 1951. Reprinted by permission of Prentice-Hall, Inc., Englewood Cliffs, N.J., U.S.A.

GORDON & CO., INC.

33 WINTER STREET
NEW HAVEN, CONN. 06501

November 6, 19..

Mrs. J. A. Hudson
133 Laurel Road
Stamford, Conn. 06903

Dear Mrs. Hudson:

Now you can enjoy serving perfect, crunchy toast at any time - for breakfast, for dinner, for tea, for late-evening snacks. It's so easy to make, and the countless ways you can serve it provide variety and zest for every meal.

How simple it is to make Toastmaster Toast! Merely put the bread in the Toastmaster and press down the lever. When the toast is done just the way you like best, up it pops, ready to serve, and the current shuts off automatically. That's all there is to making perfect toast - always crisp and golden outside, hot and tender inside. It's never hard, never dry, never scorched. And it stays hot till you're ready to serve it.

For its beauty, as well as its convenience, you will want to see the Toastmaster on your dining table. The simple, modern design and the rich chromium finish lend attractiveness to any setting. Know the inimitable flavor of Toastmaster Toast, and the matchless ease of making it.

You will find the new Toastmaster at Black & Brown in your city. Stop in and see it!

Yours very truly,

GORDON & CO., INC.

Walter F. Markers

Walter F. Markers

WFM/DT

In a letter with *closed punctuation* (see p. 20), punctuation marks are placed after the date, the salutation [1] and the complimentary close, as well as after each line of the typed heading (if any), the inside address [2] and the signature.

When *open punctuation* is used (see p. 21), the punctuation marks mentioned above are omitted, except for full stops after abbreviations.

Mixed punctuation (see p. 22) is similar to open punctuation, except that a comma (or colon) is put after the salutation, and a comma after the complimentary close.

No Problem

Mother: "*Jim, did you post those letters for me?*"

Jim: "*Yes, but just as I was going to drop them into the pillar-box, I noticed that you had put the stamps on wrong. The foreign letter had a cheaper stamp than the home letter. But I put it right.*"

Mother: "*But how did you change the stamps?*"

Jim: "*I didn't—I changed the addresses.*"

---

[1] In American business letters a colon is put after the salutation instead of a comma.

[2] The comma after the house number is now usually omitted.

Part Two
Types of Business Letters

I. Inquiries

1. Introduction

The most important inquiry in business is the inquiry relating to goods.

Inquiries of this type are addressed to suppliers by prospective customers (also called "prospects" in business). They can be made orally or in writing. Many firms have printed inquiry forms. An inquiry is without any obligation for the inquirer.

Businessmen usually send inquiries to several likely suppliers, as they want to find out which of these suppliers offers the best quality, the most favourable prices and terms and/or the shortest delivery dates.

Often the buyer, in his inquiry, merely asks the supplier to furnish literature or to send his representative (*general* or *routine inquiry*). If the customer wants a detailed offer, or if he has a special problem, his inquiry must contain full details of his requirements (*special* or *specific inquiry*).

Sometimes drawings, patterns, or the like have to be added.

2. Specimen Letters

a. Inquiry for Scotch Tweeds

Dear Sirs,

Please send us patterns of Scotch Tweeds of good quality and quote your lowest prices for cash within 30 days.

If we place an order, we shall furnish you with the usual trade references.

Yours faithfully,

---

b. Inquiry from American High School to Publisher of Textbooks

---

Gentlemen:

We consider adopting the Voix et Images system of teaching languages in our French department for the 19 . . term. Therefore, we would [1] be most interested in any sample film strips, tapes and records that you might be able to send us. Also, our instructors would be interested in the teacher training program [2] offered by your staff.

We hope to hear from you soon.

Sincerely yours,

---

[1] Anstelle von *shall* und *should* in der 1. Person verwendet man – nicht nur im amerikanischen Englisch – immer häufiger *will* und *would*.

[2] *US for* programme

c. Inquiry from Canadian Importer to German Manufacturer of Toys

---

Gentlemen:

We have learned [1] from our representative in New York that your Construction Kits for boys have proved very popular in the United States.

As they should also be of interest to Canadian customers, we would be glad to receive samples and quotations.

Please include in your quotation full information on packing, quantities and shipping weights, as well as prices, terms and probable delivery dates.

We are one of the leading importers of toys in this country and are therefore very much interested in learning if you are prepared to grant us the sole agency for your products in Canada. There is a considerable demand for German toys here, and we are convinced that good business could be developed.

Yours very truly,

---

[1] *or:* learnt

d. Another Inquiry for German Toys

Dear Sirs,

We are looking for a reliable supplier of mechanical toys in Germany.

Your firm has been recommended to us as one of the leading manufacturers of these articles, and we should be glad if you would[1] send us your catalogue together with quotations for large quantities. Please also state your terms of payment and the earliest delivery dates.

The following firms will be glad to furnish information as to our financial standing and reputation:

. . .

. . .

We hope that you will facilitate business by quoting your keenest prices.

Yours faithfully,

---

[1] *would* nach *if* ist nur dann zulässig, wenn *would* die Bedeutung *wanted* hat: *if you would* = *if you wanted to* oder *if you were kind enough to,* dt. *wenn Sie so freundlich wären*

e. Inquiry from London Agent of German Chemical Company

Dear Sirs,

We have received an inquiry from Murphy & Williamson Ltd., London, for the following:

30 tons of Activated Bleaching Earth for shipment to their associates in Teheran.

As far as we know, this material is to be used in a new refinery for the treatment of cottonseed oil.

We shall be very grateful to receive your recommendations, together with your lowest price C. & F. Khorramshahr and an indication of the earliest possible date of shipment.

Yours faithfully,

---

f. Inquiry from Indian Department Store to German Export Merchant

Gerhardsen & Co.
Export/Import
Bremen

Dear Sirs,

Your name was given us by the German Embassy in New Delhi.

We are the proprietors of a medium-sized department store in Bombay. Up to now we have been supplied by importers in Bombay, but, as our sales are steadily rising, we are now thinking of obtaining merchandise from overseas direct.

We enclose a list of the goods we intend to buy from German manufacturers and should be much obliged if you would send us quotations and samples.

We are also sending you some references, including the names of our bankers, our principal suppliers in India, and the name of a manufacturer in Leeds who knows the undersigned personally.

Your prompt reply will be appreciated.

> Yours faithfully,
> Sivaraman Stores Ltd.
> K.V. Sivaraman
> Director

Encl. 2

HENRY CHAPMAN & COMPANY LIMITED

Telephone: GLAdstone 2266
Telegrams: Chapco, London

★ NORTH CIRCULAR ROAD, LONDON, N.W.2

Your Ref.
Our Ref. HE/NJ

5th February, 19..

Firma
Greimel & Söhne
46 Dortmund
Ruhrstrasse 267
W. Germany

Dear Sirs,

We have received an inquiry from

International Trading Company
Tehran, Iran.

Their main activity is participation in government tenders and they enjoy good relations with most government purchasing organizations.

They would like to receive your offers and descriptive literature regarding the following:

15 two-wheel trailer unit air compressors providing approximately 60 bhp and controlled by pneumatic speed governor

20 tilting drum concrete mixers with a capacity of approximately 3 cu.ft.

Their local reference is the Iran Credit Bank, Tehran. Foreign references may be obtained from Messrs. Holmes Bros., 611 Theobald's Road, London W.C.1, and Corram Engineering Works Ltd., Edinburgh.

We trust that you will be able to quote these clients of ours and protect our interests by crediting us with any business which may be received from them.

Yours faithfully,
HENRY CHAPMAN & COMPANY LIMITED

Harold Ellison

Harold Ellison
Sales Manager

h. Inquiry for Filing Cabinets

CALDWELL PRODUCTS CORPORATION

PRODUCERS AND DISTRIBUTORS
322 CONSTITUTION AVE.
BOSTON, MASS. 02101

May 26, 19..

Modern Office Furniture Company
730 Madison Avenue
New York, N.Y. 10017

Gentlemen:

We are in the market for filing cabinets and would like to see your
newest models. Will you please send us your latest catalogue that
gives full information about them.

The cabinet shown in your advertisement in the May issue of the
"Office Equipment Journal" seems to be what we want. Please send
complete details on that model.

Yours very truly,

L. B. Plumber

L. B. Plumber
Purchasing Agent

LBP:ld

G. HUNTER (LONDON) LIMITED

DIRECTORS: DENNIS J. HUNTER, · E. J. HUNTER · G. J. HUNTER *Makers of Mechanical Handling Equipment*

MAIN WORKS

**GUMLEY ROAD,
GRAYS
ESSEX**

TELEPHONES: GRAYS THURROCK 5155 (5 lines)
TELEGRAMS : HUNTER GRAYS

YOUR REF.

OUR REF.

CRANES

ELECTRIC HOISTS

OVERHEAD RUNWAYS

FORK LIFT TRUCKS

CHAINS

PULLEY BLOCKS

MOBILE GANTRIES

STACKERS

WINCHES

JACKS

CONVEYORS

SHACKLES

HOOKS AND GRABS

LORRY LOADING DEVICES

CONSTRUCTIONAL STEELWORK

ALL STRAINING AND LIFTING GEAR

TESTERS AND ANNEALERS

MAINTENANCE AND REPAIRS

INSPECTIONS AND TESTS "ON SITE"

URGENT HOME/EXPORT/SHIP STORES ENQUIRY

Dear Sirs,

Please quote us your best Resale Terms and quickest delivery, for the following. Your price to include packing and carriage to:—

Delivery C. & F. Karachi

Battery-operated 2 1/2 ton Lift-Truck with solid rubber tyres, conforming to the following principal specifications, for inter-shop transport of material:

Platform:	Length 60"
	Width 30"
Speed:	Laden 5 to 6 miles per hour (either direction)
Ground Clearance:	Minimum 3"

The Truck should be suitable for operating in rough and dusty gangways of 5' 6" width; it should be able to negotiate turns of minimum radius of 7' 6" and scale ramps of 1-in-10 gradient. The Truck should be supplied complete with tool box and spares for normal maintenance for a period of at least 3 years. The electrical equipment should be designed to suit most tropical conditions, the maximum ambient temperature being 120 degrees F.

MEMBER

ESTABLISHED 1803
GH.760

ALSO AT LONDON. BIRMINGHAM AND MANCHESTER

3. Terms and Phrases

a. Reference to Advertisement, etc.

We refer to your advertisement in "Export News."

Wir beziehen uns auf Ihre Anzeige in der Zeitschrift „Export News".

We have seen your stand at the Hanover Fair.

Wir haben Ihren Stand auf der Hannover-Messe besucht.

We hear that you have put a new electric shaver on the market.

Wir hören, daß Sie einen neuen Elektrorasierer auf den Markt gebracht haben.

As we have learned from Messrs. Miller & Sons, you are manufacturers of hydraulic pumps.

Wie wir von der Fa. Miller & Sons erfahren haben, stellen Sie hydraulische Pumpen her.

Your firm has been mentioned to us as one of the leading importers of textiles.

Sie wurden uns als einer der führenden Textilimporteure genannt.

b. Reasons for Inquiring

We need . . ./We are in need of . . ./We require . . . / We are in the market for . . .

Wir benötigen . . . / Wir haben Bedarf an . . .

We are interested in importing German cutlery.

Wir sind daran interessiert, deutsche Schneidwaren einzuführen.

As we have received many inquiries from customers for . . .

Da wir viele Anfragen von Kunden wegen . . . erhalten haben . . .

Our stock is running low / Our stock is nearly exhausted / depleted.

Unser Lagerbestand geht zu Ende / Unser Lager ist fast völlig geleert.

c. Asking for Particulars with Regard to Goods, Prices, etc.

Please send us complete details on . . . / We should appreciate full particulars concerning . . . / We should welcome detailed information on . . .

Bitte senden Sie uns vollständige Angaben über . . .

Will you please send us patterns of your tweeds.

Bitte senden Sie uns Muster Ihrer Tweed-Stoffe.

We should be pleased to receive your illustrated catalogue.

Für die Zusendung Ihres illustrierten Katalogs wären wir Ihnen dankbar.

We should be obliged / We should be grateful / if you would arrange for a demonstration of your machine.

Wir wären Ihnen dankbar, wenn Sie veranlaßten, daß uns Ihre Maschine vorgeführt wird.

Please let us know the earliest date of delivery.

Bitte teilen Sie uns mit, wann Sie frühestens liefern können.

... whether you can supply from stock.

... ob Sie ab Lager (d. h. *sofort*) liefern können.

A visit from your representative would be appreciated.

Der Besuch Ihres Vertreters wäre uns angenehm.

d. Giving References

Information about our company can be obtained from ... / For information about our company please refer to / write to / contact ...

Auskünfte über unsere Firma können von ... eingeholt werden.

Should you wish to make any inquiries, we refer you to / direct you to ...

Falls Sie über uns Erkundigungen einziehen wollen, verweisen wir Sie an ...

Messrs. Brown & Smith will be glad to give any information about us you may desire.

Die Fa. Brown & Smith wird Ihnen gerne jede gewünschte Auskunft über uns erteilen.

First-class British and German references can be furnished.

Wir können Ihnen erstklassige englische und deutsche Referenzen nennen.

If we give you an order, we shall supply references.

Bei Auftragserteilung erfolgt Angabe von Referenzen.

e. Suggesting Future Business

If your prices are competitive / favourable / reasonable ...

Wenn Ihre Preise konkurrenzfähig / günstig / angemessen sind ...

If your products are of first-class quality ...

Wenn Ihre Erzeugnisse von erstklassiger Qualität sind ...

If the quality of the goods comes up to / meets / our expectations ...

Wenn die Qualität der Waren unseren Erwartungen entspricht ...

If the samples find / meet with / our customers' approval ...

Wenn die Muster (bzw. Proben) unseren Kunden zusagen ...

If the goods meet our requirements . . .	Wenn die Waren unseren Anforderungen genügen . . .
If you can guarantee delivery of the goods within two weeks . . .	Wenn Sie uns die Lieferung der Waren innerhalb von 2 Wochen fest zusagen können . . .
. . . we should be prepared to place a trial order.	. . . wären wir bereit, Ihnen einen Probeauftrag zu erteilen.
. . . we should be in a position to place substantial orders.	. . . wären wir in der Lage, größere Aufträge zu erteilen.
. . . your products should find / meet with / a ready market / a ready sale / your products should sell readily in this market.	. . . dürften Ihre Erzeugnisse guten Absatz finden / sich hier gut verkaufen lassen.

4. Exercises

Please translate the following letters into English:

a. Modehaus Küfer, Düsseldorf, an McDonald & Co., Ltd., Glasgow

Im Vorjahr kauften wir bei Ihnen einen Posten Lambswool-Pullover, mit denen wir sehr zufrieden waren.

Da wir dabei sind, unsere Aufträge für die kommende Saison zu vergeben, bitten wir Sie, uns so bald wie möglich ein ausführliches Angebot vorzulegen.

Wie wir aus Ihrem letztjährigen Angebot ersehen, stellen Sie auch Twinsets her. Bitte senden Sie uns eine Farbmusterkarte und teilen Sie uns die Qualitäten und Mengen mit, die Sie liefern können.

Wenn Ihre Bedingungen günstig sind, sind wir gerne bereit, künftig unseren gesamten Bedarf an Lambswool-Strickwaren bei Ihnen zu decken.

b. Sporthaus Meister, München, an J. E. Baker Corporation, Los Angeles, Calif.

Wir entnehmen Ihrer Anzeige in der Zeitschrift „Foreign Trade News" vom 6. 3., daß Sie Geräte für Sporttaucher (*skin-diving equipment*), wie Atemgeräte (*aqualungs*), Tauchermasken (*diving masks*) und Schwimmflossen (*flippers, fins*) herstellen und exportieren.

Bitte senden Sie uns ausführliche Beschreibungen und Abbildungen der von Ihnen hergestellten Artikel unter Angabe Ihrer Exportpreise.

Falls Sie in Süddeutschland noch nicht vertreten sind, möchten wir anfragen, ob Sie evtl. bereit wären, uns den Alleinverkauf für dieses Gebiet zu übertragen. Wir verfügen über gute Verbindungen in unserer Branche und könnten den Markt intensiv bearbeiten.

Über unsere Vermögensverhältnisse erteilt Ihnen die Bayerische Vereinsbank in München jederzeit Auskunft.

c. Metallwarenfabrik Wagner & Co., Eßlingen (Neckar), an Harrison & Smith, Ltd., London

Wie uns unsere gemeinsamen Geschäftsfreunde, die Firma Swanson & Green, London, mitteilen, haben Sie ein neuartiges Rostschutzmittel (*rust-proofing compound*) entwickelt.

Als Hersteller von Metallwaren sind wir sehr an Rostschutzmitteln interessiert und möchten daher gerne nähere Einzelheiten erfahren. Wodurch unterscheidet sich das neue Produkt von den bereits auf dem Markt befindlichen Rostschutzmitteln? Welche Versuche wurden bisher angestellt und welche Ergebnisse sind dabei erzielt worden?

Da wir Ihnen einen Probeauftrag erteilen wollen, wären wir auch um Angabe Ihrer Preise dankbar.

d. Bauer & Co., Nürnberg, an Taylor & Brown, Birmingham

Wir besuchten Ihren Stand auf der letzten Hannover-Messe und erfuhren dabei von Ihrem Verkaufsleiter, Mr. Mills, daß Sie auch Spezialanfertigungen übernehmen.

Wir benötigen bis spätestens 1. März eine vollautomatische Bohr- und Gewindeschneidmaschine (*fully automatic drilling and tapping machine*) nach beiliegenden Zeichnungen. Bitte teilen Sie uns mit, ob Sie die Maschine bis zu diesem Termin liefern können. Für die Mitteilung des Preises und Ihrer Verkaufsbedingungen wären wir Ihnen ebenfalls dankbar.

Wenn Sie sich über uns erkundigen wollen, wenden Sie sich bitte an die Birmingham Lathe Company in Birmingham, von der wir bereits mehrere Maschinen bezogen haben, oder an die Deutsche Bank in Nürnberg.

Anlagen

Please draft letters in English from the following particulars:

e. Müller & Co. in München haben die Anzeige von Barney & Sons Ltd., Sheffield, in der Zeitschrift „Trade Channel" gelesen. Sie bitten diese Firma um Zusendung ihres Werkzeugkatalogs und um Mitteilung ihrer günstigsten Exportpreise sowie ihrer Verkaufsbedingungen.

f. Unter der Überschrift „Products from U.S." findet sich in der letzten Nummer des „Journal of Commerce" folgende Mitteilung:

THREE-WAY CAN OPENER. The Model CKP can opener by Cary Corp., 3200 West Peterson Street, Chicago 45, Ill., also serves as a sharpener for knives and scissors. The unit is a counter-top appliance that opens any can automatically. It turns itself off when the can is opened, and holds it firmly in position until the handle is raised and the opened can is removed.

Ihre Firma, ein Importhaus in Hamburg, das vor allem Neuheiten einführt, interessiert sich für den neuartigen Dosenöffner.

Entwerfen Sie auf Grund des obigen Zeitungsausschnitts eine englische Anfrage, in der Sie die amerikanische Firma bitten, Ihnen einen illustrierten Prospekt zu senden und den niedrigsten Exportpreis anzugeben.

Ihre Firma verfügt über gute Geschäftsverbindungen zu mehreren Warenhäusern. Wenn das Gerät zuverlässig und der Preis konkurrenzfähig ist, dürften gute Verkaufsaussichten bestehen.

g. Die Epikur-Importgesellschaft, Hamburg, sucht einen Lieferanten von Ahornsirup (*maple syrup*). Von der kanadischen Botschaft in Bonn wurde ihr u. a. die Delta Foods Ltd., Delta, Ontario, genannt.

Epikur bittet um umgehende Zusendung von 10 Flaschen Sirup (Inhalt: *1 pint* = *ca.* *1/2 l*) zur Probe und Angabe des niedrigsten Preises bei einer Bestellung über 2000 Flaschen. Wenn der Sirup von erstklassiger Qualität und der Preis günstig ist, könnte eine laufende Geschäftsverbindung angebahnt werden. Es besteht große Nachfrage nach ausländischen Spezialitäten in Deutschland, und die Epikur glaubt, daß auch der Absatz von Ahornsirup noch gesteigert werden könnte. Bei laufendem Bezug wäre es aus Gründen der Frachtersparnis vorteilhaft, den Sirup in größeren Behältern zu verschiffen und in Hamburg in Flaschen abzufüllen.

h. In der europäischen Ausgabe der Zeitschrift „Machinery Lloyd" vom 17. Juni finden Sie eine Anzeige der Firma Markham & Co. Ltd., London, die Gabelstapler (*fork-lift trucks*) verschiedener Größen herstellt.

Das kleinste Modell, der „Minilift", interessiert Sie besonders. Sie würden gern nähere Einzelheiten darüber erfahren und bitten um Zusendung eines ausführlichen Prospekts und Preisangabe.

In Ihrem Betrieb — Sie sind Lebensmittelgroßhändler — muß täglich eine große Anzahl von Kisten verladen und gestapelt werden. Ein Gabelstapler, der so klein und wendig ist, daß er in den ziemlich engen Gängen Ihres Lagers eingesetzt werden kann, würde ein schnelleres und rationelleres Arbeiten ermöglichen.

What's the Price?

Ill-at-ease amidst big-city surroundings, an elderly farm couple approached one of the ticket windows in a railroad station.

"What's the fare to Plattsville?" asked the woman.

"That's $4.65, Ma'am," responded the clerk. Turning to her husband she said, "Well, Dad, we might as well buy the tickets here. I've asked at all these windows and they all charge the same."

II. Offers

Replies to Inquiries—Offers and Sales Letters

1. Introduction

Replies to Inquiries. Every inquiry holds the promise of future business and should therefore be answered promptly. In his reply to an inquiry, the supplier gives the desired information, sends the price list, catalogue, etc. that the prospective customer asked for, or submits a detailed offer.

If a delay in answering the inquiry is inevitable, the seller should send a brief acknowledgment to inform the prospect that his inquiry is receiving attention. Sometimes the seller has to ask for additional information before he can answer the inquiry. Should it be necessary to refer the inquiry to an agent or distributor, both the inquirer and the agent or distributor are notified.

If the supplier is unable to quote, he should inform the inquirer immediately, suggesting, if possible, other sources of supply from which the latter is likely to obtain the goods he requires.

Offers. By submitting an offer, the seller declares his willingness to sell certain goods at certain prices and on certain terms. The price at which the seller offers the goods, and the offer containing the price, are called *quotation*. Quotations are sometimes made in the form of a *pro-forma invoice* (see p. 86). A *tender* (US: *bid*) is a quotation for the supply of goods or the performance of work, made in response to an *invitation to tender*. (The term is also loosely applied to the whole system of awarding contracts on a tender basis.)

Offers can be made orally or in writing. Verbal and telegraphic offers should be confirmed by letter. Frequently offers are prepared on printed forms (*quotation forms*), which are mailed either with or without a covering letter.

Offers may be submitted in answer to an inquiry (*solicited offers*), or without an inquiry having been made (*unsolicited* or *voluntary offers*).

Unsolicited offers are sent to old customers to inform them of a special opportunity, or "to revive inactive accounts," that is, to win back old customers who have ceased sending orders. To create new business, businessmen send unsolicited offers and sales letters to a carefully chosen list of potential customers (*mailing list*).

An offer is *firm*, that is, binding on the seller, unless it contains a clause to the contrary. If the seller makes a firm offer, he undertakes to supply the goods in question at the prices and on the terms stated, provided the offer is accepted within reasonable time. The seller often fixes a time limit for acceptance, for example, *I offer you firm until noon Friday next* or *This offer is firm subject to acceptance by 10th June.*

A firm offer can be withdrawn at any time before the buyer has mailed his acceptance (order). Once the acceptance has been mailed, the seller can revoke his offer only with the buyer's consent.

If the seller does not want to be bound, he states that his offer is *without engagement* or is *subject to confirmation*. He may also stipulate that *the prices are subject to change without notice*, that the goods are *subject to being unsold*, etc.

A complete offer should cover the following points:
1. Nature and quality of the goods offered.
2. Quantity.
3. Prices and discounts (if discounts are granted).
4. Delivery period.
5. Terms of delivery.
6. Terms of payment.

If necessary, the offer is supplemented by printed material, illustrations, samples or patterns. An order form may be enclosed for the customer's convenience in ordering.

Should the offer fail to produce a response, *follow-up letters* may be sent.

Sales Letters. Sales letters are usually unsolicited. They do not necessarily ask for orders; their purpose may be to produce inquiries, to prepare the ground for the representative, or to build goodwill.

Sales letters may be personal letters or duplicated letters (*circulars*) distributed to a large number of private individuals or firms. Since a personal letter is more likely to receive attention than a mimeographed one, mass mailings are often "personalized," that is, given the appearance of personal letters. This is done, for example, by using automatic typewriters or a printing typeface imitating typewriting.

Many sales letters are prepared in series of two, three or more letters (*sales series*).

2. Specimen Letters

a. Brief Acknowledgment—Inquiry is Receiving Attention

Gentlemen:

Thank you for your inquiry of August 6.

It will probably take a few days until our engineer has prepared the necessary technical data. As soon as this information is available, we will [1] send you our quotation.

Yours very truly,

---

[1] see footnote on p. 25

b. Request for Additional Information

Dear Sirs,

Thank you very much for your inquiry of the 16th October concerning an Automatic Car Washing Plant.

We appreciate your interest in our equipment and shall be pleased to submit a detailed quotation. Before we can do so, however, we must have some more details from you.

We enclose Form No. 17 which we would [1] ask you to fill in and return to us. On receipt of this information we shall quote you for an Automatic Car Washing Plant which is strictly in line with your particular requirements.

Please send us the completed form without delay. We look forward to the pleasure of serving you.

Yours faithfully,

Encl.

---

[1] *would* hat hier die Bedeutung *möchten: we would ask you = wir möchten Sie bitten*

c. Reply to Inquiry for Teaching Material

Dear Miss Jones:

We have received your letter of November 18 inquiring about the "Voix et Images de France" student records and books.

We are sending you our catalog [1] for your convenience in ordering. We believe the information you require will be found on pages 94 and 95.

We thank you for your interest in our materials and look forward to serving you.

Sincerely yours,

Enclosure

---

[1] *US variant of* catalogue

FAIRFAX & WHITE (LADIES FABRICS) LTD.

DIRECTORS: J.D.FAIRFAX   T.L.R.WHITE   A.H.WHITE   M.MILLER

LONDON, W. 1.

CABLES:
FAIRFAX, LONDON

TELEGRAMS:
FAIRFAX, PICCY, LONDON.

86, SHERWOOD STREET,
LONDON, W.I.

TELEPHONE: GERRARD 1322
(6 LINES)

Our Ref.: ALL/BS   19th October, 19..

Tuchhandlung
    Otto Stoltz K.G.,
        8 München 2,
            Brienner Strasse,
                Germany.

Dear Sirs,

    In reply to your letter dated 10th October, we have
pleasure in enclosing patterns of our Quality 2349, which
may be of interest to you. The composition of this quality is 75% camel hair and 25% wool, while the weight is
20/21 ounces.

    We have a limited number of pieces of each shade
available for immediate delivery, but these are, of course,
subject to their being unsold on receipt of your order.

    Today's price of this cloth is £2.10 per yard.

                            Yours faithfully,

                            A. L. Lewis

                            A. L. LEWIS,
                            Manager.

Encls.

G. HUNTER (LONDON) LIMITED.

DIRECTORS: DENNIS J. HUNTER · E. J. HUNTER · G. J. HUNTER

Makers of Mechanical Handling Equipment

MAIN WORKS

GUMLEY ROAD,
GRAYS
ESSEX

L. C. Morrow Ltd.,
399 Regent Street,
Nottingham.

TELEPHONES: GRAYS THURROCK 5155 (10 lines)
TELEGRAMS: HUNTER GRAYS

4th August, 19..

Dear Sirs,

We thank you for your inquiry concerning our 'Europa'
Belt Conveyors.

This new range of light portable Conveyors has been
specifically designed by G. Hunter (London) Limited to meet
the need for a simple and inexpensive Conveyor. Production
costs have been kept to a minimum by limiting the range of
sizes and by employing a novel, robust type of construction.
The result is a Conveyor, called the 'Europa', which can be
wheeled out into the yard by one man. The boom of the Conveyor consists basically of a rigid, rectangular, hollow
section which also houses the self-lubricating ball bearings,
thus achieving simple, strong construction with clean lines.
These Conveyors can be used for very steep angles and are
highly suitable for loading lorries with, say, parcels up
to 50 lbs. The 'Europa' is ideal for Grocers, Warehouses,
Distributors and Retailers. It gives you speed, with posi-
tive grip, at the very reasonable price of £217.

In addition we are also manufacturing a stationary ver-
sion of the 'Europa' mounted on adjustable legs, and a 'Low-
Loader' model mounted on front and rear castors.

If you require any further information, please do not
hesitate to contact us.

Yours faithfully,
G. HUNTER (LONDON) LIMITED,

Sales Department.

DJH/rw

f. Quotation for Electric Boiler

Dear Sirs,

We thank you for your letter of 8th February and are pleased to submit the following quotation:

> "BUMO" A 375 Electric Boiler in accordance
> with the attached specifications
> Price: £ ... less 25 % and 15 %
> Terms: 30 days net
> Carriage paid on all orders exceeding £10
> Delivery 2/3 weeks
> Guaranteed 12 months
> Subject to price ruling at time of dispatch

We trust that our terms will be acceptable to you and enclose a leaflet illustrating the boiler.

Yours faithfully,

Enc.

---

g. Reply to Inquiry for Holiday Caravans

Dear Sirs,

We thank you for your inquiry of 17th December and are sending you our latest catalogue.

The Midland Motors Holiday Caravans combine the greatest comfort and convenience with excellent road-holding and manoeuvring qualities. No wonder they are fabulously popular in Great Britain and on the Continent. A new engine steps up performance considerably: better acceleration, higher cruising speed, better hill climbing.

As you will see from the catalogue, we offer four different models with prices ranging from £... to £... In order to facilitate the introduction of our caravans, we are prepared to grant you a special discount of 10 % on our catalogue prices.

The quotation is without obligation until final confirmation. Our terms of payment are cash against documents. At present our time of delivery is two to three months.

Any orders you entrust to us will receive our most careful attention.

Yours faithfully,

Encl.

---

h. Follow-Up Letter to Prospect

Dear Mr. Cooper:

It is obvious—you are interested in our new Phoenix Charge Posting Cash Register. That's why you asked for our catalogue, which we sent you last month.

A few weeks ago one of our representatives, Mr. Black, demonstrated our system to Mr. Bauer of Bauer's Food Fair in your city. The system has now been installed, and Mr. Bauer writes "My new Phoenix Charge Posting Cash Register makes the handling of charge accounts as easy as the recording of cash sales. It helps me save a lot of time, and my charge accounts are always up to date. I'm very pleased with its operation . . ."

You will realize, no doubt, that a catalogue cannot answer all your questions. Only an expert can do so, after he has carefully studied your particular requirements. Mr. Black would be pleased to show you how a Phoenix Charge Posting Cash Register can help you, too, save a lot of time—and money. Just fill out and mail the enclosed card.

There will, of course, be no obligation for you.

Yours very truly,

Encl.

---

i. Unsolicited Offer from American Packer

Gentlemen:

We are continually receiving orders from Germany for

ROYAL 3 1/4 lbs. Whole Chicken.

The price per case of one dozen cans [1] is \$ . . . F.O.B. vessel New York, less 2 % broker's commission, payment net upon arrival in Hamburg. ROYAL is one of the best-known brands in Germany for chicken, and we hope that you will add this item to your line.

43

We are also in a position to supply ROYAL Fancy Sweet Peas at $ ... per case of 24 cans, F.A.S. vessel Portland, Ore. We are accepting orders subject to license[2] by September 5, shipment September/early October. The freight for the peas to Hamburg is approx. $ ... per case.

Very truly yours,

---

[1] *US for* tins
[2] *US for* licence (n.)

k. Unsolicited Offer of Tools

Gentlemen:

The German Consul General in this city has given us your name as one of the leading importers of power tools. We understand that you are mainly interested in electric drills.

As export agents for the Standard Tool Company, we can make you a very favorable[1] offer:

$1/2$-inch Drill, $1/2$ HP—$23.00 each

$1/4$-inch Drill, $1/5$ HP—$14.00 each

We enclose illustrated literature on these drills, which can also be used as sanders and polishers.

The prices stated above are net, C.I.F. Hamburg, and include export packing. Shipment can be effected within two to three weeks after receipt of order. Our terms are cash against documents, or 2 % discount if an irrevocable letter of credit is opened through a New York bank.

This offer is subject to confirmation.

Under separate cover we are sending you our latest catalogue, which will give you full information on the complete range of power tools handled by us.

We look forward to the pleasure of serving you and assure you that your orders will have our best attention.

Yours very truly,

Encl.

---

[1] *US for* favourable

1. Sales Letter

NEW HAVEN INSTRUMENT CO., INC.
NEW HAVEN, CONN. 06501

March 16, 19..

John Blake & Co.
88 Appleton Street
Providence, R.I. 02901

Gentlemen:

We have been testing and distributing electric tools and electronic devices for more than 30 years and therefore believe we can state with authority that the Multi-Vox Wireless Intercom described in the enclosed circular is the finest, easiest-to-use unit of its type ever produced.

Multi-Vox Wireless Intercoms may be plugged into an electric line with no connection or wiring of any kind required. These devices use the electric wiring to transmit and receive sound.

In our opinion, the Multi-Vox represents the greatest advance ever achieved in the design and production of a wireless intercom and, because we know it is better than any competitive product, we unhesitatingly offer to supply two or more units to you at our risk for your free use for a period of 30 days.

Why not take advantage of our introductory offer and either mail the enclosed authorization-to-ship card or send us your formal purchase order if you prefer. If the latter, you may include the following statement on your purchase order "this order is placed on the understanding that the Wireless Intercoms are to be shipped to us for a 30-day free use period. After the 30-day term, we will either return the unit or authorize payment of your invoice."

Yours sincerely,

NEW HAVEN INSTRUMENT CO., INC.

Richard Dobson

Richard Dobson

Enclosure

THE FINANCIAL TIMES

Incorporating THE FINANCIAL NEWS

Telephone
City 8000
Telegrams
Finantimo, London, Telex

Bracken House
Cannon Street
London, E. C. 4

LFS/GS

26th October, 19...

Dear Sir,

Although you must surely know THE FINANCIAL TIMES, you may not know it as a regular daily reader. Yet it is for European business leaders such as yourself that the regular reading of THE FINANCIAL TIMES can be of most value. It will equip you with the extra knowledge on British and international matters which you require as a supplement to your own national press reading.

The enclosed brochure will give you some idea of the kind of paper we are publishing, but nothing can take the place of handling the paper in your office, or your own home, and judging its usefulness to YOU solely on its merits, over a period. This is what we would like you to do, at our expense, and without the slightest obligation on your part. Please complete the enclosed postcard and return it to us and we will do the rest.

We will be really disappointed if you cannot see your way to co-operate with us by affording us the very real pleasure of sending you a complimentary copy of THE FINANCIAL TIMES for two weeks.

Yours faithfully,
For THE FINANCIAL TIMES,

Leonard F. Shapland.

Leonard F. Shapland,
CIRCULATION MANAGER.

P. S. There will be others in your office who will benefit - not least in their knowledge of Commercial English usage - by reading our newspaper day by day.

n. Reviving Inactive Account

Dear Sirs,

We note that you have not entrusted us with your orders for some time. This is a matter of great concern to us, and we are wondering if in any way we failed in our efforts to please you. Should this be the case, you would do us a great favour by letting us have your frank comments. You may be sure that we will make every effort to set things right.

Under separate cover we are sending you our latest catalogue, from which you will see that we can now offer an even wider range of first-class kitchen utensils and appliances. We have recently extended and modernized our factory. These improvements have enabled us to increase our output and to shorten delivery dates.

We look forward to a renewal of our cordial business relations and assure you that we will do our best to give you efficient service.

Yours faithfully,

o. Inquiry Referred to Distributor

Gentlemen:

Thank you for your recent inquiry regarding laboratory equipment.

We are asking our distributors in your area, Gernot & Koch KG, Düsseldorf, to see that descriptive literature is made available to you at the earliest possible date. Should you desire additional information on specific applications of this equipment, please do not hesitate to contact them at any time.

Your interest in our products is sincerely appreciated.

Very truly yours,

p. Supplier Unable to Quote

Dear Sirs,

Thank you for your letter of 10th February.

We regret to inform you, however, that we cannot quote you for the equipment you require, as it is not included in our line.

We would suggest that you write to the BELCO Company Ltd., in this city, which will, no doubt, be able to submit the quotation requested.

We enclose some literature giving you an outline of the complete range of our products and shall be glad to hear from you whenever you are in the market for any of the equipment manufactured by us.

Yours faithfully,

Encl.

---

3. Terms and Phrases

a. Opening Phrases

We thank you/Thank you/We are obliged/for your inquiry of . . .

Wir danken Ihnen für Ihre Anfrage vom . . .

Many thanks/Thank you very much/for your letter of . . . As requested/As desired/we are sending you . . .

Besten Dank für Ihr Schreiben vom . . . Wunschgemäß senden wir Ihnen . . .

We have received your letter of . . ., from which we are pleased to note that you are interested in our products.

Wir haben Ihr Schreiben vom . . . erhalten, dem wir zu unserer Freude entnehmen, daß Sie Interesse an unseren Erzeugnissen haben.

We refer to your inquiry of . . . and are glad to quote as follows/to submit the following quotation: . . .

Wir beziehen uns auf Ihre Anfrage vom . . . und bieten Ihnen gerne wie folgt an / unterbreiten Ihnen gerne folgendes Angebot: . . .

The German Consul General has kindly provided us with your address.

Das deutsche Generalkonsulat hat uns freundlicherweise Ihre Anschrift zur Verfügung gestellt.

We have been advised by the German-American Chamber of Commerce that you are interested in . . .	Die Deutsch-Amerikanische Handelskammer hat uns mitgeteilt, daß Sie sich für . . . interessieren.

b. Prices and Discounts

Our prices are . . ./Our prices are quoted F.O.B. London.	Unsere Preise verstehen sich fob London.
packing included	einschließlich Verpackung
packing not included/packing extra	ausschließlich Verpackung
packing at cost	Verpackung zum Selbstkostenpreis
gross for net	**brutto für netto**
We grant a trade discount of 33$^1/_3$ % on our list prices.	Wir gewähren einen Händlerrabatt von 33$^1/_3$ % auf unsere Listenpreise.
The quantity discounts indicated in our price list vary according to the size of the order.	Die in unserer Preisliste angegebenen Mengenrabatte richten sich nach der Größe der Bestellung.
Our catalogue prices are subject to a special discount of 10 %.	Auf unsere Katalogpreise gewähren wir Ihnen einen Sonderrabatt von 10 %.

c. Terms of Delivery

ex works/ex factory	ab Werk/ab Fabrik
ex warehouse	ab Lager
F.O.R./F.O.T. *or* f.o.r./f.o.t. (free on rail/free on truck)	frei Waggon
F.A.S. *or* f.a.s. (free alongside ship)	fas (frei Längsseite Schiff)
F.O.B. *or* f.o.b. (free on board)	fob (frei an Bord)
C.I.F. *or* c.i.f. (cost, insurance, freight)	cif (Kosten, Versicherung, Fracht)
C. & F. *or* c. & f. (cost and freight)	c & f (Kosten und Fracht)
freight or carriage paid to . . .	frachtfrei . . .
franco frontier (*or*: border)	frei Grenze
carriage paid to frontier (*or*: border)	frachtfrei Grenze

franco domicile, free ... (buyer's address); *US*: F.O.B. buyer's warehouse	frei Haus
carriage (*or*: freight) paid; *US*: freight prepaid	frachtfrei, Fracht bezahlt
carriage (*or*: freight) forward; *US*: freight collect	unfrei, Fracht zu Lasten des Empfängers

d. Delivery Period

The goods can be delivered immediately on receipt of your order.	Die Waren können sofort nach Eingang Ihrer Bestellung geliefert werden.
Delivery will be effected as soon as possible/at the earliest possible date.	Die Lieferung erfolgt so bald wie möglich.
Machines made to buyer's specifications can be supplied within 4–6 months.	Die Lieferzeit für Maschinen, die in Sonderanfertigung hergestellt werden, beträgt 4–6 Monate.
We cannot promise delivery within the period stated in your inquiry, unless we receive your order by Monday next.	Wir können Lieferung innerhalb der in Ihrer Anfrage genannten Frist nur dann zusagen, wenn wir Ihren Auftrag bis nächsten Montag erhalten.

e. Terms of Payment

payment in advance	Vorauszahlung
cash with order (C.W.O. *or* c.w.o.)	Barzahlung bei Auftragserteilung
payment on receipt of invoice/payment on invoice	Zahlung bei Erhalt der Rechnung
payment by bank draft on London against pro-forma invoice	Zahlung durch Bankscheck auf London sofort nach Eingang der Proforma-Rechnung
one-third with order, one-third on delivery, and one-third within two months after delivery	$^1/_3$ bei Auftragserteilung, $^1/_3$ bei Lieferung und $^1/_3$ innerhalb von zwei Monaten nach Lieferung
cash on delivery (C.O.D. *or* c.o.d.)	gegen Nachnahme

payment on receipt of goods	Zahlung bei Erhalt der Waren
payment within 60 days from date of invoice	Zahlung innerhalb von 60 Tagen nach Rechnungsdatum
30 days net	30 Tage netto
two months' credit	2 Monate Ziel
strictly net	rein netto
2 % for cash	2 % Skonto bei Barzahlung
... less 2 % cash discount for payment within seven days	... abzüglich 2 % Skonto für Zahlung innerhalb von 7 Tagen
10 days 2 %, 30 days net (*or*: 2/10, net 30)	Zahlung innerhalb von 10 Tagen abzüglich 2 % Skonto oder innerhalb von 30 Tagen netto
against three months' acceptance	gegen Dreimonatsakzept
documents against payment (D/P), cash against documents (C.A.D)	Kasse gegen Dokumente
documents against acceptance (D/A)	Dokumente gegen Akzept
shipping documents will be surrendered against bank acceptance	Übergabe der Versanddokumente erfolgt gegen Bankakzept
payment by irrevocable and confirmed documentary letter of credit/documentary credit	Zahlung durch unwiderrufliches und bestätigtes Dokumentenakkreditiv

f. Firm Until ..., Without Engagement, etc.

This offer is firm subject to immediate acceptance, otherwise without engagement.	Dieses Angebot ist fest bei sofortiger Annahme, sonst freibleibend.
Our offer is firm subject to acceptance by 15th June/We offer you firm until .../ We give you the refusal of these goods until ...	Unser Angebot ist fest bei Annahme bis zum 15. Juni/Unser Angebot ist gültig bis .../Wir halten Ihnen unser Angebot bis ... offen.
The offer is firm for three days only.	Das Angebot ist nur drei Tage gültig.
The offer is without engagement/subject to confirmation.	Das Angebot ist freibleibend.

Prices are subject to change/alteration/ without notice.

Preisänderungen vorbehalten.

Prices are subject to market fluctuations.

Durch Marktschwankungen bedingte Preisänderungen behalten wir uns vor.

Subject to price ruling at time of dispatch.

Die Berechnung erfolgt auf Grund des zur Zeit des Versandes gültigen Preises.

Subject to prior sale/Subject to being unsold.

Zwischenverkauf vorbehalten.

... as long as our stocks last/... until our stocks are depleted/exhausted.

... solange unser Vorrat reicht.

g. Closing Phrases

Please let us know your requirements soon, if possible by cable.

Bitte teilen Sie uns bald, wenn möglich telegrafisch, Ihren Bedarf mit.

As prices are likely to rise soon, we would advise you to take prompt advantage of this offer.

Da die Preise bald anziehen dürften, möchten wir Ihnen raten, von diesem Angebot umgehend Gebrauch zu machen.

We trust that our favourable prices will induce you to place an order.

Wir hoffen, daß unsere günstigen Preise Sie veranlassen werden, uns einen Auftrag zu erteilen.

We assure you that your order will be carried out to your complete satisfaction.

Wir versichern Ihnen, daß Ihr Auftrag zu Ihrer vollen Zufriedenheit ausgeführt wird.

You may rely on the prompt and careful execution of your order.

Sie können sich auf die prompte und sorgfältige Ausführung Ihres Auftrags verlassen.

A trial order will convince you of the efficiency of our service.

Ein Probeauftrag wird Sie von unserer Leistungsfähigkeit überzeugen.

As we have not yet had the pleasure of doing business with you, we would ask you to furnish us with the usual references when sending your order.

Da wir mit Ihnen bisher noch nicht in Geschäftsverbindung standen, möchten wir Sie bitten, uns bei Auftragserteilung die üblichen Referenzen anzugeben.

4. Exercises

Please translate the following letters into English:

a. Maschinenfabrik Schultheiss AG, Göppingen, an Cooper & Co. Ltd., Birmingham

Wir danken Ihnen für Ihre Anfrage, die Sie an die Zeitschrift „Engineer's Digest" richteten und überreichen Ihnen als Anlage das gewünschte Prospektmaterial über Senkrecht-Drehmaschinen (*vertical turning mills*) zu Ihrer allgemeinen Information.

Sollten Sie in Ihrem Betrieb irgendwelche Fertigungsprobleme haben, für die eine Vertikal-Drehmaschine in Betracht käme, so bitten wir Sie, uns Zeichnungen der zu fertigenden Werkstücke mit weiteren Einzelheiten zuzusenden, damit wir Sie weiter beraten können.

Anlage: Prospekte

b. Pohlmann AG, Stuttgart, an Bricker & Co., London

Wir nehmen Bezug auf den Besuch von Mr. Summerfield auf der Hannover-Messe und übersenden Ihnen in der Anlage die erbetenen Unterlagen über unsere Elektroherde (*electric ranges*); die Preislisten sind beigefügt. Wir sind bereit, Ihnen auf diese Preise einen Rabatt von 35 % einzuräumen, vorausgesetzt, daß der Export durch uns direkt durchgeführt wird.

Die Lieferung erfolgt fob deutscher Hafen; für seemäßige Verpackung werden DM 35,— pro Gerät auf den Nettopreis aufgeschlagen.

Unsere üblichen Zahlungsbedingungen sind: Unwiderrufliches Akkreditiv zu unseren Gunsten, auszahlbar bei der Deutschen Bank, Stuttgart.

Die Lieferzeit für die angebotenen Herde beträgt im Augenblick ca. 2 Monate.

Wir würden uns freuen, bald von Ihnen zu hören.

Anlagen

c. Optische Werke GmbH, München, an Davidson & Co. (Pty.) Ltd., Kapstadt

Wir danken Ihnen für Ihr Schreiben vom 10. 2. und freuen uns, daß Sie sich für unsere Projektionsapparate (*projectors*) interessieren.

Als Drucksache senden wir Ihnen Prospektmaterial über alle Geräte, die wir zur Zeit liefern. Die Prospekte enthalten Abbildungen und Beschreibungen sowie die Maße und Gewichte der einzelnen Geräte.

Die Preise sind in der beiliegenden Exportpreisliste enthalten. Sie verstehen sich fob deutscher Hafen oder Flughafen, einschließlich Verpackung. Preisänderungen behalten wir uns vor.

Unsere Zahlungsbedingungen lauten: Bei Erstaufträgen Eröffnung eines unwiderruflichen Akkreditivs zu unseren Gunsten, auszahlbar bei der Dresdner Bank in München; bei Nachbestellungen und Angabe von Referenzen Kasse gegen Dokumente durch eine Bank an Ihrem Wohnort.

Gegenwärtig benötigen wir für alle unsere Geräte eine Lieferzeit von 6–8 Wochen.

Mit Auskünften über Verschiffungsmöglichkeiten, Frachtsätze usw. sowie mit Proforma-Rechnungen zur Einholung von Importlizenzen stehen wir Ihnen auf Wunsch gerne zur Verfügung.

Wir sind seit 1950 auf die Herstellung von Projektoren spezialisiert. Unsere Geräte haben sich auf Grund ihrer Präzision und Zuverlässigkeit im In- und Ausland einen guten Namen gemacht.

Wir hoffen, bald einen Probeauftrag von Ihnen zu erhalten, den wir prompt und sorgfältig erledigen werden.

Anlage

d. Bayerische Maschinenfabrik AG, München, an Bandra Manufacturing Company, Bombay

Wir danken Ihnen für Ihr Schreiben vom . . . und übersenden Ihnen mit gleicher Post unseren Katalog 19 . . sowie unsere z. Z. gültigen Preislisten.

Unser allgemeiner Katalog hat vor allem den Zweck, unseren künftigen Kunden in großen Zügen ein Bild unseres Fabrikationsprogramms zu geben, und deshalb sind, wie Sie bemerken werden, die technischen Einzelheiten und die Beschreibungen kurz gefaßt.

Da wir annehmen, daß Sie besonders an den Maschinen interessiert sind, die in dem kürzlich in der Fachzeitschrift „Machinery" erschienenen Artikel ausdrücklich erwähnt wurden, fügen wir über dieselben ausführlichere Prospekte bei.

Falls Sie weitere Informationen über irgendeine der von uns hergestellten Maschinen wünschen, stellen wir Ihnen gerne zusätzliche Unterlagen zur Verfügung.

Wie Sie aus unseren Preislisten ersehen werden, sind alle Preise fob Hamburg kalkuliert. Auf Wunsch können wir Ihnen natürlich auch ein cif-Angebot unterbreiten.

Alle Maschinen und Zubehörteile, die in den Preislisten 1–5 aufgeführt sind, können je nach dem verfügbaren Schiffsraum innerhalb von 3–4 Wochen versandt werden. Leider sind wir nicht in der Lage, für die größeren Maschinen eine genaue Lieferzeit zu nennen, da mit deren Herstellung gewöhnlich erst begonnen wird, wenn ein fester Auftrag vorliegt, und wir daher nur eine sehr beschränkte Anzahl auf Lager haben. Es ist uns jedoch im allgemeinen möglich, Lieferung innerhalb von 4–6 Monaten nach Auftragseingang vorzunehmen.

Wir sind bereit, Ihnen für alle Aufträge, die . . . übersteigen, einen Rabatt von 5 % auf die Listenpreise zu gewähren. Zahlung soll durch unwiderrufliches und bestätigtes Dokumentenakkreditiv zu unseren Gunsten bei der Bayerischen Hypotheken- und Wechsel-Bank, München, erfolgen.

Wir sind in Indien nicht vertreten, würden jedoch im Falle einer Auftragserteilung veranlassen, daß einer unserer Ingenieure die erste Lieferung begleitet und in Ihrem Werk verbleibt, bis die Maschinen aufgestellt und in Betrieb genommen worden sind. Außerdem könnten einige Ihrer Betriebsangehörigen in unserem Werk ausgebildet werden.

Wir hoffen, daß wir bald Gelegenheit haben, Sie von unserer Leistungsfähigkeit zu überzeugen.

Please draft letters in English from the following particulars:

e. Gerber & Co., München, erhalten von der Maschinenfabrik Müller & Söhne in Dortmund eine an diese gerichtete Anfrage der Firma Davis & Henderson Ltd., Toronto (Kanada), wegen Brauereimaschinen (*machinery for breweries*). Da Müller & Söhne keine derartigen Maschinen herstellen, haben sie die Anfrage zuständigkeitshalber an Gerber & Co. weitergeleitet.

Gerber & Co. übersenden Davis & Henderson Ltd., wie gewünscht, Proforma-Rechnung dreifach. Die Prospekte (englisch) und sonstigen Unterlagen erhält die kanadische Firma mit getrennter Post.

Gerber & Co. sind eine Spezialfabrik für Brauerei- und Mälzereianlagen (*brewery and malting-plant installations*), die namhafte Brauereien im In- und Ausland beliefert. Ihre Maschinen sind von bewährter Konstruktion, erstklassiger Verarbeitung und darüber hinaus — wie die kanadische Firma aus der Proforma-Rechnung ersehen wird — sehr preisgünstig.

Gerber & Co. würden sich freuen, einen Auftrag zu erhalten, und sichern Davis & Henderson Ltd. pünktliche und sorgfältige Ausführung zu.

f. Die Puppenfabrik Zeidler & Co. in Bad Tölz hat von der Industrie- und Handelskammer in München erfahren, daß die Delany Doll Company, Raleigh, N.C. (USA), daran interessiert ist, Original-Trachtenpuppen (*costume dolls*) aus Bayern zu beziehen.

Zeidler & Co. wenden sich an die Delany Doll Company und bieten ihre Trachtenpuppen an. Die Größe der Puppen beträgt 20 cm, der Kopf ist aus Holz geschnitzt, die Tracht im Tölzer Stil ist aus Original-Trachtenstoffen gefertigt. Die Puppen können einzeln oder als Pärchen geliefert werden. Der Stückpreis pro Puppe beträgt $ . . . Die Puppen werden in Spezialkartons zu je einem Dtzd. verpackt und mit Luftpost oder gewöhnlicher Post versandt. Was die Zahlungsbedingungen betrifft, so schlagen Zeidler & Co. zunächst „Kasse bei Auftragserteilung" vor.

Zeidler & Co. sind gerne bereit, der Delany Doll Company ein Musterpärchen zu senden und hoffen, bald von dieser Firma zu hören.

g. Die Firma Ludwig Schmitt in München erfährt von Weber & Braun, ihren Geschäftsfreunden in Hamburg, daß Morley & Co., Niagara Falls, Ont. (Kanada), an der Einfuhr von Manikür-Garnituren (*manicure sets*), Reisenecessaires (*travel kits, utility kits*) und Kleinlederwaren interessiert sind.

Schmitt hat eine große Auswahl an Artikeln dieser Art, die er zu konkurrenzfähigen Preisen liefern kann. Er unterbreitet Morley & Co. ein Angebot, dem er seine z. Z. gültige Preisliste beilegt. Gleichzeitig übersendet er seinen allgemeinen Katalog als Drucksache. Er ist auch gerne bereit, der kanadischen Firma auf Wunsch Muster vorzulegen.

Die in der Preisliste aufgeführten Preise verstehen sich fob Hamburg einschließlich Exportverpackung. Preisänderungen behält sich Schmitt vor. Bei cif-Lieferungen werden die jeweils gültigen Fracht- und Versicherungssätze berechnet. Die Mengenrabatte für größere Bestellungen sind ebenfalls in der Preisliste angegeben.

Die Zahlungsbedingungen bei Erstaufträgen sind Eröffnung eines unwiderruflichen Akkreditivs oder Kasse gegen Dokumente. Bei Zahlung durch Akkreditiv wird ein Nachlaß von 2 % gewährt.

Die Verpackung für den Export erfolgt in festen, mit Stahlbändern versehenen Pappkartons oder, falls erforderlich, in Holzkisten.

Die Lieferung erfolgt im allgemeinen innerhalb von 14 Tagen nach Eingang der Bestellung bzw. Mitteilung der Bank, daß das Akkreditiv eröffnet worden ist.

Schmitt bittet die kanadische Firma, ihm bald ihren Bedarf mitzuteilen. Er würde sich freuen, mit ihr in Geschäftsverbindung zu treten, und verspricht sorgfältige Ausführung ihrer Aufträge.

h. Herr Schmiedel von der Georg Deister KG, Spielzeugfabrik in Nürnberg, war kürzlich in England, um Mr. Billmore, den Chefeinkäufer der Diamond Stores Ltd., einer Warenhausfirma in Liverpool, mit den Erzeugnissen seiner Firma bekannt zu machen. Nach Herrn Schmiedels Rückkehr schreibt die Georg Deister KG an die englische Warenhausgesellschaft.

Zuerst bedankt sie sich für das Herrn Schmiedel gezeigte Entgegenkommen. Sollte Mr. Billmore einmal Nürnberg besuchen, so wird sie sich ihrerseits bemühen, ihm in jeder Weise behilflich zu sein.

Wie Herr Schmiedel mitteilte, interessiert sich die englische Firma für mechanische Spielwaren, befürchtet jedoch, die deutschen Erzeugnisse könnten gegenüber den aus Japan und den USA eingeführten Artikeln nicht konkurrenzfähig sein.

Dazu stellt die Nürnberger Firma fest, daß die meisten ihrer mechanischen Spielwaren patentierte Neuheiten sind, die auf dem englischen Markt wohl kaum auf Konkurrenz stoßen dürften.

Um die Einführung ihrer Spielwaren auf dem englischen Markt zu erleichtern, ist die Georg Deister KG bereit, der englischen Firma bei Aufträgen von mindestens £ ... einen Rabatt von 10 % auf alle in ihrem neuesten Katalog aufgeführten mechanischen Spielwaren einzuräumen.

Die Nürnberger Firma hofft, daß die englische Warenhausgesellschaft von diesem günstigen Angebot umgehend Gebrauch machen wird.

The Modern Way to Do It

One corporation wrote to another: "Our electronic brain has computed that the cost of the work you want done will be $25,650.50."

The following reply was received a few days later: "As this is more than we anticipated, we would like to suggest that your electronic brain make an appointment with our electronic brain to discuss ways and means of cutting costs."

III. Orders

Replies to Offers—Orders

1. Introduction

Replies to Offers. When a prospective buyer receives an offer, he will examine it carefully and perhaps compare it with offers from other suppliers. If the terms of the offer suit him, he will place an order.

An order following a firm offer, provided it is placed on time and constitutes an unqualified acceptance of the offer, results in a contract. If the offer was made without engagement, there is no contract unless buyer's order is accepted by the seller.

Sometimes certain points in the offer have to be clarified or additional information has to be obtained from the supplier before the buyer can place an order. (By making his offer clear and complete, the supplier can save his customer and himself time and trouble.)

If the buyer cannot make use of the offer, he should, as a matter of politeness, inform the seller of his refusal.

Perhaps the buyer is interested in the goods offered, but does not agree to the prices or terms proposed by the seller. In such cases he may try to obtain concessions from the supplier or make a *counter-offer*. When the supplier receives a counter-offer, he must decide whether or not he wants to accept it.

Orders. Orders are placed either in response to an offer, as mentioned above, or on the buyer's own initiative, without a preceding offer. In the latter case, the buyer declares that he is prepared to buy certain goods if they can be supplied at the prices and on the terms stated.

The order which opens business between two firms is called the *first order* or *initial order*. Orders for goods previously bought from the same firm are *repeat orders* or *re-orders*. A *trial order* is an order for a small quantity for testing purposes, which is followed by a larger order if the buyer is satisfied with the quality of the goods, or if he finds that there is a market for them. *Advance orders* are placed in advance of the time when delivery is desired. A *standing order* is an arrangement with the supplier, according to which the supplier delivers goods in specified quantities at certain intervals until further notice.

Orders can be placed orally or in writing. Verbal or telegraphic orders should be followed up by a written confirmation. The order letter is being replaced more and more by printed forms (*order forms, order blanks, purchase order forms*). Order forms are numbered to facilitate reference; they are usually accompanied by a brief note.

A complete order should cover the same points as those listed under offers. Orders following a detailed offer or placed with a regular supplier need not be so specific. In the latter case the supplier will assume that the goods are to be delivered as usual. Generally speaking, however, it is advisable to repeat in the order the main points of the offer.

After the order has been placed, follow-up letters may have to be written. The buyer may want to know when the goods will be delivered, he may want to increase or reduce his order, change his original instructions, give additional information, etc.

Follow-up is also necessary if the supplier fails to acknowledge the order or does not deliver the goods on time (see Delays in Delivery p. 122).

Sometimes unforeseen circumstances arise which force the buyer to revoke his order. (The cancelled order may be replaced by a new one.)

When an order has to be cancelled, this should be done as quickly as possible, if necessary by telegram. The supplier will, as a rule, accept the cancellation if it does not cause him any loss. (On the other hand, the cancellation of an order may also be the consequence of the seller's failure to perform his contractual duties.)

2. Specimen Letters

a. Request for a Sample

Dear Sirs,

Thank you for your letter dated 18th June regarding your DECO Glue for Plastics.

Before making a decision as to whether we should place an order for a quantity, I should be pleased if you could arrange for a sample to be sent to me in order that we may test the suitability of the glue for the application we have in mind.

Yours faithfully,

---

b. Counter-Offer (Price Too High)

Dear Sirs,

We thank you for your offer of 15th May and the patterns of Cloth No. D 677.

The terms of your offer have our approval, but we feel that the price of £ 1.50 per yard is rather high. The cloth is for export to a market where competition is very keen, and

59

at this figure our profit would be only nominal. However, if you could reduce the price to £ 1.25 per yard, we should be glad to place an order for some 30,000 yards.

We trust that in view of the size of this order you will see your way to making this concession.

Yours faithfully,

---

c. Refusal of Quotation

Dear Sirs,

We regret that we cannot make use of your quotation of 19th October for Tinplate, as we have been able to obtain this material at a lower price from another supplier.

Many thanks for the trouble you have taken in this matter.

Yours faithfully,

---

d. Order for Office Supplies

Gentlemen:

Thank you for your quotation of June 12 for office supplies. Will you please send us the following articles by parcel post:

Order No.	Quantity	Description	Unit Price	Amount
H 717	500 Pcs.[1]	Spiral-Bound Note Books	. . .	. . .
L 332	200 Sets	Colored [2] Pencils	. . .	. . .
L 734	300 Bxs.[3]	Colored Crayons	. . .	. . .
G 211	100 Pcs.	Staplers	. . .	. . .
G 612	50 Pcs.	Pencil Sharpeners	. . .	. . .

The shipment is to be invoiced to us subject to the usual terms of 2/10, n. 30.

As we are out of some of these items, we shall appreciate early shipment.

Very truly yours,

---

[1] pieces   [2] *US for* coloured   [3] boxes

e. Order Form

PHONES: GRAYS THURROCK 5155 (5 lines)

DATE

ORDER

G. HUNTER (LONDON) LTD.

Central Buying Office : GUMLEY ROAD, GRAYS, ESSEX
ALSO AT LONDON, BIRMINGHAM, MANCHESTER. ESTABLISHED 1803

YOUR NAME NOT TO APPEAR EITHER ON
GOODS OR PACKAGES

ALL GOODS TO BE SUPPLIED UNDER PLAIN LABELS
CLEARLY MARKED WITH OUR ORDER NUMBER

NO GOODS TO BE SUPPLIED EXCEPT TO OUR
OFFICIAL ORDER

PLEASE SUPPLY THE FOLLOWING SUBJECT TO THE CONDITIONS DETAILED HEREON

QUANTITY	DETAILS	PRICE

CARRIAGE PAID TO :	NOT LATER THAN	ROUTE

CONDITIONS OF PURCHASE

We reserve the right to inspect these goods before delivery, such inspection not absolving you from your
liability to supply goods free from defect and in accordance with this order.

Advice Notes and Invoices bearing our Order No. to be sent to us with each delivery.

The right is reserved to reject any goods not in accordance with this order and to cancel this order if these
general conditions are not complied with, or if delivery is not effected within the stipulated time.

If the conditions of this Order are not acceptable, information to that effect must be sent by return of post.

SEPARATE INVOICE IN DUPLICATE REQUIRED FOR EACH ORDER

DIRECTOR.

GH 103/760

f. Order Form

PURCHASE ORDER

VOLKSWAGEN DISTRIBUTOR
FOR
MICHIGAN AND INDIANA

IMPORT MOTORS LTD.

P. O. BOX NO. 184 ● GRAND RAPIDS 8, MICH.
telephone: CHerry 1-2672

10169
THIS NUMBER MUST APPEAR
ON ALL INVOICES, PACKAGES,
AND SHIPPING PAPERS.

TO:

SHIP TO:

PLEASE ENTER OUR ORDER FOR THE FOLLOWING:

WHEN WANTED	DEPARTMENT	TERMS	SHIP VIA	F.O.B.	P.O. DATE

QUANTITY	DESCRIPTION	UNIT PRICE	AMOUNT

SHIP AS PER INSTRUCTIONS.
DO NOT BACK ORDER UNLESS WE ADVISE.

BY

ORIGINAL—VENDOR

g. Confirmation of Order Placed by Telephone

Dear Mr. Smith:

We enclose Purchase Order No. 1787 in confirmation of the order we placed with you over the phone this morning.

As agreed, delivery is to be made not later than October 1. We are relying on you to see that this order is filled promptly and in accordance with our instructions.

Sincerely yours,

Encl.

---

h. Buyer Gives Marking Instructions

Dear Sirs,

With further reference to our order of the 12th August, we are giving you our marking instructions below:

BAL
16727
MWANZA Via
DARESSALAAM
MADE IN WEST GERMANY

Gross weight of package to be marked on two sides of every package.

We await your official confirmation and indication of the name of the steamer by which this consignment will be shipped.

Yours faithfully,

---

i. Cancellation of Order

Gentlemen:

We regret having to cancel Order No. 387 of January 18.

Our customer has just informed us that he has bought the furniture from a local supplier.

We hope that we shall soon be able to make good to you the loss of this order.

Yours sincerely,

---

3. Terms and Phrases

a. Opening Phrases

We thank you for your quotation of ... and should be glad if you would send us ...

Wir danken Ihnen für Ihr Angebot vom ... und bitten um Zusendung von ...

We enclose/We are sending you enclosed/Purchase Order No. ...

Wir legen Bestellung Nr. ... bei.

Please enter/book/the following order for immediate delivery: ...

Bitte merken Sie folgenden Auftrag zur sofortigen Lieferung vor: ...

Please send me the following articles and charge them to my account: ...

Bitte senden Sie mir folgende Artikel unter Belastung meines Kontos: ...

b. Buyer's Instructions and Conditions

Please acknowledge this order promptly, giving earliest delivery date.

Wir bitten um prompte Bestätigung dieses Auftrags und Angabe des frühesten Liefertermins.

The goods must be delivered, without fail, by the end of next week.

Die Waren müssen unbedingt bis Ende nächster Woche geliefert werden.

Please see that the goods are shipped by the first available steamer.

Bitte veranlassen Sie, daß die Waren mit dem ersten verfügbaren Dampfer verschifft werden.

The delivery dates in our order must be strictly adhered to.

We reserve the right to cancel the order if delivery is not made by 1st March.

We must hold you responsible for all losses which may arise as a result of any delay in delivery.

The goods must be up to/correspond to/conform to/agree with/the sample.

Goods of inferior quality will be returned at supplier's risk and expense.

If you cannot match our sample, please send us the nearest substitute you have in stock.

Please ensure that the goods are well packed.

Careful packing is essential.

Packing must be strong enough to afford the goods adequate protection.

Detailed instructions regarding packing and shipping marks will follow.

Marks as usual.

Insurance to be effected from warehouse to warehouse, covering the invoice value plus 10%.

This order is subject to our General Terms and Conditions.

Die in unserer Bestellung genannten Liefertermine müssen genau eingehalten werden.

Wir behalten uns das Recht vor, die Bestellung zurückzunehmen, wenn die Lieferung nicht bis zum 1. März erfolgt.

Für alle Verluste, die uns bei einer eventuellen Lieferverzögerung entstehen, müssen wir Sie verantwortlich machen.

Die Waren müssen dem Muster entsprechen.

Waren minderer Qualität werden auf Kosten und Gefahr des Lieferanten zurückgesandt.

Falls Sie keine unserem Muster entsprechenden Waren liefern können, senden Sie uns bitte die dem Muster am nächsten kommende Qualität, die Sie vorrätig haben.

Bitte sorgen Sie für gute Verpackung der Waren.

Sorgfältige Verpackung ist unbedingt erforderlich.

Die Verpackung muß so fest sein, daß sie den Waren ausreichenden Schutz bietet.

Genaue Anweisungen bezüglich Verpackung und Beschriftung / Markierung / folgen.

Übliche Beschriftung.

Versicherung ist von Haus zu Haus über den Rechnungswert plus 10% abzuschließen.

Diese Bestellung wird auf Grund unserer Allgemeinen Geschäftsbedingungen erteilt.

c. Closing Phrases

We trust that you will give this order your usual prompt attention.

Wir hoffen, daß Sie diesen Auftrag mit der gewohnten Pünktlichkeit erledigen werden.

Your careful attention to our instructions will be appreciated.

Für genaue Beachtung unserer Anweisungen wären wir Ihnen dankbar.

If this first transaction is satisfactory, we are prepared to place a standing order.

Bei zufriedenstellender Abwicklung dieses ersten Geschäftes sind wir bereit, einen Dauerauftrag zu erteilen.

d. Cancellation of Orders

We are sorry that it is necessary/We regret being compelled/We regret having/to cancel our order of . . .

Wir bedauern, unsere Bestellung vom . . . widerrufen zu müssen.

Please cancel our order for . . . and send us instead . . .

Bitte stornieren / streichen / Sie unsere Bestellung über . . . und senden Sie uns statt dessen . . .

As the buyer of the goods has withdrawn from the contract, we have no alternative but to cancel our order.

Da der Käufer dieser Waren vom Vertrag zurückgetreten ist, bleibt uns keine andere Wahl, als unsere Bestellung zu widerrufen.

We have just learned that the firm for which these goods were intended has gone bankrupt.

Wir haben soeben erfahren, daß die Firma, für die diese Waren bestimmt waren, in Konkurs gegangen ist.

We shall not fail, however, to let you have our instructions for any further requirements.

Bei weiterem Bedarf werden wir Ihnen jedoch bestimmt wieder Aufträge zukommen lassen.

We hope that we shall soon be able to make up for the inconvenience caused by placing another order.

Wir hoffen, daß wir Sie bald durch Erteilung eines anderen Auftrages für die Ihnen entstandenen Unannehmlichkeiten entschädigen können.

e. Refusal of Offers—Counter-Offers

We regret that we are unable to make use of/to avail ourselves of/your offer at present.

Leider können wir z. Z. von Ihrem Angebot keinen Gebrauch machen.

As your prices are too high, we cannot take your offer into consideration.	Da Ihre Preise zu hoch sind, können wir Ihr Angebot nicht berücksichtigen.
We have been able to obtain the goods at a more favourable price.	Wir konnten diese Waren zu einem günstigeren Preis bekommen.
These articles are not suited for our market.	Diese Artikel eignen sich nicht für unseren Markt.
We have a sufficiently large stock.	Wir verfügen über ein ausreichend großes Lager.
We have just replenished our stock.	Wir haben unser Lager soeben aufgefüllt.
We cannot expect to achieve satisfactory sales, unless you reduce your prices by at least 10 %.	Wir können nur dann mit einem zufriedenstellenden Absatz rechnen, wenn Sie Ihre Preise um mindestens 10 % senken.
If you can accommodate us with regard to the price, we shall be glad to give you an order.	Wenn Sie uns im Preis entgegenkommen können, erteilen wir Ihnen gerne einen Auftrag.
We cannot do regular business on the basis of the terms suggested by you.	Zu den von Ihnen vorgeschlagenen Bedingungen können wir keine laufenden Geschäfte durchführen.
We require at least 30 days' credit.	Wir müssen mindestens 30 Tage Ziel beanspruchen.

4. Exercises

Please translate the following letters into English:

a. Weidemann & Co., Köln, an Thomas & Son Ltd., Preston, Lancs. (England)

Wir haben Ihr Angebot vom 18. 6. erhalten und danken Ihnen für die uns als Postpaket übersandten Muster.

Da die Qualität der Muster unseren Erwartungen entspricht, bestellen wir auf Grund der in Ihrem Angebot genannten Preise und Bedingungen:

1. . . . . .
2. . . . . .
3. . . . . .

Bitte achten Sie darauf, daß nur solche Waren geliefert werden, die genau den Mustern entsprechen.

Wir benötigen die Waren dringend und müssen daher auf Lieferung innerhalb der von Ihnen genannten Frist von 4 Wochen bestehen. Zahlung erfolgt innerhalb von 10 Tagen nach Eingang Ihrer Rechnung durch Überweisung auf Ihr Konto bei der Lloyds Bank.

Da wir laufend Bedarf an diesen Waren haben, sind wir bereit, Ihnen weitere Aufträge zu erteilen, wenn die erste Lieferung zu unserer Zufriedenheit ausfällt.

b. Spinnerei AG, Rheydt, an Wool Export & Import Company Ltd., London

Wir danken Ihnen für Ihr Angebot über Merinowolle sowie für die Zusendung von Mustern, die wir sorgfältig geprüft haben. Da wir uns bei dieser Prüfung davon überzeugen konnten, daß die Wolle von guter Qualität ist, kabelten wir Ihnen heute morgen wie folgt:

BESTELLEN 100 BALLEN MERINOWOLLE QUALITÄT A
LAUT ANGEBOT LIEFERUNG ANFANGS MAI

Als Anlage zu diesem Schreiben senden wir Ihnen unsere Bestellung Nr. 267/66.

Wir weisen ausdrücklich darauf hin, daß die Lieferung pünktlich erfolgen muß, da sonst Gefahr besteht, daß eine Stockung in unserer Produktion eintritt. Für die Folgen einer Lieferverzögerung müßten wir Sie haftbar machen.

Bei zufriedenstellender Abwicklung dieses Auftrags könnten sich weitere Geschäftsmöglichkeiten ergeben.

Anlage

c. Dircks & Co., Hamburg, an Lewis Engines Ltd., Birmingham

Wir beziehen uns auf Ihr Angebot vom 12. 4. und bestellen einen Dieselmotor (*diesel engine*) vom Typ SM zum Preis von £ . . . c & f Hamburg einschließlich seemäßiger Verpackung. Die Versicherung wird hier gedeckt. Die Lieferung muß bis spätestens Ende Juli erfolgen.

Wir haben inzwischen die Dresdner Bank in Hamburg angewiesen, ein bis zum 31. Juli befristetes unwiderrufliches Akkreditiv zu Ihren Gunsten, zahlbar bei der Midland Bank in London, zu eröffnen.

Bitte benachrichtigen Sie uns, sobald der Motor verladen worden ist.

Für sorgfältige Erledigung unserer Bestellung wären wir Ihnen dankbar.

d. Maschinen-Import-GmbH, Stuttgart, an John Herbert Ltd., Halifax, Yorks. (England)

Wir kabelten Ihnen heute morgen wie folgt:

WIDERRUFE BESTELLUNG PRÄZISIONSDREHBANK
MODELL HLV BRIEF FOLGT

Es tut uns leid, daß wir Sie bitten müssen, den Auftrag zu streichen. Unser Kunde ist nicht in der Lage, die Präzisionsdrehbank (*precision lathe*) abzunehmen, da die Werkshalle, in der sie aufgestellt werden sollte, letzte Woche abgebrannt ist.

Wir hoffen, Ihnen in nächster Zeit einen anderen Auftrag übermitteln zu können.

Please draft letters in English from the following particulars:

e. Die Firma Müller & Co. in München hat von der Westland Tool Company Ltd. in Sheffield ein Angebot erhalten und bestellt zur Probe folgende Werkzeuge:

1 Lötgarnitur (*soldering kit*) Nr. 18, 1 Schleif- und Poliergerät (*sander-polisher*) Nr. 377, 1 Heimdrehbank (*turning lathe*) Nr. A 76, 1 Bandsäge (*band saw*) Nr. G 79, 1 Laubsägemaschine (*jig saw*) mit Elektromotor Nr. G 83.

Lieferung so bald wie möglich. Zahlung erfolgt nach Erhalt der Sendung durch Bankscheck.

Müller & Co. weisen darauf hin, daß eine beträchtliche Nachfrage nach Werkzeugen besteht. Wenn die Qualität der bestellten Geräte ihren Anforderungen entspricht, werden sie einen größeren Auftrag erteilen.

f. Die Firma Feinkost Hauser in Stuttgart hat vor 10 Tagen bei Brooke & Sons Ltd., London, 10 Kisten Ceylon Pekoe bestellt.

Heute schreibt Hauser an Brooke & Sons Ltd. und bittet diese Firma, der Sendung, wenn möglich, auch noch 3 Kisten Flowery Orange Pekoe Nr. A312 beizufügen, dessen Preis laut Angebot £ . . . je Pfund beträgt. Wenn diese Sorte z. Z. nicht verfügbar ist, wolle die Firma Brooke & Sons Ltd. umgehend mitteilen, wann mit der Lieferung gerechnet werden kann. Auf jeden Fall soll sie aber die 10 Kisten Ceylon Pekoe innerhalb der vereinbarten Zeit liefern.

Hauser bittet Brooke & Sons Ltd. bei dieser Gelegenheit auch um ein Angebot über Kenia Kaffee der Qualitäten AA und A.

g. Müller & Co. in München senden der Firma Hawkins & Westcott Ltd., Manchester, von der sie bereits früher Waren bezogen haben, Bestellung Nr. 683 über verschiedene Baumwollartikel. Die auf dem Bestellformular angegebenen Bestellnummern und Preise haben Müller & Co. dem letztjährigen Katalog von Hawkins & Westcott entnommen. Sollten sich die Preise inzwischen geändert haben oder die bestellten Waren nicht mehr vorrätig sein, so bitten Müller & Co. um sofortige Benachrichtigung.

h. Hamm & Co. KG, München, bedankt sich bei Harding Machine Tools Ltd., Coventry, für ihr Angebot vom 25. 7. über die Sonderanfertigung einer automatischen Fräsmaschine (*automatic milling machine*).

Die Münchener Firma ist mit den Bedingungen des Angebots einverstanden, nur dürfte die Lieferzeit — die englische Firma nannte 8–10 Monate — einige Schwierigkeiten bereiten, da die Maschine unbedingt bis März des nächsten Jahres zur Verfügung stehen muß. Wenn die englische Firma die rechtzeitige Lieferung der Maschine verbindlich zusagen kann, ist die Hamm & Co. KG gerne bereit, ihr den Auftrag zu erteilen.

Die Harding Machine Tools Ltd. soll daher sofort mitteilen, ob sie diesen Termin einhalten kann.

i. Braun & Co. in Schweinfurt bestellten vor 1½ Monaten lt. Auftrag Nr. A/3002 ein elektronisches Kugellager-Prüfgerät (*electronic bearing tester*) bei der Electronic Instruments Company in Detroit, Mich. (USA).

Sie wenden sich heute erneut an diese Firma und fragen an, wann sie mit der Lieferung dieses Geräts rechnen können.

k. Breuermann & Co., eine Kaffee-Importfirma in Bremen, haben von Edwards & Smith Ltd., London, ein Angebot über Santos-Kaffee erhalten. Da sie soeben eine größere Menge dieses Kaffees gekauft haben, können sie von dem Angebot zur Zeit keinen Gebrauch machen. Bei künftigem Bedarf werden sie jedoch auch Angebote von Edwards & Smith Ltd. einholen.

A Confusing Order

A milkman, while on his rounds one morning, found the following note from a customer:

"Dear Milkman:
We don't want milk every day. We want milk like this: Today we want milk. Tomorrow we don't. And the next day will be just like the day before the day after tomorrow.

Mrs. Jones"

IV. Acknowledgments
Replies to Orders—Acknowledgments

1. Introduction

Replies to Orders. This chapter deals with acknowledgments and refusals of orders, sellers' counter-offers, as well as with sellers' replies to buyers' counter-offers.

When an order is received, it is customary for the seller to send the buyer a written acknowledgment.

The acknowledgment of an order placed on the basis of a firm offer, in good time, and without any qualifications, is sent merely "for order's sake," as a final confirmation of a contract already in existence. In all cases where the seller is free to accept or refuse the buyer's order,[1] the acknowledgment constitutes the seller's formal acceptance of the order, which results in a contract between buyer and seller.

Occasionally, however, a supplier is compelled to refuse an order. Perhaps the buyer's terms are not acceptable, the goods ordered are no longer manufactured or carried in stock, or the firm which placed the order is known to be financially embarrassed. Manufacturers selling through agents or dealers often have to refuse orders received at the factory.

Whenever possible, the supplier does not refuse an order outright, but makes a counter-offer, for example by recommending substitutes. Should the goods be only temporarily out of stock, the supplier may place the order on file and inform the customer that it will be executed as soon as a new supply is received. (If the customer is unable to wait that long, he will cancel his order.)

Acknowledgments. Acknowledgments of orders may be either letters or printed forms. (Many purchase order forms have an acknowledgment copy or counterfoil, which is filled in by the supplier and returned to the customer.)

In his acknowledgment, the supplier thanks the customer for his order and informs him of the date on which the goods will be delivered. In the case of immediate delivery, the acknowledgment includes an advice of dispatch. If the order is incomplete or not clear, the supplier asks the customer to furnish further details or to specify his wishes. The acknowledgment may also contain a request for references or credit information.

In order to avoid misunderstandings, it is often advisable to repeat in the acknowledgment the most important points of the order. The acknowledgment may also be a detailed confirmation of the sale concluded (*sales note, contract note*). Sometimes the seller sends the buyer a contract in duplicate and asks him to return one copy with his signature.

---

[1] If a firm offer is accepted too late, or an order is placed in response to an offer without engagement, if buyer's order is a qualified acceptance of seller's offer (that is, a counter-offer), or if it was not preceded by an offer.

2. Specimen Letters

a. Acknowledgment and Dispatch Advice

Gentlemen:

Thank you very much for the order you gave our salesman, Mr. Colbert, on November 7.

Enclosed you will find the bill of lading [1] and invoice for the complete order, which was shipped by rail this morning. You will note from the invoice that we have allowed you a 'quantity discount of 10 %.

We hope that the goods will arrive in good condition and look forward to the pleasure of serving you again soon.

Yours sincerely,

Encl.

---

[1] railroad bill of lading

b. Motorcar Dealer Thanks Customer for His Order

Dear Mr. Cooper:

We're [1] glad that you decided to become a Volkswagen owner. Thank you for buying your new VW from us.

After all, you might have bought it in any of the other 49 states, or in any of 135 other countries around the world. That's how many places you can travel to and still get service from factory-trained mechanics.

It has been a pleasure helping you pick out your new VW. We wish you many years and many miles of enjoyable driving.

Sincerely,
Murray Motors Inc.

---

[1] Contractions are sometimes used for the sake of informality but, on the whole, they should be avoided in business letters.

c. Acknowledgment Form

PHONE:
GRAYS & THURROCK
5155 (10 Lines)

ESTABLISHED 1903

ACKNOWLEDGMENT

G. HUNTER (London) LTD.

GUMLEY ROAD, GRAYS, ESSEX

MEMBER FBI

Acceptance of this order is subject to our standard Conditions of Sale.
G. HUNTER (LONDON) LTD.

INVOICE TO:

DELIVER TO (IF DIFFERENT)

YOUR ORDER No.	DATED	TERMS	JOB No.	INVOICE No.	DATED

DISTIN-GUISHING NUMBER OR MARK	DESCRIPTION	PRICE EACH

DESPATCH BY

PACKING

PACKING

CARRIAGE

TOTAL

We acknowledge with thanks receipt of your order as detailed hereon. If these particulars differ in any way from your requirements will you please let us know by return. Please quote our job number in any correspondence.

Form No. 2

ASHTON-UNDER-LYNE, LYE, BELFAST, CAMBRIDGE, DUBLIN, GLASGOW, LEEDS, NEWCASTLE, ANTWERP, AUGSBURG, MILAN, PARIS, ROTTERDAM, VIENNA, ZÜRICH

73

d. Scottish Knitting Mill Acknowledges Order from German Fashion Shop

---

Dear Sirs,

Thank you very much for the order you gave our German representatives, Müller & Co., in Bielefeld. We have entered it as follows:

18 Men's Sport Shirts, L.Slvs. [1]

		40″	42″	44″	46″	48″	50″	52″
3101	Black	2	2	2	2	—	—	—
3004	Cedarwood	1	1	1	2	1	—	—
3044	Antique Bronze	1	1	1	1	—	—	—
				. . . . 6.21	7.03			

50 Men's "Galloway" Pullovers, L.Slvs.

		40″	42″	44″	46″	48″
3001	Barn Red	2	2	2	2	2
3093	Lt. [2] Natural	2	2	2	2	2
3004	Cedarwood	2	2	2	2	2
3113	Slate Blue	2	2	2	2	2
3102	City Grey	2	2	2	2	2
		. . . . .5.27	6.02	6.40		

21 Men's "Galloway" Cardigans, L.Slvs., No Pkts. [3]

		40″	42″	44″	46″	48″
3093	Lt. Natural	1	2	2	2	1
3102	City Grey	1	2	2	2	1
3107	Flannel Grey	1	1	1	1	1
		. . . . .5.83	6.27	7.03		

Date of shipment from Scotland: 15th August/30th September, 19 . . .

This order is subject to our Conditions of Sale of which we enclose a copy.

Yours faithfully,

Enc.

---

[1] long sleeves
[2] light
[3] no pockets

Conditions of Sale

Force Majeure: The Company accepts no liability for any delay in the execution of orders arising from wars, strikes, lock-outs, fire, flood, unavailability of raw materials and other circumstances beyond its control.

Carriage paid to Port of Shipment only or to Packing House in Great Britain.

Payment: Settlement of accounts is to be made in Sterling. $2^{1}/_{2}$ % discount for payment within 60 days, or 120 days net.

The above terms also apply when payment is made by Bills of Exchange, and all charges and expenses thereon will be payable by the customers.

---

e. Letter Accompanying Acknowledgment Form and Invoice

Gentlemen:

Thank you very much for your order of December 20, 19 . ., for

2 C–2H High Capacity Air Cleaners.

Enclosed you will find Acknowledgment No. 328 and invoice in quintuplicate.

We will do everything we can to ship the Air Cleaners by January 17, 19 . . .

Should you require prints or additional literature, please let us know and we will rush them to you immediately.

Very truly yours,

Encl. 2

---

f. Acknowledgment of Order and Request for Credit Information

---

Gentlemen:

Thank you for your order for

5 No. 18 Steel Safes, beige finish,
3–number combination lock, $ . . . each.

75

As this is our first transaction with you, we must ask you to fill in and return the enclosed blank form from our credit department. This is part of our routine in handling new accounts.

Your order will be shipped as soon as we receive this information. However, if you are in urgent need of the safes, you may instruct us by wire to ship them on a C.O.D. basis.

Very truly yours,

Encl.

---

g. Chemical Company Acknowledges Order Superseding Previous One

---

Dear Sirs,

Thank you for your letter of the 19th July and Order No. AN 3775, which supersedes your previous order No. AN 3482.

We have accordingly cancelled Order No. AN 3482 and booked Order No. AN 3775 as follows:

500 lbs. Resin BE 28 @ £ 0.57 per lb., F.O.B. U.K. Port.

The consignment will be ready for shipment in approximately 10 days' time.

Yours faithfully,

---

h. Manufacturer Acknowledges Order—Customer Referred to Dealer

---

Dear Mrs. Myers:

Thank you very much for your order of April 7 for a 15 cu.ft. BLUESPOT Frostless Freezer.

We would like to send you the freezer, but as manufacturers we sell only through dealers and never supply appliances direct from the factory. May we therefore suggest that you visit one of the following dealers in your city:

Kendall Appliances Store, 411 Woodbury Ave.
Harper & Smith, Inc., 66 Union Street

You will receive courteous and prompt service at either of these stores, and we are sure that you will be satisfied with your BLUESPOT Frostless Freezer. The sealed refrigeration system is guaranteed for five years. All other parts carry a similar one-year guarantee.

Yours sincerely,

---

i. Maker of Tweed Skirts Acknowledges Order from Private Customer—Cannot Promise Delivery Within the Time Desired

---

Dear Mrs. Grey,

Thank you for your order of 6th November. Much as we should like to help you, we are sorry to say that we cannot promise delivery by 23rd November.

At this time of the year we are exceptionally busy in all departments. As you know, we make everything individually and specially to order, which naturally takes time, and we normally require about six weeks for delivery.

We would rather tell you this now than disappoint you later and hope that you will instruct us to put your order in hand for delivery as soon as possible.

In the meantime we shall hold your order in our pending file and should be grateful if you would quote the reference AJ/CD/018 in your reply.

Yours sincerely,

---

k. Stock Temporarily Depleted

Dear Sirs,

Thank you very much for your order of the 5th February for Wall Paper.

There has been such a demand for Patterns 88/377, 88/867 and 89/310 that our stock is temporarily depleted. However, a new supply is expected early next month, and when it arrives we shall lose no time in sending you the patterns desired.

By the same post you will receive from us a selection of our latest patterns. Orders for these patterns can be executed immediately.

Yours faithfully,

---

l. Exporter in Hong Kong Offers Substitutes

Dear Sirs,

Your Order No. 06687

We have just received a letter from our suppliers informing us that they have discontinued the production of Quality No. 2366, Tsingtao Pongee (machine-made). In substitution they have offered us Qualities No. 2369 AA and 2369, which are their latest products.

We are enclosing our price list for these two qualities and also sample cuttings for your inspection. Will you please let us know by return of post which quality you prefer us to substitute, so that we can inform our suppliers accordingly.

Yours faithfully,

Encl.: Price List
Sample Cuttings of
Qualities 2369 AA and 2369

m. Refusal to Supply at Buyer's Price

Dear Sirs,

Thank you for your order for 2,000 yards of Cloth No. 112 at £ 0.70 per yard.

We regret, however, that we are unable to accept your order at this figure. You will find, on referring to our previous correspondence, that we quoted a price of £ 0.75 per yard. This is our keenest price, on which we cannot grant you any further concession. Besides, it is generally expected that prices will rise in the near future.

We shall, of course, be pleased to carry out your order if you confirm it at £ 0.75 per yard, 30 days net.

Yours faithfully,

3. Terms and Phrases

a. Acknowledgment of Orders

We thank you for your order, which we acknowledge as follows: ...

Wir danken Ihnen für Ihren Auftrag, den wir wie folgt bestätigen: ...

Your order has been put in hand, and we shall do our best to have the goods ready by the end of next week.

Wir haben mit der Ausführung Ihres Auftrags bereits begonnen und werden uns bemühen, die Waren bis Ende der nächsten Woche fertigzustellen.

We shall do our utmost to expedite the completion of your order.

Wir werden uns nach Kräften bemühen, die Fertigstellung Ihres Auftrags zu beschleunigen.

We shall notify your forwarding agent as soon as the consignment is ready for collection.

Wir werden Ihren Spediteur benachrichtigen, sobald die Sendung abholbereit ist.

We assure you that your instructions will be carefully observed.

Wir versichern Ihnen, daß wir Ihre Anweisungen genau beachten werden.

Special care will be devoted to the execution of your order.

Wir werden der Ausführung Ihres Auftrags besondere Sorgfalt widmen.

We hope that this first order will lead to further business.

Wir hoffen, daß dieser Erstauftrag zu weiteren Geschäften führen wird.

... represents the first step in the establishment of/marks the commencement of/is the beginning of/a long and mutually satisfactory business relationship.

... der Anfang einer dauerhaften und für beide Teile zufriedenstellenden Geschäftsverbindung ist.

We trust that we may have the pleasure of serving you again soon.

Wir hoffen, Ihnen bald wieder zu Diensten sein zu können.

We should be glad if you availed yourselves of our services in the event of further requirements.

Wir würden uns freuen, wenn Sie bei weiterem Bedarf auf uns zurückkämen.

b. Refusal of Orders—Counter-Offers

We regret being unable to supply the goods ordered.

Leider sind wir nicht in der Lage, die bestellten Waren zu liefern.

We must ask you to excuse us from accepting your order.	Wir müssen Sie um Verständnis dafür bitten, daß wir Ihre Bestellung nicht annehmen können.
We cannot execute your order at the prices stipulated.	Wir können den Auftrag zu den von Ihnen vorgeschriebenen Preisen nicht ausführen.
As we cannot supply our motor scooters direct from the factory, we refer you to . . ., our authorized dealers in your area.	Da wir unsere Motorroller nicht direkt ab Fabrik liefern können, verweisen wir Sie an unseren für Ihr Gebiet zuständigen Vertragshändler, die Fa. . . .
We have passed your order on to our agents.	Wir haben Ihre Bestellung an unsere Vertretung weitergegeben.
We no longer stock this item.	Wir führen diesen Artikel nicht mehr.
These sizes are no longer available.	Diese Größen sind nicht mehr vorrätig/lieferbar.
We are out of these blouses/These blouses are out of stock.	Diese Blusen sind ausgegangen.
Our stocks have been sold out/have been cleared/are depleted/are exhausted.	Unser Lager ist geräumt/geleert/erschöpft.
A new supply will not be available until . . .	Eine neue Lieferung wird nicht vor . . . erwartet.
Unless you instruct us to the contrary, shipment will be made on receipt of new supplies.	Wenn Sie uns keine gegenteiligen Weisungen erteilen, erfolgt die Lieferung, sobald wir eine neue Sendung erhalten.
For article No. 223 we could substitute articles No. 226 or No. 228, which are very similar to the quality ordered.	Anstelle von Artikel Nr. 223 könnten wir Artikel Nr. 226 oder Nr. 228 liefern, die der bestellten Qualität sehr ähnlich sind.
If you raise your order to . . ., we shall be glad to supply the material at the price requested.	Wenn Sie Ihre Bestellung auf . . . erhöhen, liefern wir Ihnen den Stoff gern zum gewünschten Preis.
The prices stated in your order have been taken from our price list of 1st January 19 . ., which has in the meantime been superseded by a new one.	Die in Ihrer Bestellung genannten Preise sind unserer Preisliste vom 1. Januar 19 . . entnommen, die in der Zwischenzeit durch eine neue ersetzt worden ist.

4. Exercises

Please translate the following letters into English:

a. Gerhard & Co., Offenbach, an Griffith & Co., Ltd., Brockville, Ontario (Kanada)

Wir danken Ihnen für Ihren Probeauftrag vom 6. 6. und legen unsere Auftragsbestätigung Nr. E-73651 bei.

In Ihrem Auftrag ist die Versandart nicht erwähnt. Soll die Ware auf dem Seeweg oder per Luftfracht versandt werden?

Da die Verladung gegebenenfalls mit D. „Barbara" erfolgen könnte, der am 20. 6. aus Hamburg ausläuft, bitten wir um telegrafischen Bescheid.

Anlage

b. Primus Werke AG, Erlangen, an Gillott Corporation, Los Angeles, Calif. (USA)

Wir danken Ihnen für Ihren Auftrag, den wir zusammen mit Ihrem Schreiben vom 8. 5. erhielten.

Als Anlage senden wir Ihnen einen von uns unterzeichneten Liefervertrag in doppelter Ausfertigung und bitten Sie, ein Exemplar mit Ihrer Unterschrift zu versehen und an uns zurückzusenden. Ihre Anweisungen bezüglich Verpackung und Versand werden wir genau befolgen.

Obwohl wir zur Zeit mit Aufträgen überhäuft sind, werden wir unser möglichstes tun, die Waren bis Anfang Juni zur Verschiffung bereitzustellen.

Anlage: Liefervertrag

c. Tankbau AG, Karlsruhe, an Lebanese Trading Company Ltd., Beirut

Ihre Bestellung Nr. 4119

Wir danken Ihnen für den uns mit Ihrem Schreiben vom 4. 5. übermittelten Auftrag, den wir unter Zugrundelegung unserer umstehenden Bedingungen gebucht haben.

Um prompte und sorgfältige Erledigung Ihres Auftrags werden wir uns bemühen.

Mit freundlichen Grüßen
Tankbau AG

10 Stück Zweitakt-Gemischsäulen (*petrol/oil mixing pumps*)
Mischungsverhältnisse (*mixing proportions*): 1 : 12, 1 : 20,
1 : 25 und 1 : 40, genau wie Kommissions-Nr. 538/872

5 Säulen mit Drehstrommotor (*three-phase motor*)	DM . . . per Stck.
5 Säulen mit Wechselstrommotor (*A.C. motor*)	DM . . . per Stck.
	cif Beirut

Lieferzeit: September/Oktober

Zahlung: Kasse gegen Dokumente bei einer Bank in Beirut

Provision: 10 % auf den fob-Preis

d. Hammer & Söhne, Osnabrück, an Peterson & Co., London

Besten Dank für Ihren Auftrag vom 27. 5. Leider müssen wir Ihnen mitteilen, daß die
von Ihnen gewünschte Qualität ausgegangen ist und wahrscheinlich erst wieder in ca.
2 Monaten lieferbar sein wird. Wir möchten deshalb anfragen, ob Ihnen evtl. mit einer
ähnlichen Qualität, z. B. Nr. 866 auf S. 14 unseres Katalogs, gedient wäre. Sollte dies
der Fall sein, so bitten wir Sie, uns umgehend Bescheid zu geben.

e. Huber & Co., Fürth, an Howell & Smith, Liverpool

Wir sind im Besitze Ihres Schreibens vom 8. 11., in welchem Sie um einen weiteren
Nachlaß von 10 % auf die Preise unseres Angebots vom 18. 10. bitten.

Nachdem wir unsere Preise nochmals überprüft haben, müssen wir Ihnen zu unserem
Bedauern mitteilen, daß es uns nicht möglich ist, Ihnen weitere Rabatte zu gewähren.
Wenn Sie unsere Erzeugnisse mit anderen Fabrikaten vergleichen, werden Sie fest-
stellen, daß unsere Waren in Anbetracht ihrer hohen Qualität sehr preisgünstig sind.
Eine Reduzierung unserer Preise wäre nur bei einer Qualitätsverschlechterung möglich,
die aber sicher nicht im Sinne unserer Kunden wäre.

Wir würden uns freuen, Ihren Auftrag zu erhalten, und erwarten Ihre baldige Antwort.

Please draft letters in English from the following particulars:

f. Die Maschinenfabrik Maier & Co. in Nürnberg hat von Baker & Smith Ltd. in
Southampton einen Auftrag auf Lieferung einer automatischen Drehbank erhalten, die
nach Angaben des Bestellers angefertigt werden soll.

Die Maschinenfabrik bestätigt den Eingang dieses Auftrags und weist darauf hin, daß — wie bereits in ihrem Angebot erwähnt — die Lieferzeit bei Sonderanfertigungen mindestens 5–7 Monate beträgt. Da die Drehbank jedoch sehr dringend benötigt wird, ist die Maschinenfabrik bereit, den Auftrag der Baker & Smith Ltd. als vorrangig zu behandeln. Sie hofft, daß die Drehbank bis zum 20. Mai versandbereit sein wird, und verspricht, die englische Firma sofort nach Fertigstellung derselben zu benachrichtigen.

g. Auf der letzten Büromaschinenmesse in München besuchte Mr. John D. Brown von Jenkinson & Co., London, den Stand der Firma Müller & Co. Er unterhielt sich mit dem Verkaufsleiter der Firma Müller, Herrn Hoyer, und bestellte 200 Diktiergeräte XR 325.

Die Firma Müller bestätigt diesen Auftrag in einem Schreiben an Jenkinson & Co. Die Geräte sind voraussichtlich in ca. 3 Wochen versandfertig. Die Lieferung erfolgt wunschgemäß c & f London.

Da Mr. Brown in seinem Gespräch mit Herrn Hoyer auch die Frage der Alleinvertretung anschnitt, stellt die Fa. Müller fest, sie sei grundsätzlich bereit, Jenkinson & Co. ihre Vertretung zu übertragen. Zunächst wäre jedoch zu klären, ob Jenkinson & Co. auf Provisionsbasis oder für eigene Rechnung tätig sein möchten.

h. Die Werkzeugmaschinenfabrik Gießen AG hat der Phoenix Manufacturing Company in New York am 29. 7. ein Angebot über zwei Hochleistungsfräsmaschinen (*heavy-duty milling machines*) Typ S900 unterbreitet, das von letzterer am 11. 8. telegrafisch angenommen wurde.

Nach Eingang des Telegramms sendet die Werkzeugmaschinenfabrik der amerikanischen Firma eine Bestätigung des Vertragsabschlusses. In dieser Bestätigung bezieht sie sich auf ihr Angebot und die telegrafische Annahme durch den Käufer, nennt die zu liefernden Maschinen und wiederholt die für die Lieferung vereinbarten Bedingungen. Diese lauten:

Preis: $ . . . je Maschine cif New York
Zahlungsbedingungen: 90 % des Rechnungsbetrages durch unwiderrufliches Akkreditiv gegen Vorlage der Versanddokumente, die restlichen 10 % innerhalb von 2 Monaten nach Ankunft der Maschinen in New York.
Verpackung: Die Maschinen werden wasserdicht verpackt und in Holzverschlägen mit Bandeisensicherung versandt.
Versicherung: Die Versicherung wird bei der Allianz Versicherungs-AG gegen alle Gefahren von Haus zu Haus abgeschlossen.
Lieferung: Februar/März 19 . . mit direktem Dampfer.

Die Werkzeugmaschinenfabrik erklärt in einer angefügten Klausel, daß sie in Fällen höherer Gewalt keine Haftung für Lieferungsverzögerungen bzw. Nichtlieferung übernimmt. Eventuelle Streitigkeiten zwischen den Vertragspartnern sollen nach der Vergleichs- und Schiedsordnung der Internationalen Handelskammer [1] entschieden werden.

Tit for Tat

An elderly American farmer wrote to a mail-order house as follows: "Please send me one of the gasoline engines you show on page 877, and if it's any good, I'll send you a check." [2]

In time he received the following reply: "Please send check. If it's any good, we'll send the engine."

[1] See Glossary of Commercial Terms under *Arbitration*.
[2] *US for* cheque

V. Delivery
Execution of Orders—Invoices, Statements, Debit and Credit Notes

1. Introduction

Execution of Orders. The seller executes buyer's order by delivering the goods according to the terms of the contract.

Before delivery can be made, the goods have to be carefully packed to ensure safe arrival. Adequate packing is of particular importance in the case of overseas shipments. The packing containers must be strong enough to withstand rough handling and the stresses of transport, but, on the other hand, they should be as light and compact as possible.

Export packages have to be provided with distinctive marks, which make it possible to identify the individual shipments. Caution marks (words or symbols) are usually added. The marks should be shown on at least two sides of each package. Buyer's instructions with regard to packing and marking, as well as the regulations of the importing country, must, of course, be strictly complied with.

Unless it has been agreed that the buyer is to collect the goods, the seller has to make arrangements for transport. For this purpose he enlists the services of forwarding agents and carriers. Small packages may be sent by parcel post.

To protect the goods from the risks of loss or damage in transit, insurance is taken out by the seller or the buyer. In the case of overseas shipments, marine insurance is necessary. Ordinarily, marine insurance covers the goods only as long as they are on board the carrying vessel, but it can also be effected on a warehouse-to-warehouse basis (*warehouse-to-warehouse insurance*).

After execution of the order, the seller sends the buyer his *invoice*. He may also send the buyer a *dispatch* or *shipping advice* and a *packing list* showing the contents of the individual packages.

Sometimes the supplier has to advise the customer when the goods are ready for dispatch, or send him progress reports from time to time, informing him how his order is getting along and when he may expect delivery.

Invoices. Invoices or bills [1] are usually rendered when the goods are delivered, but they may also be made out before or after delivery. Most invoices are prepared on printed forms with the firm's letterhead (*invoice forms*, US: *billheads*). A complete invoice contains the following details:
1. Name and address of buyer.
2. Date and number of invoice.
3. Date and number of order.

---

[1] The words *invoice* and *bill* are often interchangeable. *Bill* is the broader term; it is defined as "an account that states the costs of goods sold, services rendered, or work done (Webster)." The term *invoice* is applied mainly to accounts relating to goods.

4. Quantity and description of the goods; marks, numbers, etc., of packages.

5. Unit price and extension;[1] deductions, additional charges, etc.; total invoice amount.

6. Miscellaneous details, such as method of transport, terms of payment, etc.

(It should be noted that terms stated on the invoice which deviate from those agreed upon in the contract are not legally valid.)

In foreign trade the regular invoice is known as a *commercial invoice* to distinguish it from a *customs invoice* and a *consular invoice*. It has to be made out with great care, as it forms the basis on which the other export documents are prepared. Commercial invoices are often required for customs and other official purposes and must therefore conform to the regulations of the importing country. These regulations may require that the commercial invoice be signed by the exporter, be made out in a certain number of copies, bear a special declaration by the exporter, be certified by a chamber of commerce, etc.

A special kind of invoice is the *pro-forma invoice*. It is used when the buyer is required to pay in advance, when goods are sent on approval, or consigned to an agent for sale. A foreign buyer may need a pro-forma invoice in order to be able to apply for an import licence, or to instruct his banker to open a documentary credit. A pro-forma invoice is often sent to a customer to show him what the cost of the goods would be if he decided to buy them. In this case the pro-forma invoice is merely a special form of quotation.

Statements. Customers who have a current account with a supplier receive statements of account at regular intervals, for example, once a month or once every quarter. The statement is, in effect, a copy of the customer's account since it was last balanced. It shows the balance at the beginning of the period, all invoices rendered and payments received during the period (including debit and credit notes, if any), and the balance at the end of the period. The statement enables the two firms to compare the entries in their books; it also acts as a reminder to the debtor that money is still owing.

Statements often bear an indication of the terms, as, for example: *Account net and payable within 30 days.—Account subject to* $2^1/2 \%$ *discount if paid on or before April 10.*

Debit and Credit Notes. Debit and credit notes (US: *debit* and *credit memoranda, debit* and *credit memos*) are exchanged between two firms when faulty goods or empty containers are returned by the customer, or when an error or omission in an invoice or statement has to be corrected.

When a debit note has been received and found correct, it is acknowledged by a credit note, and vice versa.

---

[1] *To extend,* in connection with invoices, means to multiply the unit price by the quantity. *Extension* is the product of this multiplication.

2. Specimen Letters

a. Dispatch Advice—Bill of Exchange Drawn

Dear Sirs,

We are pleased to inform you that your order of the 10th February has today been dispatched by rail.

As agreed, we have drawn on you for the amount of our invoice at one month. We enclose the draft, which please furnish with your acceptance and return to us.

Yours faithfully,

Encl.

---

b. Shipping Advice

Dear Sirs,

Your Order No. 177, dated 17th October

This is to advise you that the above-mentioned order was shipped on board the vessel "Ubana" from London to Mombasa on 25th November.

We are pleased to hand you enclosed copy of commercial invoice amounting to . . ., as well as non-negotiable copy of the bill of lading.

The original shipping documents (commercial invoice in triplicate, customs invoice in duplicate, full set of clean on-board bills of lading and certificate of insurance) have been presented to our bankers for collection through Barclays Bank, International Ltd. Nairobi, Kenya, on a sight draft basis.

We shall be glad to hear that the goods have arrived safely and in good order.

Yours faithfully,

Encl.

---

c. Invoice

INVOICE

TELEPHONE: HAMILTON 2833 TELEGRAMS: MACDONALD HAMILTON	**MACDONALD & CO. LTD.** **TARTAN SPECIALISTS** **GORDON STREET** **HAMILTON SCOTLAND**	CODE: BENTLEY'S SECOND

Messrs. Kohler & Schmitt   10th December, 19..
Bayerstrasse 196
Munich
Germany

Sent by rail to the order of: The General Transport Ltd.
                                  9 St. Clare Street
                                  London, E.C.3
            Consigned to: Danzas & Cie. GmbH
                                  Munich, Germany

Order 7/2698 d/d 22/9/19..

1 Bale marked: K & S MUNICH GERMANY 83/1	Class 300-54" Pure New Wool:			
	842/4x2	61 1/2 yards		
	842/4x3	64 1/4 "		
	842/4T1	61 1/2 "		
		187 1/4 yards	122p	£228.45
	Class 51-54" Pure Worsted:			
	Black	29 1/2 yards	122p	£ 35.99
				£264.44
		Canvas		£ .95
				£265.39

Net net wt.[1] 117 lbs. Net wt. 119 lbs.
Gross wt. 121 lbs.
Net wt./sq.yd. 5 2/3, 6 1/2 ozs.
Sq.yds. 325 1/8
Measurements: 28"x26"x17"

Terms:
3 3/4% discount for payment by 20/12/19..
3 % " " " " 10/ 1/19..
2 1/2% " " " " 10/ 2/19..
Thereafter net. Payment must be made within
90 days after date of invoice.

Bankers:
Please send all remittances to: Bank of Scotland
                                        George Square
                                        Glasgow, Scotland

We hereby certify this invoice to be true and correct.

                                MACDONALD & CO. LTD.

                                      SECRETARY

ALL COMMUNICATIONS TO BE ADDRESSED TO THE COMPANY AND NOT TO INDIVIDUALS.

---

[1] weight

d. Invoice

H. ANDREWS & CO. LTD.
DIRECTORS: H. ANDREWS C. ANDREWS

COFFEE

TELEGRAMS:
ANDCO, LONDON.

CODES:
A.B.C. 5ᵀᴴ & 6ᵀᴴ EDNˢ
BENTLEYS.
UNIVERSAL TRADE.
ACME.

TELEPHONES: MINCING LANE 8667.
„ „ 8668.

TELEX 26691.

PLANTATION HOUSE,
MINCING LANE,

LONDON,...................... 12th June, 19 ..
E.C.3.

Contract No. 4254............ *Dated* 11th February, 19 ..

INVOICE *of* ..... 500 bags coffee[1].... *Shipped by S.S.* ..."Hornfels"

from ... Port Limon .... *to* .... Bremen .... *by order of*

and for account and risk of .... Messrs. Tiedemann & Sohn, Bremen ....

CAFE DE COSTA RICA LA VERBENA OTIS 550 BREMEN	500 bags washed Costa Rica coffee LA VERBENA 1958/59 crop		
	Net weight 34,500.00 kilos		
	☉ U.S.$54.20 per 50 kilos		
	Cost & Freight Bremen	U.S.$	37,398.00
	Net shipping weights.		
	Payment: Net cash against documents on first pres- entation.		
E.& O.E.			

[1] *telegram style for:* **500 bags of coffee**

e. Packing List

Customer Code	Salesman 99	Date	Terms 30 Days No Cash Discount	Chilton Shipping Number 23206	Customer Order Number

DATE MUST BE DELIVERED:

VIA:

THIS IS NOT AN INVOICE

This is your packing list. Please check the contents of this shipment against this list.
Kindly notify us at once of any discrepancy.
Thank you for your order. Your invoice will follow.
Film strips, tapes and records billed by component items in each set.
Prices shown are catalogue list. You will be billed at your regular discount or net.

SHIPPING LABEL & PACKING SLIP

QUAN.	LESSONS	CATALOGUE LIST PRICE	BOOK CODE	AUTHOR—TITLE—EDITION	%	NET PRICE	Tax	HANDLING

Order prepared by _____
Checked by _____
Order packed by _____
Checked by _____

f. Statement

CHILTON BOOKS

A DIVISION OF CHILTON COMPANY

STATEMENT

EAST WASHINGTON SQUARE • 525 LOCUST STREET
PHILADELPHIA 6, PENNA., U.S.A.

REMIT TO CHILTON BOOKS, P. O. BOX 7271, PHILADELPHIA 1, PA., U.S.A.

OLD BALANCE	DATE	REFERENCE	DEBIT	CREDIT	BALANCE

CC 905

PLEASE NOTIFY US IMMEDIATELY
IF THIS STATEMENT IS NOT CORRECT.
CHILTON BOOKS

g. Debit Memo and Credit Memo

DEBIT MEMO

VOLKSWAGEN OF AMERICA, INC.
ENGLEWOOD CLIFFS, N. J.

No 2330

DATE: ....
REF.: ....
....

YOUR ACCOUNT WAS CHARGED TODAY WITH:

$

CREDIT ACCT. #

DEBIT ACCT. #

FORM VWOA 9048A-3-62-2M

CREDIT MEMO

VOLKSWAGEN OF AMERICA, INC.
ENGLEWOOD CLIFFS, N. J.

No 2850

DATE: ....
REF.: ....
....

YOUR ACCOUNT WAS CREDITED TODAY WITH:

$

CREDIT ACCT. #

DEBIT ACCT. #

SALES DEPARTMENT

FORM VWOA 9048A-3-62-2M

h. Manufacturer Advises Exporter of Impending Completion of Order

Dear Sirs,

The Wire-Drawing Machine you ordered on the 15th May for an overseas customer will be completed in about a fortnight.

We should therefore be glad to receive your packing and marking instructions. Perhaps you would also let us know whether measurements, gross weights and net weights are to be stencilled on the cases.

We understand that you will arrange for the collection of the shipment at our Sheffield Works, and we shall advise you as soon as the machine has been packed.

Yours faithfully,

i. Covering Letter

Dear Sirs,

We enclose Statement of Account for the first quarter of 19 . ., which shows a balance of £ 44.47 in our favour.

Will you please let us have your cheque for this amount after verification.

Yours faithfully,

Encl.

3. Terms and Phrases

a. Advising Dispatch

This is to inform you that we have to-day sent you the following goods: . . .

Wir teilen Ihnen mit, daß heute folgende Waren an Sie abgegangen sind: . . .

We are pleased to advise that the goods you ordered have been dispatched by rail this morning.

Wir freuen uns, Ihnen mitteilen zu können, daß die von Ihnen bestellten Waren heute morgen mit der Bahn versandt wurden.

The consignment has been shipped by M.S. "Martha" leaving London on ...

Die Sendung wurde mit M. S. „Martha" verschifft, das am ... aus London ausläuft.

S.S. "Eastern Trader" is scheduled/due/ to arrive in Singapore on ...

Der Dampfer „Eastern Trader" soll am ... in Singapur eintreffen.

We hope the consignment will arrive safely/reach you in good condition.

Wir hoffen, daß die Sendung wohlbehalten/in gutem Zustand/bei Ihnen ankommt.

b. Sending Invoice—Requesting Payment

We enclose invoice in duplicate/triplicate/quadruplicate/quintuplicate.

Wir legen Rechnung in zweifacher/dreifacher/vierfacher/fünffacher Ausfertigung bei.

A copy of the invoice is enclosed; the original together with the other documents will be surrendered/released/to you by the Mercantile Bank on payment of our draft for ...

Rechnungskopie liegt bei. Die Originalrechnung wird Ihnen zusammen mit den anderen Dokumenten von der Mercantile Bank bei Zahlung unserer Tratte über ... ausgehändigt.

Please remit the invoice amount by bank draft, as arranged.

Wir bitten um Zahlung des Rechnungsbetrages durch Bankscheck, wie vereinbart.

Please remit by bank transfer to our account with either of the following banks ...

Wir bitten um Überweisung auf unser Konto bei einer der beiden nachstehend aufgeführten Banken ...

We enclose a three months' sight draft, which please return to us after accepting.

Wir legen einen 3 Monate nach Sicht fälligen Wechsel bei und bitten Sie, diesen nach Annahme zurückzusenden.

c. Notations and Declarations on Invoices

Please advise us if the goods are not delivered within 14 days from date of dispatch, as otherwise the carrier may refuse payment for loss.

Bitte benachrichtigen Sie uns, wenn die Auslieferung der Waren nicht innerhalb von 14 Tagen nach Versanddatum erfolgt, da sonst der Frachtführer bei Verlust die Schadensersatzleistung verweigern könnte.

All unearned discounts will be charged back.

Bei unberechtigtem Skontoabzug erfolgt Rückbelastung.

Cartons are non-returnable.	Pappkartons werden nicht zurück-genommen.
Packing containers, if returned in good condition and carriage paid, will be credited in full.	Bei frachtfreier Rücksendung der Versandbehälter in gutem Zustand wird der volle, dafür in Rechnung gestellte Betrag gutgeschrieben.
Complaints will be considered only if made within 7 days from receipt of goods.	Reklamationen finden nur innerhalb von 7 Tagen nach Empfang der Ware Berücksichtigung.
We hereby certify that this invoice is in all respects true and correct.	Wir bestätigen hiermit, daß diese Rechnung in jeder Hinsicht in Ordnung ist.
This is to certify that these goods are of United Kingdom origin.	Es wird hiermit bestätigt, daß diese Waren britischen Ursprungs sind.

d. Packing

wooden case, wooden box	Holzkiste
crate	Lattenkiste, Holzverschlag
carton, cardboard box	Pappkarton
plywood box	Sperrholzkiste
chest	(Tee-)Kiste
sack, bag	Sack
bale	Ballen
drum	zylindrischer Behälter
cask, barrel	Faß
carboy, demijohn	Korbflasche
case lined with oilpaper	mit Ölpapier ausgelegte Kiste
tin-lined case	Kiste mit Blecheinsatz, mit Blech ausgelegte Kiste
soldered zinc lining	verlöteter Zinkblecheinsatz
case with metal strapping/steel strapping; metal-strapped/steel-strapped/case; case bound with metal bands/steel straps	mit Metallband/Stahlband gesicherte Kiste

wrapping paper, kraft paper	Packpapier
corrugated cardboard	Wellpappe
wood wool; *US*: excelsior	Holzwolle

e. Marking

Shipping Marks:

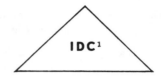

3320²
COLOMBO³
1/10⁴
GROSS WT. ... NET WT. ...⁵
DIMENSIONS................

MADE IN ENGLAND⁶

¹ consignee's mark	Kennmarke des Empfängers
² order number	Auftragsnummer
³ port of destination	Bestimmungshafen
⁴ number of package and total number of packages	Nummer des Kollos und Gesamtzahl der Kolli
⁵ weight and dimensions (not always required)	Gewicht und Ausmaße (nicht immer erforderlich)
⁶ mark of origin (not always required)	Ursprungsbezeichnung (nicht immer erforderlich)

Caution Marks:

GLASS—HANDLE WITH CARE	VORSICHT GLAS
FRAGILE	ZERBRECHLICH
INFLAMMABLE; *US:* FLAMMABLE	FEUERGEFÄHRLICH
POISON	GIFT
KEEP DRY	VOR NÄSSE SCHÜTZEN
KEEP IN COOL PLACE	KÜHL AUFBEWAHREN
USE NO HOOKS	KEINE HAKEN GEBRAUCHEN
THIS SIDE UP; TOP	OBEN
BOTTOM	UNTEN
LIFT HERE	HIER ANHEBEN

Some Symbols:

4. Exercises

Please translate the following letters into English:

a. Kurt Seidel OHG, München, an McKearney & Co., Dublin

Wir beziehen uns auf Ihren Auftrag Nr. 6777 vom 3. 7. und freuen uns, Ihnen mitteilen zu können, daß die bestellten Waren mit M/S „Cynthia" verschifft wurden, das morgen nach Dublin ausläuft.

In der Anlage senden wir Ihnen eine Abschrift unserer Rechnung, über deren Betrag wir auf Sie per 90 Tage Sicht gezogen haben. Den Wechsel und die Versanddokumente haben wir unserer Bank, der Dresdner Bank in München, übergeben und diese angewiesen, die Aushändigung der Dokumente bei Akzeptierung des Wechsels zu veranlassen.

Wir hoffen, daß dieses Geschäft zu Ihrer vollen Zufriedenheit durchgeführt wurde, und würden uns freuen, bald weitere Aufträge von Ihnen zu erhalten.

Anlage

b. Landmaschinenwerke AG, Hof (Saale), an F. Özkök, Istanbul

Betr. Ihr Auftrag Nr. C/2234 vom 18. Februar

Wir freuen uns, Ihnen mitteilen zu können, daß — wie Ihrem Vertreter, Herrn Maurer, anläßlich seines kürzlichen Besuches zugesagt — eine weitere Teilsendung am 24. April mit D. „Michael" in Triest verladen wurde.

Für Ihre Akten erhalten Sie anbei eine Kopie der Handelsrechnung Nr. 8179 und eine nicht begebbare Kopie des Konnossements.

Der volle Satz Versanddokumente wurde unserer Hausbank zum Inkasso über die Akbank T.A.S., Succ. Bahçekapi, Istanbul-Bahçekapi, übergeben.

Anlagen

Please draft letters in English from the following particulars:

c. Die Firma Johann Hauser in Aachen benachrichtigt Black & Sons, Ltd., London, daß die Sendung laut Auftrag Nr. B433 heute der Bahn übergeben worden ist. Sie legt dem Schreiben ihre Rechnung sowie eine 3-Monats-Sichttratte über £ 2660.50 bei und bittet die englische Firma, die Tratte mit ihrem Akzept zu versehen und zurückzusenden. Die Firma Hauser ist überzeugt, daß die Waren guten Absatz finden werden, und hofft auf Fortsetzung der Geschäftsbeziehungen.

d. Gessner & Co. in München schreiben an A. P. Kondogouris in Limassol (Cypern), daß die von ihm bestellten Ersatzteile am 7. 4. mit Luftpost versandt wurden.

Ihrem Schreiben legen Gessner & Co. folgende Dokumente bei: 1. Handelsrechnung Nr. 8334 vom 6. 4. über DM 290,—, ordnungsgemäß unterschrieben, 4fach; 2. Combined Certificate of Value and Origin, 3fach; 3. Packliste Nr. 46216.

Gessner & Co. bitten Kondogouris, so bald wie möglich die Überweisung des Rechnungsbetrages auf ihr Konto Nr. 24464 bei der Dresdner Bank, München, zu veranlassen.

e. Braun & Söhne in Hannover teilen am 14. November der Eastern Trading Company in Bangkok mit, daß die bestellten Elektromotoren (Auftrag B 8336 vom 2. Oktober) heute in Hamburg mit D. „Hansa" verladen wurden.

Die Verpackung der Motoren erfolgte in seefesten Kisten mit Bandverschluß. Jeder einzelne Motor wurde vor Versand nochmals sorgfältig geprüft. Der Vertreter der Firma Braun & Söhne in Bangkok, Paiboom & Co. Ltd., ist gerne bereit, den Kunden in allen technischen Fragen zu beraten. Er unterhält auch ein großes Ersatzteillager.

Wie vereinbart, haben Braun & Söhne die Versanddokumente (Handelsrechnung vier-fach, voller Satz Konnossemente und Versicherungspolice) zusammen mit einer Sicht-tratte ihrer Bank zur Weiterleitung an die Bank of Thailand in Bangkok übergeben, die der Eastern Trading Company die Dokumente bei Einlösung der Tratte aushändigen wird. Eine Kopie der Handelsrechnung legen Braun & Söhne ihrem Schreiben bei.

Braun & Söhne hoffen, daß die Sendung wohlbehalten ankommen wird. Über weitere Aufträge würden sie sich freuen.

Substitution

A customer ordering a box of men's handkerchiefs initialled "H" from a large mail-order house received a box of handkerchiefs with the initial "I" and the following explanatory enclosure slip: "We regret that we are at present out of the merchandise you ordered. The enclosed is the nearest thing to it and we trust that the substitution will be satisfactory."

VI. Payment
Acknowledging Receipt of Goods and Making Payment—Acknowledging Receipt of Payment

1. Introduction

Acknowledging Receipt of Goods and Making Payment. When the buyer receives the goods delivered by the seller, he will examine them carefully; if he finds them to be in order, he will, in many cases, send the seller an acknowledgment of receipt. Should a remittance be made at the same time, an advice to this effect is included in the acknowledgment.

Before payment is effected, the buyer carefully checks the seller's invoice or statement and compares it with his own records. If he discovers any error or discrepancy, he will notify the seller immediately. The matter is then investigated by the latter and, if it is found that the buyer was right, a correction is made.

In settling indebtedness the following means of payment may be used: 1. cash, 2. postal orders and money orders, 3. cheques and bank drafts, 4. bank transfers, 5. bills of exchange and promissory notes, and 6. documentary credits.

The means of payment most commonly used in foreign trade are bank transfers, bank drafts, bills of exchange and documentary credits.

Payments in foreign trade involve the conversion of one currency into another. Means of payment which represent a claim to the payment of a certain sum in a foreign currency are collectively known as *foreign exchange*.

A sum of money sent in the form of cash, a cheque, bank transfer, etc., to a person at another place is known as a *remittance*. (The word is also applied to the act of sending the money.) Remittances are accompanied by a *remittance advice*, or they are sent together with the order or the letter acknowledging receipt of the goods. If the sender of the remittance does not have any proof of payment, he will ask the recipient to send him a receipt.

Acknowledging Receipt of Payment. It is not necessary for the seller to acknowledge the buyer's remittance unless the buyer asks for a receipt. To many suppliers, however, such an acknowledgment is a welcome opportunity to build goodwill and to solicit further business.

Errors, misunderstandings and other difficulties in connection with payment have to be called to the buyer's attention. For example, the buyer may have made an error in remitting, he may have misunderstood the terms of payment, or he may have forgotten to mention the number and date of the invoice he is paying.

Sometimes buyers take discounts at an incorrect rate or after the discount period has elapsed. This is called "taking unearned discounts." The practice of taking unearned discounts purposely is known among American businessmen as "discount piracy"; it is of course incompatible with good business methods.

2. Specimen Letters

a. Acknowledging Receipt of Goods

Dear Sirs,

Today we have received the consignment of which you advised us on the 7th March. We have examined the goods and have found them to be in order.

In payment of your invoice we enclose cheque for £... on the District Bank Ltd. Manchester. Please send us your official [1] receipt.

Yours faithfully,

Encl.

---

[1] properly signed

b. Advising Settlement by Bank Transfer

Dear Sirs,

We are pleased to inform you that we have today instructed our bankers, Lloyds Bank in London, to transfer to your account with the Bayerische Vereinsbank, Munich,

£ 367.31

in settlement of your invoice No. 1348 of July 6th.

Please acknowledge receipt.

Yours faithfully,

---

c. Buyer Acknowledges Receipt of Goods—Returns Draft with His Acceptance

---

Dear Sirs,

We thank you for your letter of the 12th September, as well as for the prompt delivery of the 100 bags of Santos Coffee which arrived here yesterday in good condition.

Your draft for £ ..., maturing on the 12th December, is being returned to you enclosed with our acceptance. We shall not fail to honour this bill when it is presented for payment.

Yours faithfully,

Encl.

---

d. Error in Invoice

Gentlemen:

We have just received your invoice No. 288 of March 15 for $..., covering the purchase of a bucket for the BROOKS L16 Loading Shovel.

As you will note when referring to your records, this bucket was a replacement for a defective one, and Mr. Thompson, your Sales Manager, agreed to grant us a 50% reduction on the new item.

We are therefore returning your invoice and are asking you to issue a corrected bill for $ ...

Very truly yours,

Encl.

---

e. Discrepancies in Statement

Dear Sirs,

We have received your quarterly statement showing a balance of £ 213.56 in your favour.

When checking your figures against our own records, we noted the following discrepancies:

1. Invoice No. 4677 for £ 21.50 was charged twice. As you will see, you debited us with this amount on the 16th September and again on the 26th September.
2. Credit Note 10063 of the 7th October for £ 9.83 is not included in your statement.

We are deducting £ 31.33 from the amount of your statement and are instructing our bank to transfer the balance of £ 182.23 to your account.

Yours faithfully,

f. Remittance Advice

TEL: HORSFORTH 4242   REMITTANCE ADVICE

UNITED MERCHANTS AND MANUFACTURERS (U.K.) LTD,

INCORPORATING ARTHUR TATE & CO., COHN HALL MARX (U.K.) & CO.,
T.A.D. TEXTILES, RIVERDALE (U.K.) & CO. AIREVALE CURTAIN CO

NEWLAY   .   LEEDS 13

DATE	REFERENCE	PAYMENTS & RETURNS	PURCHASES	BALANCE

A12

     DISCOUNT

     NETT

THE LAST AMOUNT IN THIS COLUMN IS THE AMOUNT OF THE CHEQUE ENCLOSED.

Coding

T.A. - T.A.D. TEXTILES	CS - CASH
R.D. - RIVERDALE (U.K.) & CO.	GD - GOODS
C.H. - COHN-HALL-MARX (U.K.) & CO.	RT - RETURN
S.S. - ARTHUR TATE SUITINGS DIVISIONS	DS - DISCOUNT
U.M. - UNITED MERCHANTS & MANUFACTURERS (U.K.) LTD.	TF - TRANSFER
A.D. - AIREVALE CURTAIN CO.	JE - JOURNAL ENTRY

g. Seller Acknowledges Receipt of Cheque

Dear Sirs,

Thank you for your cheque of 18th June for £ 77.53 in settlement of our invoice No. 355, dated 7th June.

We enclose our official receipt and look forward to the pleasure of serving you again.

Yours sincerely,

Encl.

h. Supplier Asks for Details of Invoice Paid

Dear Sirs,

Thank you for your cheque in the amount of £ . . .

Your payment arrived without a remittance advice. We do not know which invoice you are paying, and should appreciate it if you would give us the invoice number and date in order that we may credit your account properly.

Yours faithfully,

i. Seller Apologizes for Overcharge

Gentlemen:

We have received your letter of November 10 and regret very much the overcharge of $10.35 which you have called to our attention. The charge was incorrect and has now been cancelled.

A corrected bill for $312.55 is enclosed. Please accept our sincere apologies for this error.

Very truly yours,

Encl.

k. Publisher of Textbooks Corrects Error in Invoice

Dear Mrs. Robinson:

Thank you for your letter of February 15 regarding our invoice No. 4668.

Due to an error, you were billed incorrectly. The price of the textbook is $5.20 less 20 % discount.

We are cancelling this invoice and you should receive a credit shortly. To rectify our error we are re-billing you at the correct price.

Thank you for bringing this matter to our attention, and we apologize for any inconvenience this mistake may have caused you.

Sincerely yours,

l. Supplier Calls Customer's Attention to Unearned Discount Taken

Gentlemen:

Thank you for your remittance in the amount of $320.58 in payment of our invoice of Feb. 16 for $328.80, on which you have taken a $2^1/2$ % cash discount.

As our prices are cash prices, we cannot grant you any cash discount, and would therefore appreciate your sending us, at your convenience, a check for $8.22, the amount of the discount in question.

Very truly yours,

3. Terms and Phrases

a. Receipt of Goods, Invoices, etc.

We acknowledge receipt of the goods ordered and thank you for the prompt delivery.

Wir bestätigen den Erhalt der bestellten Waren und danken Ihnen für die prompte Lieferung.

The goods covered by your invoice of ... arrived by S.S. "Hamburg" yesterday.

Die Waren lt. Ihrer Rechnung vom ... kamen gestern mit Dampfer „Hamburg" an.

The shipment has reached us safely and has turned out to our complete satisfaction.

Die Sendung ist wohlbehalten bei uns eingetroffen und zu unserer vollen Zufriedenheit ausgefallen.

Your statement for the last quarter has been received and found correct.

Wir haben Ihren Kontoauszug für das letzte Quartal erhalten und in Ordnung befunden.

We are glad to advise you that your statement for December 19.. corresponds with our books.

Wir freuen uns, Ihnen mitteilen zu können, daß Ihr Auszug für Dezember 19.. mit unseren Büchern übereinstimmt.

b. Arranging Payment

In payment of/In settlement of/your invoice we enclose crossed cheque for £ ... on District Bank Ltd., Manchester.

Zum Ausgleich Ihrer Rechnung senden wir Ihnen in der Anlage einen gekreuzten Scheck über £ ... auf die District Bank Ltd., Manchester.

We enclose cheque for £ ..., which please credit to our account/place to the credit of our account.

Wir legen einen Scheck über £ ... bei und bitten um Gutschrift auf unser Konto.

We enclose bank draft for $ ..., which covers your invoice after deduction of 2 % cash discount.

Wir legen einen Bankscheck über $ ... bei, der Ihre Rechnung nach Abzug von 2 % Skonto deckt.

We have instructed our bank to transfer/to remit/the amount of £ ... to your account with Barclays Bank Ltd., Bedford.

Wir haben unsere Bank angewiesen, den Betrag von £ ... auf Ihr Konto bei der Barclays Bank Ltd., Bedford, zu überweisen.

We have accepted your draft and shall not fail to honour it promptly at maturity.

Wir haben Ihre Tratte akzeptiert und werden sie bei Fälligkeit prompt einlösen/honorieren.

c. Errors in Invoices and Statements

On checking your invoice, we find that an error has occurred.

Bei Prüfung Ihrer Rechnung stellen wir fest, daß Ihnen ein Fehler unterlaufen ist.

We are returning your invoice, as you have made an error in totalling.

Wir schicken Ihre Rechnung zurück, da Sie sich bei der Addition verrechnet haben.

There is a discrepancy between the goods delivered and your invoice.

Die gelieferten Waren stimmen nicht mit Ihrer Rechnung überein.

We should like to draw your attention to two credit items which have been omitted from your statement.

Wir möchten Sie auf zwei Gutschriften aufmerksam machen, die in Ihrem Auszug nicht aufgeführt sind.

We should be obliged if you would correct the statement/issue a corrected statement.

Für eine Berichtigung des Kontoauszuges wären wir Ihnen dankbar.

As we are having difficulty, owing to this error, in obtaining the release of the goods from the customs, we should be glad if you would send us an amended invoice.

Da wir wegen dieses Irrtums Schwierigkeiten haben, die Freigabe der Waren beim Zoll zu erreichen, bitten wir um Zusendung einer berichtigten Rechnung.

Please let us have a credit for the difference.

Bitte erteilen Sie uns eine Gutschrift für den Differenzbetrag.

Please confirm to us the adjusted balance of . . .

Bitte bestätigen Sie uns den berichtigten Saldo von . . .

d. Receipt of Payment

We acknowledge receipt of your cheque for . . ., which we have placed to the credit of your account.

Wir bestätigen den Eingang Ihres Schecks über . . ., den wir Ihrem Konto gutgeschrieben haben.

Our bankers have just advised us that they have received your remittance in the amount of . . .

Unsere Bank teilt uns soeben mit, daß Ihre Überweisung in Höhe von . . . eingegangen ist.

We thank your for your prompt remittance and enclose our official/formal/receipt.

Wir danken Ihnen für Ihre prompte Zahlung und legen eine rechtsgültige *(d. h. ordnungsgemäß unterschriebene* Quittung bei.

e. Errors in Payment, etc.

We are returning your cheque because it is postdated.

Wir lassen Ihren Scheck an Sie zurückgehen, da er vordatiert ist.

We have noticed that your cheque is not signed.

Wir haben festgestellt, daß Ihr Scheck nicht unterschrieben ist.

Since payment was made after expiry of the discount period, we cannot agree to your deducting a 2 % discount.

Da die Zahlung nach Ablauf der Barzahlungsfrist erfolgte, können wir uns mit dem Abzug von 2 % Skonto nicht einverstanden erklären.

| You have made a deduction of . . . from our invoice without giving any reason for it. | Sie haben von unserer Rechnung . . . abgezogen, ohne irgendwelche Gründe dafür anzugeben. |

4. Exercises

Please translate the following letters into English:

a. Export-Import GmbH, Hamburg, an Brown & Smith Ltd., London

Betr.: Unser Auftrag No. A3112 vom 10. 7.

Die mit obigem Auftrag bestellten Gummiwärmeflaschen und -handschuhe sind heute bei uns eingetroffen.

Wir bedanken uns für die prompte und sorgfältige Ausführung unseres Auftrags und senden Ihnen als Anlage einen Bankscheck zum Ausgleich Ihrer Rechnung über . . .

Anlage

b. Müller & Co., Bielefeld, an Wm. Johnson Ltd., London

Wir haben Ihren Kontoauszug für das 2. Quartal 19 . . erhalten, der einen Saldo von £ 277.53 zu Ihren Gunsten aufweist.

Wie wir anhand unserer Bücher festgestellt haben, berücksichtigt diese Aufstellung weder die Gutschrift vom 20. 4. in Höhe von £ 18.53, die wir für zurückgesandte Waren erhielten, noch den Preisnachlaß von £ 4.61, den uns Ihr Vertreter, Mr. Robinson, auf unsere Reklamation vom 5. 5. hin gewährte.

Für umgehende Berichtigung des Auszugs wären wir Ihnen dankbar.

c. Hälsen & Co., Lübeck, an John Black, Southampton

Besten Dank für Ihr Schreiben vom 29. 9., dem ein Scheck über £ 38.28 zum Ausgleich unserer Rechnung vom 20. 9. beilag.

Wir würden uns freuen, Sie bei künftigem Bedarf wieder bedienen zu können.

Please draft letters in English from the following particulars:

d. Georg Mehlen KG, Frankfurt/Main, schreibt an Baker & Co. Ltd., London, daß die ihr am 26. 5. angekündigte Sendung inzwischen wohlbehalten angekommen ist. Die

Firma hat die Waren geprüft und in Ordnung befunden. Sie hat heute ihre Bank angewiesen, den Rechnungsbetrag in Höhe von £ 367.38 auf das Konto von Baker & Co. bei der Lloyds Bank Ltd., London, zu überweisen.

e. Die Bremer Importgesellschaft mbH bestätigt den Eingang der Versandanzeige der Firma Law & Co., Bradford (England), vom 25. 5. Die 100 Ballen Flanellstoff sind am 2. 6. in gutem Zustand in Bremen eingetroffen. Die Tratte von Law & Co. sendet die Importgesellschaft mit ihrem Akzept versehen zurück und verspricht, für prompte Einlösung bei Verfall zu sorgen.

f. Schmitt & Co. in Düsseldorf haben von Pickering & Co., Ltd., Oldham (England), Waren bezogen und darüber drei Rechnungen mit den Nummern 17662, 17678 und 17695 erhalten. In diesen Rechnungen ist jedoch der von Pickering & Co. in ihrem Angebot vom 16. 3. zugesagte Rabatt von 10 % nicht berücksichtigt. Schmitt & Co. bitten daher um Berichtigung der Rechnungen bzw. Gutschrift des fraglichen Betrages.

g. Kraemer & Co. (Export–Import) in Hamburg bedanken sich bei Western Style Inc., Houston, Texas, für die prompte Lieferung der am 15. 5. bestellten Blue Jeans. Bei Prüfung der Rechnung stellten Kraemer & Co. jedoch fest, daß dem Lieferanten bei Posten No. 3 — 250 Jeans for Boys zum Preise von je $1.70 — ein Fehler unterlaufen ist. Der Gesamtpreis beträgt $425.00, nicht $452.00. Kraemer & Co. bitten um Berichtigung.

No Funds

Indignantly a daughter said to her father when he returned home one evening, "Dad, why in the world did you tell me to put my money in such a bank? Why, it's absolutely on the rocks."

"What," said her father, "that's one of the strongest banks in the country. What do you mean by such a statement?"

Waving a check in the air, his daughter replied, "Look at this. It's my check for $25.00 and it was returned today by the bank and marked 'No Funds.'"

VII. Credit Letters
Credit Inquiries and Credit Information

1. Introduction

Credit Inquiries. When a new customer asks for credit, the supplier must first find out whether the customer is creditworthy. To this end, he sends credit inquiries (*or*: status inquiries) to possible sources of information.

The most important credit information sources are: 1. the customer (he may be asked to furnish information about himself, for example, by filling in a credit application form, or by submitting a copy of his latest balance sheet), 2. the customer's trade references (other suppliers whom the customer has given as references), 3. the customer's bank references (the banks named by the customer), 4. other firms known to have done business with the customer, and 5. inquiry agencies (*US*: commercial *or* mercantile agencies). It should be noted that banks give information only to other banks. Therefore, a supplier seeking information from his customer's bank can secure this information only through his own bank.

This chapter is chiefly concerned with inquiries addressed to trade references.

When such inquiries are made, the inquirer should always be aware of the fact that he is asking a favour. Credit inquiries are often accompanied by a stamped and self-addressed envelope or, if they are sent abroad, by an addressed envelope and an International Reply Coupon.

Many letters of inquiry do not mention the name of the person or firm about whom the inquiry is made; the name is placed on a separate sheet of paper which is attached to the letter. This is done to ensure confidential treatment of the matter.

The inquirer must, of course, assure the firm he is writing to that the information given will be treated confidentially and without responsibility on the latter's part.

Credit inquiries often close with an offer to reciprocate favours. Many businessmen feel, however, that this goes without saying.

Letters requesting credit information, and the envelopes in which they are sent, are marked *Confidential, Strictly Confidential,* or *Private and Confidential.*

Credit Information. Business firms are under no obligation whatsoever to answer credit inquiries. Usually, however, they are quite willing to co-operate, knowing that they, too, have to ask similar favours from time to time.

In replies to credit inquiries, the name of the person or firm about whom information is given is often omitted; instead, reference is made to *the firm in question, the firm mentioned in your letter, the firm about which you inquire,* etc.

The information supplied should be concise. It is usually not necessary or advisable to go too much into detail. Favourable reports should never be "over-enthusiastic." If they are "too good to be true," they are likely to arouse suspicion. When unfavourable reports have to be given, this should be done in a cautious and impersonal manner.

In Anglo-Saxon countries there are very strict laws protecting individuals against oral defamation (*slander*) and written defamation (*libel*). An unfavourable report about a business firm may, under certain circumstances, give rise to an action for libel. British and American firms are therefore extremely careful when giving unfavourable information by letter. An unfavourable opinion is usually stated in rather general terms, and frequent use is made of such phrases as *it seems, we believe, according to reports received, we have learned from reliable sources*, etc. A refusal to give information is often tantamount to an unfavourable report. Such a refusal may, of course, also be necessary because the firm from which information is requested does not know the firm in question well enough to express an opinion.

Firms giving credit information usually point out in their letters that the information is supplied in confidence and that they assume no liability. Both the letter and the envelope are marked *Confidential, Strictly Confidential*, etc.

2. Specimen Letters

a. Credit Inquiry

Dear Sirs,

Private and Confidential

We have been referred to you by the firm mentioned on the enclosed slip and should be glad if you would give us as detailed information as possible regarding their financial status and business reputation. In particular, we should like to know whether, in your opinion, a credit to the extent of approx. £3,000 could be safely granted.

We thank you for your courtesy and assure you that your information will be treated confidentially. For your convenience we enclose a stamped and addressed envelope.

Yours faithfully,

Encl. 2

---

b. Credit Inquiry

Gentlemen:

Your name has been given us as a reference by the Bisdell Corporation of Rochester, N.Y., which desires to establish credit with our organization.

Will you kindly furnish us with the following information:

1. Length of time you have been dealing with this company _____

2. Highest recent credit on open account_____

3. Method of payment

   Take cash discounts _____

   Pay when due _____

   A little slow _____

   Slow _____

4. Amount now owing $ _____

5. Comments as to general management and reliability_____

_____

Any information furnished will, of course, be considered as strictly confidential. If we can reciprocate at any time, we shall be pleased to do so.

Very truly yours,

_____

c. Favourable Information

_____

Confidential

Dear Sirs,

In reply to your inquiry of the 8th June, we are pleased to say that the firm in question enjoys a good reputation. The proprietors are reported to have considerable capital at their disposal. They have always met their obligations punctually. We should therefore have no hesitation in granting them credit to the extent you mention.

This information is given without responsibility on our part and on the understanding that you will treat it as confidential.

Yours faithfully,

_____

d. Credit Inquiry

ROAD EQUIPMENT COMPANY

116 N. LA SALLE STREET, CHICAGO 1, ILL.

TELEPHONE:
RANDOLPH 8-6430

February 3, 19..

John Miles Tractor Company
619 Stonegate Road
Peoria, Ill. 61601

Re: Cooper Construction Company
    Springfield, Illinois

Gentlemen:

We understand that you are familiar with the affairs of the above company, from which we have just received a large order.

Will you kindly give us your opinion of the company's financial responsibility, credit standing, and general management. If you are granting accommodations, we should like to know the extent of the accommodation, the amount at present owing you and, if on a secured basis, the nature of the security.

Your reply will be appreciated, and we assure you that any information you may give us will be held in strict confidence. Should the occasion present itself, we shall be very glad to reciprocate the favor.

Yours very truly,

C. F. Cummings

Credit Department

CFCummings:jn

e. Favourable Information

Dear Sirs,

Messrs. Johnson & Co., about whom you inquire in your letter of 17th March, have done business with us for the past two years. Orders have been comparatively small and payments regular, with a short delay in one case. Our representative reports that the firm is sound and reliable. A credit of £400 would appear to be in order.

This information is given in confidence and without responsibility on our part.

Yours faithfully,

f. Unfavourable Information

Gentlemen:

We regret to state, in response to your letter of May 28, that our experience with the firm in question has not been satisfactory.

During the ten months they have had an account with us, we have repeatedly had difficulties in collecting bills. It seems that their financial position is not very strong.

Under these circumstances we would advise you to proceed with caution and, if possible, to do business on cash terms only.

This information is given without any obligation on our part, and we trust that it will be held strictly confidential.

Very truly yours,

g. Report by American Mercantile Agency

April 20, 1965

Nelson-Towers Trading Company   288 Broad Street
(Subsidiary of Nelson & Towers, Inc.)   New York 7, N.Y.

OFFICERS: John D. Nelson, President
              Donald A. Towers, Vice-President
              George L. Smathers, Secretary-Treasurer
DIRECTORS: The officers
RATING: NQ[1]

HISTORY

Incorporated under New York laws August 7, 1964, authorized capital
$75,000.
John D. Nelson, 60, single, native-born. Operated a partnership business
with Donald A. Towers which was succeeded by Nelson & Towers, Inc. in 1950.
Donald A. Towers, 58, married, born in Canada. Partner of John D. Nelson
before partnership was incorporated.
George L. Smathers, 41, married, native-born. Nine years employed by
National City Bank of New York. 1957 joined Peel & Co., Inc., export merchants in this city, later managed finance department of that corporation,
from which position he resigned on August 1, 1964.

OPERATION-LOCATION

Wholly-owned subsidiary of Nelson & Towers, Inc., which operates as importers of general merchandise. Twelve persons are currently employed.

The company maintains a suite of offices on the 12th floor of a 35-story office
building.

FINANCIAL INFORMATION

On April 18, 1965, A. J. Muller, office manager, reported that John D.
Nelson was abroad on a business trip and that the other officers were out of
town.
Mr. Muller stated that the subject company had been acting mainly as import
agent. However, he stated that recently the company had placed orders with
several domestic suppliers for merchandise to be exported overseas. He
stated that the company had ample capital for these commitments and had at
its own option included 50% deposits with orders to ensure prompt delivery.
Mr. Muller declined to submit balance sheet, stating he was not authorized
to give full financial information on the company.
The parent company, Nelson & Towers, Inc., on December 31, 1964, showed
net worth of $210,407 and a good financial condition, with current assets
over twice current liabilities, and a liquid condition maintained.

PAYMENTS

A. J. Muller stated that principal purchases so far had been made on a letter
of credit or sight draft basis.
Accounts are maintained at two depositories in this city, which have in three
instances made an advance to the subject company on a secured basis.

[1] *Not Quoted* in the rating book, as this firm has been established only for a rather short time.

h. Refusal to Give Information

Dear Sirs,

With reference to your inquiry of 30th January, we regret to say that we are unable to express an opinion on the financial standing of the firm in question.

Yours faithfully,

---

3. Terms and Phrases

a. Opening Phrases

Your name has been given us as a reference by Messrs. Black & Co.

Sie wurden uns von der Firma Black & Co. als Referenz genannt.

The firm whose name appears on the enclosed slip/The firm mentioned on the enclosed slip of paper/has placed a first order in the amount of . . .

Die auf dem beiliegenden Blatt genannte Firma hat uns erstmalig einen Auftrag in Höhe von . . . erteilt.

Mr. Smith is seeking an account with us with a credit limit of . . .

Mr. Smith wünscht einen laufenden Warenkredit bis zu einer Höhe von . . .

Messrs. Baker & Sons wish to enter into business relations with us.

Die Firma Baker & Sons möchte mit uns in Geschäftsverbindung treten.

As this firm is unknown to us . . .

Da uns diese Firma unbekannt ist . . .

As we have not done business/have not had any dealings/with this firm so far . . .

Da wir mit dieser Firma bisher nicht in Geschäftsverbindung standen . . .

b. Information Requested

We shall appreciate/We should be grateful to you for/any information you can give us about the firm in question.

Für jede Auskunft, die Sie uns über die betreffende Firma geben können, wären wir Ihnen dankbar.

We should be glad if you would give us some details / particulars / regarding / concerning . . .

Wir wären Ihnen dankbar, wenn Sie uns Näheres über . . . mitteilen könnten.

116

financial standing/financial status	finanzielle Lage, Vermögenslage
credit standing/credit status	Kreditwürdigkeit
ability to meet financial obligations	Zahlungsfähigkeit
turnover	Umsatz
business conduct/manner of dealing	Geschäftsgebaren
business methods	Geschäftsmethoden
reliability	Zuverlässigkeit

Do you think it would be reasonable/justifiable/in order/a fair risk/to allow them a credit of about...?

Ist Ihrer Ansicht nach ein Kredit in Höhe von etwa ... vertretbar?

To what figure do you think we could safely go?

Bis zu welchem Betrag könnten wir Ihrer Meinung nach ohne Risiko gehen?

Any other information you could supply would be appreciated.

Für jede weitere Auskunft, die Sie uns geben könnten, wären wir Ihnen dankbar.

c. Promising Confidential Treatment and Offering to Reciprocate Favours

Your reply will be treated as strictly confidential/in strict confidence/in absolute confidence.

Ihre Auskunft werden wir streng vertraulich behandeln.

You can rely on our treating your information with the utmost discretion/with the strictest discretion.

Sie können sich darauf verlassen, daß wir Ihre Auskunft mit größter Verschwiegenheit behandeln werden.

We shall always be glad to reciprocate/We shall be glad to reciprocate this favour at any time.

Zu Gegendiensten sind wir stets gern bereit.

If we can be of assistance to you in a similar case/If we can render you a similar service/, please let us know.

Wenn wir Ihnen einen ähnlichen Dienst erweisen können, so teilen Sie uns das bitte mit.

d. Favourable Information

The firm about which you inquire/The firm mentioned in your inquiry/has an excellent reputation.

Die von Ihnen genannte Firma genießt einen ausgezeichneten Ruf.

They are old-established traders who enjoy unquestionable confidence.

Es handelt sich um alteingesessene Kaufleute, die uneingeschränktes Vertrauen genießen.

They have considerable resources/considerable funds/a considerable amount of capital/at their disposal.

Sie verfügen über beträchtliche finanzielle Mittel/beträchtliches Kapital.

They have always met their obligations promptly/They have always been punctual in paying their bills.

Sie sind ihren Zahlungsverpflichtungen stets pünktlich nachgekommen.

They usually take advantage of cash discounts.

Sie zahlen meist unter Ausnutzung von Skonto.

They have been regular customers of ours for the past five years.

Seit 5 Jahren zählt die Firma zu unseren regelmäßigen Kunden.

Barney & Co. placed $ ... worth of business with us last year.

Die Firma Barney & Co. erteilte uns letztes Jahr Aufträge im Wert von $ ...

We think/believe/that you will not be taking any risk in granting them a credit up to ...

Wir glauben nicht, daß Sie irgendein Risiko eingehen, wenn Sie der Firma einen Kredit bis zu ... gewähren.

e. Unfavourable Information

In reply to your letter of ... we regret to inform you/we are sorry to inform you/ that we do not consider it advisable to grant any credit to the firm in question.

In Beantwortung Ihres Schreibens vom ... bedauern wir, Ihnen mitteilen zu müssen, daß es uns nicht ratsam erscheint, der betreffenden Firma Kredit zu gewähren.

We have learned from reliable sources/ We have it on good authority/that they are having financial difficulties.

Aus zuverlässiger Quelle haben wir erfahren, daß die Firma mit finanziellen Schwierigkeiten zu kämpfen hat.

They are reported to be in a precarious financial position.

Die Firma soll sich in einer schwierigen finanziellen Lage befinden.

Owing to the failure[1] of one of their customers they have suffered/sustained/ considerable losses.

Durch den Konkurs eines ihrer Kunden sind der Firma beträchtliche Verluste entstanden.

It seems/It appears/that the firm is insufficiently provided with capital/is undercapitalized.

Anscheinend verfügt die Firma nicht über genügend Kapital.

---

[1] *bankruptcy* is often referred to as *failure*

During the past six months they have been slow in paying their debts/there have been repeated delays in payment.	Seit den letzten 6 Monaten gehen die Zahlungen schleppend ein.

f. Requesting Confidential Treatment

May we ask that you treat this information as confidential.	Wir bitten um vertrauliche Behandlung dieser Auskunft.
This information is for your own use only and given without responsibility.	Diese Auskunft ist nur für Sie bestimmt und wird ohne jede Haftung erteilt.

4. Exercises

Please translate the following letters into English:

a. Erich Schwarz KG, München, an Fairfax & Co. Ltd., Oldham, Lancs. (England)

Die Firma Andrews & Baxter Ltd. in London hat sich um unsere Vertretung in Großbritannien beworben und Sie dabei als Referenz genannt. Bei Abschluß eines Vertretervertrages würden wir dieser Firma Konsignationswaren im Werte von ca. £5000 zur Verfügung stellen.

Wir wären Ihnen deshalb für eine möglichst genaue Auskunft über die Vermögenslage dieser Firma und den Umfang ihrer Geschäfte dankbar. Vor allem würde uns interessieren zu erfahren, ob sie Ihrer Ansicht nach in der Lage ist, den britischen Markt intensiv zu bearbeiten. Verfügt die Firma über gute Geschäftsverbindungen in ihrer Branche?

Wir versichern Ihnen, daß wir Ihre Auskunft als streng vertraulich und für Sie unverbindlich behandeln werden. Einen adressierten Umschlag sowie einen Internationalen Antwortschein legen wir diesem Schreiben bei.

Anlagen:
1. Adressierter Umschlag
2. Internationaler Antwortschein

b. Fries & Co., Bremen, an Brown-Anderson Co. Ltd., London

Die in Ihrem Schreiben vom 8. August erwähnte Firma ist uns seit längerer Zeit bekannt. Es handelt sich um ein gut fundiertes Außenhandelsunternehmen, das für eigene Rechnung und als Vertreter für einige namhafte ausländische Firmen tätig ist.

Die Inhaber sind tüchtige und zuverlässige Kaufleute, die über ausgedehnte Geschäftsverbindungen verfügen. Soweit uns bekannt ist, sind sie ihren Verbindlichkeiten stets prompt nachgekommen. Wir glauben daher, daß Sie den gewünschten Kredit ohne Bedenken gewähren können.

Wir bitten um vertrauliche Behandlung dieser Auskunft, für die wir keine Haftung übernehmen.

c. Hermann Koerner OHG, Bayreuth, an Baxter Engineering Company Ltd., Birmingham

Die in Ihrem Schreiben vom 20. Juni genannte Firma wurde erst vor 2 Jahren gegründet. Seit etwa 6 Monaten gehen die Zahlungen schleppend ein. Wir haben den Eindruck, daß die Firma mit großen Absatzschwierigkeiten zu kämpfen hat. Wie wir aus sicherer Quelle erfahren haben, hat die Firma jetzt eine Hypothek auf ihr Grundstück aufgenommen.

Unter diesen Umständen müssen wir Ihnen zur Vorsicht raten.

Wir bedauern, daß wir Ihnen keine bessere Auskunft erteilen können, und bitten um Verschwiegenheit.

Please draft letters in English from the following particulars:

d. Das Bremer Exporthaus Möller & Co. verhandelt wegen eines größeren Auftrags mit der International Trading Company Ltd. in Lagos (Nigeria). Diese Firma nannte u. a. Seymour & Smith Ltd. in London als Referenz.

Möller & Co. schreiben an diese Firma und bitten um Auskunft über die Kreditwürdigkeit, das Geschäftsgebaren und den Ruf der International Trading Company. Vor allem möchten sie wissen, ob es nach Ansicht der Londoner Firma vertretbar wäre, Waren im Werte von ca. 10 000 DM auf der Basis „Dokumente gegen Akzept" zu liefern. Für alle weiteren Hinweise, die die Londoner Firma evtl. geben könnte, wären Möller & Co. ebenfalls dankbar.

Möller & Co. legen ihrer Anfrage einen adressierten Umschlag und einen Internationalen Antwortschein bei. Sie versichern der Londoner Firma, daß sie die Auskunft mit aller Verschwiegenheit behandeln werden, und erklären sich zu Gegendiensten bereit.

e. Breese & Co. in Hannover erhalten von Knight & Co. Ltd., Manchester, eine Anfrage wegen der Firma Brockmann & Clasen, die sie als Referenz angegeben hat.

Sie teilen der anfragenden Firma mit, daß Brockmann & Clasen ein gut eingeführtes Export- und Import-Unternehmen ist, mit dem sie schon seit ca. 2 Jahren in Geschäftsverbindung stehen. Während dieser Zeit hat die Firma regelmäßig Aufträge erteilt. Die Zahlungen erfolgten stets pünktlich, meist unter Ausnutzung von Skonto. Nach den vorliegenden Informationen ist die finanzielle Lage des Unternehmens in jeder Hinsicht zufriedenstellend. Ein Kredit in Höhe von £500 scheint Breese & Co. daher vertretbar. Breese & Co. geben diese Auskunft nach bestem Wissen, aber ohne jede Verbindlichkeit.

f. Aufgabe im Anschluß an Brief f. auf S. 27

In ihrer Anfrage an Gerhardsen & Co. in Bremen gibt Sivaraman Stores Ltd. in Bombay u. a. John Thompson Ltd., Leeds, als Referenz an. (Mr. Thompson kennt Mr. Sivaraman persönlich!)

Entwerfen Sie das Schreiben, mit dem Gerhardsen & Co. Mr. Thompson von John Thompson Ltd. um Auskunft über die Sivaraman Stores Ltd. bitten.

Every Big Business Was Small Once [1]

A wholesaler in Louisiana once received an order for $12.35 worth of candy from the "Horsie Hollow Candy Shop" in a small town. As he had never heard of a firm with this name, he asked the New Orleans office of Dun & Bradstreet, the famous American mercantile agency, for a credit report. Dun & Bradstreet had no record of the firm either, so they instructed one of their reporters to investigate. $12.35 is a small sum, to be sure, but the point is that there was a new firm which was not yet on file—an intolerable state of affairs. The investigator turned in the following report:

"The Horsie Hollow Candy Shop is situated on a dirt road just off the main highway. The shop consists of a remodeled [2] turkey coop, valued at $35. A small but steady business is being done. The shop is run by two partners. Both are 11 years of age and unmarried. Their liquid assets amount to $13.25 in merchandise and cash. The owners have had two years' experience in selling cookies and lemonade. Their principal suppliers are their mothers, both of whom reported prompt payments, that is, strictly C.O.D. Although the owners are men of limited means, they have a high standing in the community."

The wholesaler was favourably impressed and sent the goods on his regular credit terms. The bill was paid promptly, and the wholesaler opened a new account in his books in the name of the Horsie Hollow Candy Shop.

[1] By courtesy of Dun & Bradstreet, Inc. and Dr. E. K. Fritschi
[2] *US for remodelled*

VIII. Delays in Delivery
Delays in Delivery and Non-Delivery—Missing Consignments

1. Introduction

Delays in Delivery and Non-Delivery. The buyer follows up his orders to make sure that the goods are delivered on time. If there is any delay in delivery, the buyer sends the seller a reminder or warns him that he will rescind the contract unless the goods are delivered within a certain period of time or by a certain date. (In many cases, the buyer sends a reminder—or even several reminders—before fixing a final deadline for delivery.)

Reminders and the allowance of additional time can, of course, be dispensed with if the buyer reserved the right to cancel his order in the case of any delay in delivery, or if it is quite obvious that the seller is not able or not willing to perform his contract.

Delays in delivery or non-delivery may result in losses for the buyer and lead to action for damages. Sometimes buyer and seller themselves, when entering into a contract, fix the amount of damages payable in the event of a breach of contract (*liquidated damages*).

If the proper performance of the contract is rendered impossible by acts of God (flood, lightning, earthquake, etc.) or other circumstances beyond the seller's control, the seller is not liable for any losses sustained by the buyer. (Many suppliers insert in their offers or sales notes a clause to the effect that they do not accept any liability in such cases.)

In his reply to a letter from a customer complaining of a delay in delivery, the supplier apologizes and explains the situation. However, if difficulties arise with regard to delivery, the supplier should not wait until he receives a reminder from the customer, but he should inform the customer of these difficulties as soon as they appear.

In any case the supplier should, if possible, tell the customer when he can expect delivery of the goods. He may send part of the goods and promise to deliver the balance later. In order to induce the customer to accept the goods when they are delivered at a later date, he may offer a price reduction or a similar concession. If the seller finds that he is unable to deliver the goods, he should ask the buyer to release him from the contract. It is better to seek a release than to commit a breach of contract and face the possibility of legal action.

Missing Consignments. Sometimes a customer complains of a delay in delivery, although the goods have been dispatched by the supplier and should already have arrived at their destination. In such cases, investigations have to be made. These investigations may reveal that the consignment has been delayed, misdirected or lost in transit. Occasionally it is also discovered that the consignment was overlooked by the customer, or that some other error has occurred.

122

2. Specimen Letters

a. English Company Reminds German Supplier of Delivery

Dear Sirs,

Our order No. 379 of 29th March, which you acknowledged on 4th April, calls for delivery of various kinds of photographic equipment.

We are in urgent need of the equipment specified in this order. Please let us know how soon we may expect this shipment to arrive in England. We would remind you that your acknowledgment states that the equipment will be delivered from stock, and we are wondering why there is such a long delay.

Yours faithfully,

---

b. British Representative of German Company Complains of Repeated Delays in Delivery

---

2nd July, 19 . .

Dear Sirs,

The long delays in the execution of our orders are causing us great concern.

From time to time we have contacted you and have been given various promises which we, on our part, have passed on to our customers. These delivery promises have in almost every instance been broken by you, with the result that our customers now no longer believe any promise we make to them.

We are now faced with cancellations of orders by many of our customers. Consequently, we shall have to put your machines into our stock when they finally arrive here in England, as we shall no longer have any customers for them.

The latest cancellation is that by Sheldon & Co., Birmingham, a firm which bought over £4,000 worth of equipment last year. The date of their order is the 10th March, and when you acknowledged it on the 23rd March you promised to send the machines "within a few weeks."

While we are on the subject of delivery dates, we also have to remind you of the spare parts we ordered on the 5th May. As these parts have not yet arrived, we have had to postpone several urgent repairs, a fact which has added to our customers' annoyance.

You will understand that we are very unhappy over this most unpleasant state of affairs, and we only hope you will realize that this loss of confidence on the part of our customers will have very serious consequences for your company as well as ours.

Yours faithfully,
NEWMAN & CO. Ltd.

Andrew D. Newman
Managing Director

---

c. Buyer Gives Warning of Cancellation

Dear Sirs,

On the 20th March we placed an order with you for 500 yds. of Harris Tweed, pointing out at that time that prompt delivery was essential. In the meantime, almost three weeks have passed, and we are still without the material.

As the tweed is urgently required for an export shipment, we shall be compelled to cancel our order if the consignment is not received here by the 15th April.

Yours faithfully,

---

d. Buyer Threatens to Claim Damages

Dear Sirs,

On the 10th May we ordered central heating radiators from you for a building currently under construction. We pointed out to your representative that the radiators were urgently needed by the 5th June, and he promised to see to prompt delivery.

We regret to say that this promise was not kept, a fact which is causing us considerable inconvenience. You will understand that, under these circumstances, your delay gives us the right to claim damages. We are reluctant to take such a step, however, and are prepared to wait for the radiators until the end of this week.

We trust that you will make every effort to meet this deadline and thus save yourselves and us a great deal of trouble and annoyance.

Yours faithfully,

---

e. Supplier Apologizes for Delay in Delivery

Dear Sirs,

We have received your letter of March 13th and offer our apologies for the delay in the execution of your order.

Unfortunately this order was overlooked in the pressure of business, but we are pleased to say that the goods are now ready for dispatch. Shipment will be effected by M/V "Norfolk" on April 29th, and the consignment should reach you about May 12th.

We hope this delay has not caused you any serious inconvenience and assure you that every effort will be made in future to ensure prompt delivery of your orders.

Yours faithfully,

f. Supplier Advises Customer of Delay by Strike

Gentlemen:

Unfortunately we will not be able to fill your order of August 5 within two weeks, as agreed in the contract.

Last week a strike was called by the Metal Workers' Union, and it is completely uncertain how long it will last. This unforeseen occurrence has upset our production schedule, and we cannot, at the present stage, make any definite promise with regard to delivery.

We will, however, keep you posted on all further developments, and assure you that we will do everything to speed up the completion of your order as soon as the strike is terminated.

Yours very truly,

g. Delay in Departure of Vessel

Dear Sirs,

We regret having to inform you that the departure of the vessel by which we have arranged shipment of your recent order, and which had originally been scheduled to sail o/a[1] 15th December, was delayed owing to bad weather. This vessel (S.S. "Martha") is now reported to sail from Southampton o/a 29th December.

We regret this delay very much, on which, however, we have no influence.

Yours faithfully,

---

[1] on or about

h. Supplier Asks to Be Released from Contract

Gentlemen:

We are very sorry that we will not be able to supply the heavy-duty compressors you ordered on September 10.

Last week a fire broke out in our plant which destroyed several buildings, including our warehouse. We have cleared away the debris, but it will probably be several months before we can resume production. Under these circumstances we are compelled to ask you to release us from the contract.

We are sure you will understand the difficulty of our situation, which is due to circumstances beyond our control. You will hear from us as soon as we are in a position to serve you again.

Yours very truly,

---

i. Parcel Missing

Dear Sirs,

We were very much surprised to learn from your letter of the 15th October that the parts you ordered on the 10th September have not yet arrived. These parts were dispatched by parcel post on the 27th September and should have reached you long ago.

We cannot understand this delay and would suggest that you ask the postal authorities to make investigations concerning the missing parcel.

Yours faithfully,

---

3. Terms and Phrases

a. Reminders and Complaints Concerning Delays in Delivery

We expressly stated in our order that the goods must reach us not later than . . .

Wir haben in unserer Bestellung ausdrücklich darauf hingewiesen, daß die Waren bis spätestens . . . hier eintreffen müssen.

Your delay in delivery places us in a difficult position.

Ihr Lieferverzug bringt uns in eine schwierige Lage.

Would you be good enough to look into the matter and advise us when the goods can be shipped.

Wir bitten Sie, der Sache nachzugehen und uns mitzuteilen, wann die Waren verschifft werden können.

We must have your definite promise that the goods will be dispatched by the end of next week.

Wir erwarten Ihre definitive Zusage, daß der Versand der Waren bis Ende der nächsten Woche erfolgt.

We must insist on your informing us by telegram of the earliest possible date of delivery.

Wir müssen darauf bestehen, daß Sie uns telegrafisch das frühest mögliche Lieferdatum mitteilen.

We must ask you to give top priority to all our outstanding orders.

Wir müssen Sie bitten, alle unsere noch nicht ausgeführten Bestellungen als vorrangig zu behandeln.

. . . to hasten delivery, as our import licence will expire on . . .

. . . die Lieferung zu beschleunigen, da unsere Importlizenz am . . . ausläuft.

Should you fail to deliver the goods by . . ., we shall be compelled to cancel the order.

Falls Sie die Waren nicht bis zum . . . liefern, sehen wir uns gezwungen, die Bestellung zu widerrufen.

. . . to obtain the goods from another supplier.

. . . die Waren anderweitig zu beschaffen.

. . . to hold you liable for any losses incurred.

. . . Sie für alle uns entstehenden Verluste haftbar zu machen.

b. Seller's Reply

We apologize for the delay and shall do our utmost to expedite delivery.

Wir entschuldigen uns für die Verzögerung und werden unser möglichstes tun, um die Lieferung zu beschleunigen.

We greatly regret the delay, which is due to circumstances beyond our control.

Die Verzögerung, die auf höhere Gewalt zurückzuführen ist, bedauern wir sehr.

On receipt of your letter we immediately got in touch with the shipping company, and they informed us that M.V. "Martha" was held up due to engine trouble.

Sofort nach Eingang Ihres Schreibens setzten wir uns mit der Reederei in Verbindung und erfuhren von dieser, daß M/S „Martha" wegen eines Maschinendefekts nicht auslaufen konnte.

The delay is due to the exceptional demand during the past few months.

Die Verzögerung ist auf die ungewöhnlich große Nachfrage während der letzten Monate zurückzuführen.

The acute shortage of qualified labour makes it increasingly difficult for us to keep pace with the rush of orders.

Der akute Mangel an qualifizierten Arbeitskräften macht es für uns immer schwieriger, mit der großen Zahl der eingehenden Aufträge Schritt zu halten.

Our forwarding agent has been unable to book the necessary shipping space at an earlier date.

Unser Spediteur konnte den benötigten Schiffsraum nicht zu einem früheren Zeitpunkt buchen.

We would ask you to accept our apologies for the inconvenience caused and hope that you will give us an opportunity to regain your confidence.

Wir möchten Sie bitten, die Ihnen entstandenen Unannehmlichkeiten zu entschuldigen, und hoffen, daß Sie uns Gelegenheit geben werden, Ihr Vertrauen wiederzugewinnen.

. . . to renew our cordial relations.

. . . unsere freundschaftlichen Geschäftsbeziehungen zu erneuern.

c. Seller Informs Buyer of Delay

We regret having to advise you of a delay in the execution of your order.

Wir bedauern, Ihnen mitteilen zu müssen, daß sich die Ausführung Ihres Auftrags verzögern wird.

We are sorry that a slight delay will be unavoidable/inevitable.

Eine geringfügige Verzögerung ist leider unvermeidlich.

Due to an unauthorized strike in our factory, it will be impossible to deliver the goods within the time agreed upon.

Wegen eines wilden Streiks in unserer Fabrik wird es nicht möglich sein, die Waren innerhalb der vereinbarten Frist zu liefern.

Owing to a delay in the delivery of raw materials, we shall probably be unable to complete your order before the end of May.	Wegen Verzögerung bei der Lieferung von Rohmaterial wird es uns voraussichtlich nicht möglich sein, Ihren Auftrag vor Ende Mai fertigzustellen.

4. Exercises

Please translate the following letters into English:

a. Walter Neubert OHG, Garmisch, an Blakeley & Co. Ltd., Knitting Mills, Leeds

Am 15. Juli bestellten wir bei Ihrem deutschen Vertreter, Herrn Bergmann, lt. Bestellschein Nr. A-23/280 Wollpullover und Wollsocken.

Wir haben damals Ihren Vertreter ausdrücklich darauf aufmerksam gemacht, daß die Ware bis Anfang Oktober in unserem Besitz sein muß. Herr Bergmann sagte uns die Einhaltung dieses Termins zu und setzte einen entsprechenden Vermerk auf den Bestellschein.

Heute ist bereits der 20. Oktober, und wir haben noch immer keine Versandanzeige von Ihnen erhalten. Bitte teilen Sie uns telegrafisch mit, wann wir mit der Ankunft der Waren rechnen können.

Wir benötigen die Sendung dringend, da die Nachfrage nach Wollsachen wegen des kalten Wetters bereits eingesetzt hat. Auch im Hinblick auf das bevorstehende Weihnachtsgeschäft müssen wir auf umgehender Lieferung bestehen.

b. Maschinenfabrik Müller GmbH, Ingolstadt, an Torrington Company Ltd., London

Vor ca. 3 Wochen sandten Sie uns die anläßlich der letzten Hannover-Messe bei Ihnen bestellte Bohrmaschine (*drilling machine*). Leider haben Sie jedoch den zum Antrieb erforderlichen Elektromotor nicht mitgeliefert.

Obwohl wir die Maschine für unseren Betrieb dringend benötigen, steht sie jetzt unbenutzt in unserem Lager, da wir auf die Lieferung des von Ihnen vorgesehenen Spezialmotors angewiesen sind.

Bei unserem Besuch auf der Messe haben wir Ihren Verkaufsleiter, Mr. Hardie, ausdrücklich darauf hingewiesen, daß unsere Bestellung nur unter der Voraussetzung pünktlicher Lieferung erteilt werde. Mr. Hardie sagte uns die Lieferung der kompletten Maschine innerhalb von 4 Wochen verbindlich zu. Sie werden daher unsere Enttäuschung darüber verstehen, daß die Maschine jetzt mehr als 2 Monate nach Auftragserteilung immer noch nicht einsatzbereit ist.

Wir setzen Ihnen nunmehr eine Nachfrist bis zum Ende dieses Monats. Sollten wir bis dahin nicht im Besitze des Motors sein, lehnen wir die Annahme ab und senden Ihnen die bereits gelieferte Maschine zu Ihren Lasten zurück. Die geleistete Anzahlung in Höhe von . . . bitten wir Sie in diesem Falle auf unser Konto (No. 633) bei der Dresdner Bank, Filiale Ingolstadt, zu überweisen.

c. Heinrich Seitz KG, Krefeld, an George & Frank Ltd., London

Wir bedauern, daß es uns nicht möglich ist, Ihren Auftrag vom 8. Mai fristgemäß auszuführen. Die Nachfrage nach unseren Erzeugnissen ist z. Z. so groß, daß wir einen beträchtlichen Auftragsrückstand haben.

Sie können sich jedoch darauf verlassen, daß wir alles tun werden, um mit der zunehmenden Anzahl von Aufträgen Schritt zu halten. Der Versand der von Ihnen bestellten Regelventile (*control valves*) kann voraussichtlich in ca. 14 Tagen erfolgen.

Wir bitten Sie, diese Verzögerung zu entschuldigen, und hoffen, daß sie Ihnen keine größeren Unannehmlichkeiten verursacht.

Please draft letters in English from the following particulars:

d. Die Lehmann AG, Berlin, kaufte vor einiger Zeit 6 Mikrowellen-Öfen von der Microwave Corporation, Newark, N.J. (USA).

Als Mr. Sanders von der Microwave Corporation letzten Monat die Berliner Firma besuchte, bat ihn diese zu veranlassen, daß ihr umgehend einige Ersatzteile für die Öfen zugeschickt würden. Mr. Sanders, der einige Tage später in die Vereinigten Staaten zurückflog, versprach, selbst für den Versand der Teile zu sorgen.

Inzwischen sind 4 Wochen vergangen, ohne daß die Lehmann AG die Ersatzteile erhalten hat. Da von den Öfen bereits 3 ausgefallen sind, sandte sie der amerikanischen Firma heute folgendes Telegramm:

NEED URGENTLY 12 SPINDLES NO. 64663   6 TURNTABLES NO. 38228
12 FUSES NO. 74763 FOR MICROWAVE OVENS SHIP AIRMAIL

Die Lehmann AG bestätigt dieses Telegramm und bittet die Microwave Corporation nochmals dringend, die an sich geringfügigen Teile, die aber in der Bundesrepublik nicht zu bekommen sind, so bald wie möglich zu liefern, damit die defekten Geräte repariert werden können und bei Auftreten weiterer Schäden Ersatzteile zur Verfügung stehen.

e. Am 10. Oktober 19 . . bestellten Kelber & Messner in München 200 elektrische Rasenmäher (*electric lawn mowers*) von Burdick & Sons Ltd., London, wobei Lieferung bis Anfang März verbindlich zugesagt wurde.

Am 15. März schrieben Kelber & Messner an die englische Firma und erinnerten sie an die fällige Lieferung. Daraufhin erhielten sie einen Anruf von Mr. Brockman, dem Verkaufsleiter von Burdick & Sons Ltd., der versprach, dafür zu sorgen, daß die bestellten Rasenmäher bis spätestens Mitte April geliefert werden. Bis heute — 25. April — haben Kelber & Messner jedoch nichts mehr von der englischen Firma gehört. Sie wenden sich nochmals an Burdick & Sons Ltd. und beschweren sich in ziemlich scharfem Ton über den Lieferungsverzug, der für sie bereits Geschäftsausfälle zur Folge gehabt hat. Mehrere Kunden wollten nicht mehr länger warten und haben ihre Rasenmäher inzwischen bei der Konkurrenz gekauft. Kelber & Messner erwähnen ausdrücklich, daß sie frühzeitig bestellt haben, um die Rasenmäher zu Beginn des Frühjahrs zur Verfügung zu haben. Burdick & Sons Ltd. haben zweimal ein gegebenes Lieferungsversprechen nicht eingehalten. Kelber & Messner teilen daher mit, daß sie sich gezwungen sehen, die englische Firma für alle entstehenden Folgen verantwortlich zu machen, wenn die Sendung nicht bis Ende Mai in München eintrifft.

f. Die Firma Krause & Co. in Herne hat am 28. 9. Schleifbänder (*sanding belts*) von der Abrasive Products Company Ltd. in Manchester bestellt. Als Lieferzeit waren 4 Wochen vereinbart. Trotz der Mahnung vom 2. 11. ist die Lieferung jedoch bis heute (5. 12.) nicht erfolgt. Da inzwischen auch die Nachfrist verstrichen ist, bitten Krause & Co., ihren Auftrag zu streichen, und verzichten auf Lieferung.

Die Firma war bisher mit den englischen Schleifbändern sehr zufrieden und bedauert, daß sie sich zu einem solchen Schritt genötigt sieht. Da die Schleifbänder jedoch dringend in der Produktion benötigt wurden, blieb keine Wahl, als sie anderweitig zu beschaffen. Abschließend erwähnen Krause & Co., daß die Nichteinhaltung des Lieferversprechens durch die englische Firma ihnen große Unannehmlichkeiten verursacht hat.

g. Aufgabe im Anschluß an Brief b. auf S. 123/124

Auf das Schreiben ihres Vertreters, der Firma Newman & Co., Ltd., London, erklärt die Maschinenfabrik AG, München, daß es ihr der Mangel an Arbeitskräften und die Arbeitszeitverkürzungen sehr schwer machen, ihren Lieferverpflichtungen so prompt nachzukommen, wie sie das gerne möchte. Sie wird jedoch die Auslandsaufträge bevorzugt ausführen und hofft, die noch ausstehenden Lieferungen an die englischen Kunden in den nächsten 14 Tagen vornehmen zu können.

Die Maschinen für Sheldon & Co., Birmingham, sind in ca. 5 Tagen versandbereit. Die Maschinenfabrik wird sich direkt an den Kunden wenden und versuchen, ihn zur Annahme der Maschinen zu veranlassen.

Die reklamierten Ersatzteile wurden am 24. Mai in 2 Kisten mit der Bahn abgesandt und müßten bereits in London angekommen sein. Vielleicht sollte sich die Firma Newman mit der englischen Eisenbahnverwaltung in Verbindung setzen und Nachforschun-

gen über den Verbleib der Sendung anstellen lassen. Eine Fotokopie des Frachtbrief-
doppels legt die Maschinenfabrik ihrem Schreiben bei.

Um das leidige Problem der langen Lieferzeiten aus der Welt zu schaffen, beabsichtigt
die Maschinenfabrik ihre Kapazität durch Rationalisierung und teilweise Automatisie-
rung zu erhöhen. Außerdem will sie in Irland einen Zweigbetrieb errichten, der dann
vor allem den englischen Markt versorgen könnte.

Die Maschinenfabrik ist sich der Schwierigkeiten bewußt, denen sich ihr englischer Vertreter gegenübersieht, versichert ihm aber, daß von ihrer Seite aus alles getan wird, um
diese Schwierigkeiten zu überwinden.

h. Die Transformatorenfabrik Hermann & Söhne in München erhält am 29. 11. eine Bestellung von der International Trading Company in Lagos. Sofort nach der Akkreditiv-
eröffnung durch die nigerianische Firma nimmt die Transformatorenfabrik die Ausführung des Auftrags in Angriff. Anfangs Januar erfährt sie jedoch von ihrem Lieferanten
für Transformatorenblech (*transformer lamination stock*), daß eine für Mitte Januar
zugesagte Lieferung wegen technischer Schwierigkeiten erst Anfang Februar erfolgen
kann. Da dies die termingerechte Auslieferung der Transformatoren in Frage stellt,
sieht sich die Transformatorenfabrik gezwungen, an die International Trading Company mit der Bitte heranzutreten, die Verlängerung des Akkreditivs bis Ende April zu
veranlassen.

Sorry, Too Late

*A New York maternity shop received this note: "Dear Sirs: You have not yet
delivered the maternity dress I ordered. Please cancel the order. My delivery was faster
than yours."*

IX. Complaints and Adjustments
Complaints Concering Goods Delivered and Adjustment of Complaints

1. Introduction

Complaints Concerning Goods Delivered. A complaint is made by the buyer if the wrong goods have been delivered, if the goods received are defective or damaged, if the quantity is not right, etc.

The *letter of complaint* (or: *claim letter*) must indicate clearly what is wrong. The seller cannot take any action unless he is informed exactly of the nature of the defect, extent of the damage, etc. The complaint should also contain such details as order number, date of order, or arrival date, to enable the seller to identify the consignment in question. The buyer usually requests a particular adjustment, but he may also ask the seller to make suggestions as to how the matter could be settled.

If the buyer has received the wrong goods, goods that are unsalable or otherwise of no use to him, he is entitled to reject them. Should he still be interested in the delivery of the proper goods, he demands a replacement.

In the case of minor defects in the goods delivered, the buyer will keep them but claim a reduction in price (*allowance*). Many small defects can be remedied by repair, or by the replacement of parts.

Sometimes the seller's failure to supply the goods as provided for in the contract gives rise to an action for damages.

In many trades it is customary for the seller or manufacturer to offer the buyer a written *guarantee* (or: *warranty*). Under the terms of his guarantee, the manufacturer undertakes to replace or repair, free of charge, any article which may prove defective during the guarantee period, provided the defect is due to faulty material or workmanship.

Adjustment of Complaints. When a complaint is received from a customer, the supplier investigates the matter. If a decision cannot be made immediately, the supplier should write a brief acknowledgment informing the customer that his letter is receiving attention.

Depending on the circumstances, the seller may grant the buyer's claim, refuse it, or offer a compromise.

If the seller finds that he is to blame, he should frankly admit his fault, offer his apologies, and make a prompt adjustment.

Should it turn out that the buyer himself is responsible for the defect, the seller will, as a rule, refuse buyer's claim. Sometimes, however, in such cases, the claim is granted, or a compromise is made, in the interest of good business. The action taken depends on seller's adjustment policy, the type of customer concerned, and the circumstances of the particular case. Unfounded complaints made by customers who try to take advantage of the supplier are, of course, always refused.

Damage or loss in transit is a matter that has to be taken up with the carrier or the insurance company. If the carrier is liable for the damage or loss, a claim is entered with the carrier. Insurance companies pay compensation in the case of accidents in transit regardless of whether the carrier or any other third person is liable, but they require the insured to assign to them any claims he may have against third parties.

In order to help his customer, the supplier is often prepared to send a replacement for the damaged or lost goods pending the settlement of a claim against an insurance company or a carrier.

Modern businessmen recognize the value of a satisfied customer. They do not regard complaints as a nuisance, but as a welcome opportunity to build goodwill. Many firms actually encourage customers to inform them whenever they are not completely satisfied with the goods or service received.

Sometimes a buyer's complaint gives rise to a dispute. This is the case, for example, if the buyer claims that the quality of the goods is not according to contract and the seller claims that it is. Should the parties be unable to settle the dispute themselves, they have to refer the matter to a court of arbitration or to a court of law. As a rule, businessmen try to avoid litigation, which is both costly and time-consuming, and therefore agree, when entering into a contract, that disputes arising from the contract are to be settled by arbitration, whereby it is understood that they will both accept the arbitrator's decision as final.

2. Specimen Letters

a. American Company Complains About Drive Belts of Sewing Machines

---

Siehl & Co. KG
Karlsruhe, Germany

Gentlemen:

In execution of our order of January 24 you sent us ten industrial sewing machines for our factory.

We have been very much surprised to find that the drive belts for these machines, which are made of some sort of plastic material, tend to disintegrate within a short time. This has rendered the machines completely useless to us and has caused us considerable inconvenience.

We are returning the ten defective belts by airmail and request you to replace them free of charge, as soon as possible.

134

Please let us have your comments regarding this matter. We hope that a repetition of the trouble can be avoided in the future.

Yours very truly,
Elite Garment Company

---

b. Canadian Agent of German Manufacturer of Cameras Complains About Defective Shutters

---

Baumann & Schmitt
Munich, Germany

Gentlemen:

Recently we have received several complaints from customers who state that the shutters in your cameras do not function properly.

You will certainly understand that the dissatisfaction of our customers with your products is a matter of great concern to us, as it might cause a decline in sales. Since the prices of German cameras are higher than those of comparable American products, we have always emphasized in our advertising the excellent workmanship and dependability of the German cameras. If they lose this reputation, it will be very difficult for us to maintain our present position on the market.

As this matter is very urgent, we hope to receive your comments by return mail.

Very truly yours,
Campbell & Co. Ltd.

---

c. London Agent of German Chemical Company Complains About Samples Damaged in Transit

---

Neckar Chemie AG
Mannheim, Germany

Dear Sirs,

We refer to our letter of 16th November, regarding the inquiry from Mr. John Buckley of the Lenham Chemical Company Ltd., London, and regret to advise you that the samples of catalysts you submitted arrived in a badly damaged condition, with the tins broken and the contents mixed together.

Unfortunately it is not possible for the Lenham Chemical Company to make use of this delivery, and we hope you will kindly arrange for further samples of Catalysts 106, 216 and 312 to be dispatched immediately.

We are wondering whether it would not be convenient for you to send the samples to our address, in which case we will ensure that they are immediately forwarded to the Lenham Chemical Company. But we will, of course, leave this entirely to your own discretion.

Yours faithfully,
Alford & Co. Ltd.

---

d. Retailer Rejects Surplus

Dear Sirs,

Today we have received, at our Quaker Street Warehouse, 1,000 tins of Premium Brand Plum Pudding instead of the 100 tins we ordered on 18th April.

We immediately checked our copy of the order and found that it states the correct quantity. It seems, therefore, that an error occurred in the execution of our order.

As we cannot sell such a large quantity of tinned Plum Pudding, we are compelled to place the surplus of 900 tins at your disposal and await your instructions.

Yours faithfully,

---

e. Supplier at Fault—Claim Granted

Dear Sirs,

Thank you for your letter of the 12th April, in which you included a cutting of the cloth you received from us some days ago.

You are quite right. The cloth is not of the quality you ordered; we sent you a thinner material by mistake. As requested, we are sending you Credit Note No. 8773 to adjust the difference in price.

We offer our sincere apologies for this oversight and hope that the matter has now been settled to your complete satisfaction.

Yours faithfully,

Encl.

---

f. Customer at Fault—Claim Refused

Dear Mr. Tower:

We have received your letter of May 19 and the Slumbertone Clock-Radio which you want us to repair free of charge under the terms of our guarantee.

Our Repair Department has carefully checked the clock-radio and reports that it has apparently been tampered with, as two tubes and the loudspeaker are damaged.

Since our guarantee covers only faulty material and workmanship, we cannot assume the repair costs ourselves. However, we would charge you only $10. If you want us to go ahead with the work at this price, please let us know at once, and we shall return your clock-radio in perfect working condition in about three to four days.

Yours sincerely,

---

g. Customer at Fault—Claim Granted

Dear Mr. Clark:

We have examined the Britebeam Flashlight you returned to us a few days ago, and have found that it was damaged by a leaky battery.

Our offer to send a new flashlight free if our batteries leak or damage your flashlight applies only to armor [1]-clad batteries. The batteries in your flashlight were paper-clad batteries which, although having a moisture-resistant paper case, are not leakproof. We cannot, therefore, be responsible for any damage caused to a flashlight by paper-clad batteries. However, in order to accommodate you, we are sending you a new Britebeam Flashlight complete with three leakproof batteries.

If you use leakproof batteries all the time, your new flashlight will give you the same dependable service that has made Britebeam Flashlights so famous all over the world.

Yours very truly,

---

[1] *US for* armour

h. Suggesting Compromise

Gentlemen:[1]

We are glad that you notified us immediately of the mistake in the letterheads which we forwarded to you on October 15.

Another thousand are being printed with the correct letterhead, and we will forward them to you tomorrow by special delivery in order that you may not be inconvenienced by any further delay.

In looking over our records, we find that the proof of the letterhead was O.K.'d by your Mr. Black. Apparently he also overlooked the misspelling of the street name.

Of course, we are standing the expense of running the extra number, but since the mistake was only partly ours, we think that it would be only fair for you to pay for the additional stock required. Another thousand sheets of this same grade of paper would cost $4.45.

We believe you will agree that this is a fair way of handling the matter, and we shall be looking forward to hearing from you.

Yours very truly,

---

[1] By courtesy of Harper & Row, Publishers, *Business Letters*

i. Damage in Transit

Dear Sirs,

We are sorry to hear that 58 jars of our most recent shipment of McMuir Marmalade were broken when they arrived in Hamburg. Your order was properly packed and shipped in good condition, as evidenced by the clean bill of lading issued by the shipping company. The damage must therefore have occurred in transit.

We are sending you today a replacement for the broken jars. Please let us have the survey report made out by Lloyd's Agent in Hamburg, so that we can report the damage to the insurance company.

We hope that the new consignment will arrive safely and in good time.

Yours faithfully,

---

k. Motorcar Dealer Invites Complaints

Dear Mr. Moore:

Have we done anything wrong?

The last time you had your Volkswagen in for service was ten months ago. And although we sent you two reminders that your VW was due for a check-up, you haven't been back since.

We're beginning to think you're avoiding us.

If you have a complaint about our service, please tell us what it is. We'll do everything possible to give you satisfaction.

If you were treated discourteously, we owe you an apology.

If you found an error in our billing, we owe you some money.

If you can show us where our service has been less than what it should be, we'll make good.

Please use the enclosed postage-free reply card to tell us why you haven't been in. We can fix any Volkswagen ever made so there's no reason why we can't patch this up.

Sincerely,
Fielding Motors Inc.

Encl.

The reply card enclosed with the previous letter is shown below:

Gentlemen:

I haven't been in to have my VW serviced because
☐ I've moved out of the area.
☐ I'm going to a VW dealer more conveniently
located to me.
(Please explain any of the following reasons in detail.)
☐ Discourteous treatment _____

_____

_____

☐ Unsatisfactory repairs _____

_____

_____

☐ Car not ready when promised _____

_____

_____

☐ Actual cost higher than estimate _____

_____

_____

☐ Other _____

_____

_____

Name _____
(Please Print)
Address _____
City _____

1. Guarantee Clause

Warranty

The Company warrants each machine for a period of six months from the date of delivery. Should any parts prove defective within this period, they should be returned to the Company's Works at . . ., carriage paid. The Company will examine such parts carefully and, if satisfied that the defect is due to faulty material or workmanship, will repair the defective parts or supply new ones, free of charge.

3. Terms and Phrases

a. Making Complaints

We are sorry to tell you that your last consignment has not turned out to our satisfaction.

Zu unserem Bedauern müssen wir Ihnen mitteilen, daß Ihre letzte Sendung nicht zu unserer Zufriedenheit ausgefallen ist.

Upon opening the case, which showed no signs of damage from the outside, we discovered that 25 plates were broken.

Beim Öffnen der Kiste, die äußerlich keine Anzeichen von Beschädigungen aufwies, entdeckten wir, daß 25 Teller zerbrochen waren.

We have noticed a shortage in weight of . . .

Wir haben ein Fehlgewicht von . . . festgestellt.

Part of the goods have been damaged in transit/during transport.

Ein Teil der Waren ist auf dem Transport beschädigt worden.

The damage seems to have been caused by inadequate packing.

Es scheint, daß der Schaden auf ungenügende Verpackung zurückzuführen ist.

The samples taken from each of the three bags will show you that my claim is justified.

Die jedem der 3 Säcke entnommenen Proben werden Sie davon überzeugen, daß meine Beschwerde berechtigt ist.

We have no use for the poor quality you sent us.

Wir haben für die schlechte Qualität, die Sie uns sandten, keine Verwendung.

We place the faulty goods at your disposal.

Wir stellen Ihnen die mangelhaften Waren zur Verfügung.

We are holding the shipment pending the receipt of your instructions.

Wir werden die Sendung bei uns aufbewahren, bis wir Ihre Anweisungen erhalten.

We are returning the blouse for your inspection.

Wir senden Ihnen die Bluse zur Prüfung ein.

We are prepared to keep the goods if you reduce the price by 20 %.

Wir sind bereit, die Waren zu behalten, wenn Sie uns eine Preisermäßigung von 20 % gewähren.

We should be glad to hear of the allowance you are prepared to make.

Bitte teilen Sie uns die Höhe des Preisnachlasses mit, den Sie uns zu gewähren bereit sind.

Please send us replacements for these goods as soon as possible.

Bitte senden Sie uns so bald wie möglich Ersatz für diese Waren.

Please let us know what you intend to do in this matter.

Bitte teilen Sie uns mit, was Sie in dieser Sache zu tun gedenken.

This has been a matter of great annoyance to me.

Diese Angelegenheit hat mir viel Verdruß bereitet.

We expect you to devote more care to the execution of our orders in future.

Wir erwarten, daß Sie unsere Bestellungen in Zukunft mit größerer Sorgfalt ausführen werden.

Your efforts to avoid similar occurrences in the future will be appreciated.

Wir würden es begrüßen, wenn Sie sich bemühten, ähnliche Vorkommnisse in Zukunft zu vermeiden.

b. Granting Claims

Thank you for writing us about your experience with . . .

Wir sind Ihnen dankbar, daß Sie uns über Ihre Erfahrungen mit . . . berichtet haben.

. . . for calling this error to our attention.

. . . daß Sie uns auf dieses Versehen aufmerksam gemacht haben.

We are sorry to learn from your letter of . . . that one of our transistor radios, which you bought several months ago, has ceased to operate.

Zu unserem Bedauern ersehen wir aus Ihrem Schreiben vom . . ., daß einer unserer Transistor-Empfänger, die Sie vor einigen Monaten gekauft haben, nicht mehr funktioniert.

We are prepared to exchange the goods for those of another quality.

Wir sind bereit, die Waren gegen solche einer anderen Qualität umzutauschen.

A new consignment is being rushed to you today.

We are sending you ... to replace the goods mentioned in your letter of ...

Please return the goods at our expense for credit.

Enclosed you will find cheque for ..., representing a refund on the shirts you recently returned to us.

We shall enter a claim with the railway so that you will not be troubled further.

We are anxious to settle the matter to your entire satisfaction.

We trust that the arrangement suggested will meet with your approval.

Please accept our apologies for the inconvenience caused you by this oversight.

We shall take all possible steps to ensure that such a mistake is not made again.

Eine neue Sendung geht Ihnen heute auf schnellstem Wege zu.

Wir senden Ihnen ... als Ersatz für die in Ihrem Schreiben vom ... erwähnten Waren.

Bitte senden Sie die Waren auf unsere Kosten gegen Gutschrift zurück.

Anbei erhalten Sie einen Scheck über ... als Rückerstattung für die kürzlich zurückgesandten Hemden.

Um Ihnen weitere Mühe zu ersparen, werden wir den Schaden der Bahn melden.

Es liegt uns sehr viel daran, die Angelegenheit zu Ihrer vollen Zufriedenheit zu regeln.

Wir hoffen, daß die vorgeschlagene Regelung Ihre Zustimmung findet.

Wir bitten Sie, die Unannehmlichkeiten, die Ihnen durch dieses Versehen entstanden sind, zu entschuldigen.

Wir werden alles tun, damit ein solcher Fehler nicht wieder vorkommt.

c. Refusing Claims, Compromise, etc.

Since the inspection did not reveal any faulty material or workmanship, we feel that we cannot make the adjustment you request.

We regret that we cannot accept the return of the goods in this case.

You will agree that under these circumstances we cannot be made responsible for the loss.

Da die Prüfung keine Material- oder Verarbeitungsfehler ergab, sehen wir uns nicht in der Lage, die Angelegenheit Ihrem Wunsche gemäß zu regeln.

Wir bedauern, daß wir in diesem Fall die Waren nicht zurücknehmen können.

Sie werden zugeben müssen, daß wir unter diesen Umständen für den Verlust nicht verantwortlich gemacht werden können.

We cannot assume any liability in this case.

In diesem Falle können wir keine Haftung übernehmen.

We would suggest that you report the damage to the insurance company.

Wir möchten vorschlagen, daß Sie den Schaden der Versicherungsgesellschaft melden.

If you follow our operating instructions, we are confident that the machine will give satisfactory service.

Wenn Sie unsere Betriebsanleitung beachten, glauben wir bestimmt, daß die Maschine zu Ihrer Zufriedenheit arbeiten wird.

Although the guarantee period has already expired, we are willing to accommodate you and make the necessary repairs free of charge.

Obwohl die Garantiezeit bereits abgelaufen ist, sind wir bereit, Ihnen entgegenzukommen und die notwendigen Reparaturen kostenlos durchzuführen.

To satisfy both parties, we suggest that we share the expenses.

Um beide Teile zufriedenzustellen, schlagen wir vor, daß wir uns in die Kosten teilen.

4. Exercises

Please translate the following letters into English:

a. Müller & Co., Lübeck, an Thomas & Marsh, Stoke-on-Trent, Staffs. (England)

Die am 30. 8. bestellte Sendung Porzellanwaren kam gestern endlich mit M/S „Cynthia" an.

Es stellte sich jedoch heraus, daß statt der auf der Rechnung aufgeführten 15 Kisten nur 13 geliefert wurden. Nach einem Vermerk auf dem Konnossement sind die Kisten Nr. 8 und 11 nicht zur Verladung gekommen. Außerdem wurde beim Auspacken der Sendung festgestellt, daß ein Teil des Inhalts der Kisten 6, 7 und 9 während des Transports beschädigt wurde, da das Porzellan nicht sorgfältig genug verpackt war.

Wir müssen Sie darauf aufmerksam machen, daß wir mit der Ausführung unseres Auftrags äußerst unzufrieden sind. Erstens wurde die in Ihrer Auftragsbestätigung genannte Lieferzeit von 4 Wochen nicht eingehalten, so daß wir zweimal mahnen mußten, und zweitens ist die gelieferte Sendung unvollständig und teilweise beschädigt.

Wir bitten Sie daher dringend, uns die beiden fehlenden Kisten sowie Ersatz für die beschädigten Waren, über die wir eine Aufstellung beilegen, umgehend zu liefern. Eine Fortsetzung unserer Geschäftsbeziehungen müssen wir von der prompten Erledigung unserer Beschwerde abhängig machen.

Anlage

b. Weiß & Co., Hamburg, an Dixon Manufacturing Company Ltd., Toronto (Kanada)

Durch Ihr Schreiben vom 22. 9. haben wir erfahren, daß unsere letzte Sendung beschädigt ankam und ein Teil der Waren unbrauchbar ist.

Wir bedauern dieses Vorkommnis sehr, können jedoch kein Verschulden unsererseits feststellen, da wir wie immer auf sorgfältige Verpackung geachtet haben. Unserer Meinung nach kann der Schaden nur durch ein außergewöhnliches Ereignis entstanden sein.

Wir schlagen deshalb vor, daß Sie den Schaden unter Vorlage der Versicherungspolice, des Havarie-Zertifikats, des Konnossements und der Handelsrechnung der dortigen Vertretung der Hamburger Seeversicherungs-AG melden. Sollten Sie aber vorziehen, daß wir für Sie die Schadensmeldung in Hamburg vornehmen, so sind wir gern dazu bereit. In diesem Falle müßten wir Sie jedoch bitten, uns die dafür erforderlichen Unterlagen zur Verfügung zu stellen. Nach der Regulierung des Schadens würden wir Ihnen dann eine Gutschrift erteilen.

Please draft letters in English from the following particulars:

c. Schübbe & Co. in Hamburg bestellten am 15. 10. bei Simpson & Co. Ltd., Nairobi (Kenia), 150 Sack Kaffee, die gestern mit D. „Raja" eingetroffen sind. Sofort nach Ankunft haben Schübbe & Co. Proben entnommen und dabei festgestellt, daß der Kaffee nicht dem vorliegenden Muster entspricht. Es wurde bestenfalls mittlere Qualität und nicht, wie vereinbart, erstklassige Qualität geliefert. Außerdem wurde bei 14 Säcken Verunreinigung durch Ratten festgestellt. Schübbe & Co. haben für die Sendung keine Verwendung und bitten um Anweisung, was damit geschehen soll. Falls die Fa. Simpson dies wünscht, werden Schübbe & Co. das Gutachten eines Sachverständigen über die Qualität des gelieferten Kaffees einholen. Da Schübbe & Co. den Kaffee auf Grund des Musters bereits weiterverkauft haben, bitten sie Simpson & Co. dringend, unverzüglich dem Muster entsprechende Ware zu liefern. Die Fa. Simpson soll telegrafisch mitteilen, wann die Ersatzlieferung erfolgen kann.

d. Die Fa. Riess & Co. in Düsseldorf, die regelmäßig englische Stoffe von Blythe & Carr in Bradford bezieht, ist mit der letzten Sendung — 10 Stück Tweed Nr. 6677 — nicht zufrieden und beschwert sich bei der Lieferfirma.

Der Stoff ist zu lose gewebt und verzieht sich leicht. Riess & Co. legen ihrem Schreiben ein Muster des beanstandeten Stoffes und zum Vergleich ein Gegenmuster des gleichen Materials aus einer früheren Lieferung bei. Der Unterschied in der Struktur der beiden Stoffe ist augenfällig. Der zuletzt gelieferte Stoff eignet sich nicht für die Verarbeitung zu Damenkostümen, da diese nach kurzer Zeit aus der Form geraten würden. Riess & Co.

müssen deshalb die Sendung dem Lieferanten wieder zur Verfügung stellen. Gleichzeitig fragen sie an, ob Blythe & Carr kurzfristig 10 Stück Nr. 6677 von der gleichen Qualität wie das früher bezogene Material liefern können. Riess & Co. benötigen den Stoff sehr dringend, da sonst Schwierigkeiten in der Produktion auftreten. Sie hoffen, daß Blythe & Carr alles tun werden, um ihnen in ihrer schwierigen Lage zu helfen.

e. Während Ihres letzten Aufenthaltes in London kauften Sie einen Gabardinemantel bei Swanson & Baker Ltd.

Nach Ihrer Rückkehr aus England nehmen Sie den Mantel zu Hause näher in Augenschein und entdecken, daß das Futter an mehreren Stellen, vor allem im linken Ärmel, Mottenschaden aufweist. Der Schaden kann unmöglich in der kurzen Zeit entstanden sein, in der Sie den Mantel besitzen. Außerdem haben Sie ihn in England fast täglich getragen. Wahrscheinlich war der Mantel, bevor Sie ihn kauften, längere Zeit unsachgemäß gelagert worden.

Sie sind nicht gewillt, die durch den Mottenfraß verursachte Wertminderung in Kauf zu nehmen und beschweren sich bei Swanson & Baker. Welche Regelung schlagen Sie vor?

f. Aufgabe im Anschluß an Brief a. auf S. 134/135

Die Nähmaschinenfabrik Siehl & Co. in Karlsruhe bestätigt das Schreiben der Elite Garment Company in New Orleans, La. (USA), und teilt mit, daß sie die 10 schadhaften Elcolan-Antriebsriemen erhalten hat.

Sie hat heute 10 neue Riemen mit Luftpost abgeschickt und bedauert die Unannehmlichkeiten, die dem Kunden entstanden sind.

Die Fabrik gibt zu, daß tropisches oder subtropisches Klima die Festigkeit der Antriebsriemen zuweilen beeinträchtigt, macht den Kunden jedoch darauf aufmerksam, daß sich derartige Schäden durch Einfetten der Riemen leicht vermeiden lassen. Die Fettschicht verhindert, daß das Material zuviel Feuchtigkeit aufnimmt und sich auflöst. Zum Einfetten soll ein gutes, säurefreies Fett, am besten Vaseline, verwendet werden.

Die Fabrik ist überzeugt, daß die neuen Riemen lange halten, wenn der Kunde diesen Rat befolgt.

g. Aufgabe im Anschluß an Brief b. auf S. 135

Hier liegt folgender Sachverhalt vor: Baumann & Schmitt erhielten vor einiger Zeit von ihrem Lieferwerk eine Sendung Verschlüsse, die Mängel aufwiesen. Aus Versehen wurde ein Teil dieser Sendung ohne vorherige Prüfung an das Werk weitergegeben, wo die Verschlüsse in Kameras eingebaut wurden. Da der kanadische Vertreter von Baumann & Schmitt, die Firma Campbell & Co. Ltd. in Toronto, damals dringend eine neue Sendung Kameras angefordert hatte, wurden sofort alle greifbaren Apparate, darunter auch die mit den defekten Verschlüssen, nach Toronto gesandt. Als der Fehler entdeckt wurde, sandten Baumann & Schmitt ihrem Vertreter 37 einwandfreie Kameras mit Luftpost und kabelten wie folgt:

HOLD CAMERAS SERIAL NUMBERS 1134653—1134689 SHUTTERS DEFECTIVE NEW SHIPMENT FORWARDED BY AIR TODAY

Dieses Telegramm kreuzte sich mit dem Schreiben des Vertreters.

Baumann & Schmitt bestätigen nun das Schreiben von Campbell & Co. Ltd. sowie das obige Telegramm. Sie erklären kurz den Sachverhalt und entschuldigen sich für die Unannehmlichkeiten, die diese Angelegenheit dem Vertreter verursacht hat.

Baumann & Schmitt hoffen, daß die Ersatzsendung inzwischen in gutem Zustand angekommen ist. Die Kameras mit den im Telegramm genannten Seriennummern soll die kanadische Firma zurücksenden; die dabei entstehenden Kosten gehen zu Lasten von Baumann & Schmitt.

Die Münchener Firma hat volles Verständnis für die schwierige Lage ihres Vertreters und hat Maßnahmen getroffen, die eine Wiederholung dieses Vorkommnisses in Zukunft verhindern sollen.

h. Aufgabe im Anschluß an Brief c. auf S. 135/136

Die Neckar Chemie AG in Mannheim schreibt ihrer Vertreterfirma, Alford & Co. Ltd., London, auf ihre Beschwerde, daß die Proben der Katalysatoren 106, 216 und 312 mit großer Sorgfalt verpackt wurden und sie sich daher nicht erklären kann, wie der Schaden entstanden ist.

Wie vom Vertreter erbeten, wird die Neckar Chemie AG sofort eine weitere 5-kg-Probe jeder der 3 Qualitäten absenden, diesmal jedoch an seine Adresse. Jeder Behälter wird in einem Polyäthylen-Beutel mit Juteumhüllung (*polythene bag with jute cover*) verpackt.

Die Neckar Chemie AG hofft, daß die Proben diesmal unversehrt ankommen.

Not Satisfied

An elderly spinster bought a television set in a department store. A few weeks later the adjustment manager of the store received the following letter from this lady:

"Dear Sir: The television set I bought in your store works all right, but the program is very bad. Could you exchange the set for one with a better program?"

From an advertisement in a San Francisco newspaper: "We guarantee in writing that our famous LIFETIME SOLE will wear at least three months."

X. Collection Letters
Delays in Payment and Non-Payment—Reminders and Collection Letters

1. Introduction

Delays in Payment and Non-Payment. Just as the buyer follows up his orders, the seller keeps an eye on his customers' unpaid invoices.

When a customer fails to pay his debts on time, the seller sends him a *reminder*. If necessary, the reminder is followed by increasingly urgent *collection letters* (or: *dunning letters*).

Should the customer fail to respond to these letters, steps have to be taken to collect the account. This may be done by entrusting a *collection agency* or bank with the collection, or by bringing legal action against the debtor.[1]

Collection agencies are commercial establishments specializing in the collection of bills. (Inquiry agencies usually are collection agencies at the same time.)

Collection through banks is effected, in most cases, by means of a sight draft. The creditor draws a sight draft on the debtor and hands it to his bank with instructions to pass it on to the debtor's bank for presentation for payment. Although the debtor cannot be forced to pay the sight draft, he will usually honour it if he is able to do so, as he knows that his refusal to pay will give the banker notice that he is in financial difficulties, with the result that the banker will demand repayment of outstanding loans and refuse to grant the debtor any new loans.

Legal action is the last resort in the collection of outstanding accounts. When this step appears to be inevitable, the account is turned over to a lawyer. The lawyer may try once more to induce the debtor to pay but, if also this very last attempt to bring about an amicable settlement fails, he will institute legal proceedings.

The customer's reply to a reminder or collection letter is either a letter of apology announcing payment, or a request for an extension.

However, a debtor who experiences temporary financial difficulties should not wait until he receives a reminder from the creditor, but he should ask for an extension as early as possible. To show his good will, the debtor may make a part payment (*payment on account*) and ask the creditor to grant him an extension for the balance. Sometimes debtors offer to accept a bill of exchange for the amount owing, in order to give the creditor the assurance that the amount will be paid. On the other hand, it also happens that a customer who was supplied on a draft basis is unable to honour his acceptance at maturity and is therefore forced to ask the drawer for a prolongation. (When an extension or prolongation is granted, the creditor is entitled to charge interest on the debt for the additional time allowed.)

---

[1] The German *Mahnbescheid* is unknown in the Anglo-Saxon countries.

Reminders and Collection Letters. When an account becomes overdue, it is first assumed that it has been overlooked by the customer. Therefore the account is brought to the customer's attention by means of a copy of the invoice or statement, a printed notice, a letter, etc. These are called *reminders*. When sending invoice copies or statements as reminders, many firms add a rubber-stamped notation (*Past due—please remit*), a printed card, or a gummed label (*collection sticker*). The letters employed as reminders are usually form letters. Sometimes a reminder is included in an offer or sales letter sent to a customer (*hidden reminder*).

If the reminder does not produce any results, it is followed by two or more *collection letters*. In these letters various arguments and appeals are used to obtain payment or at least an explanation from the customer.

In each letter that is written the request for payment becomes more insistent and urgent than in the previous one. The final collection letter demands payment and warns the debtor that drastic steps will be taken unless payment is made immediately. Such steps may be: reporting the case to a trade or credit association, drawing a sight draft for collection through the debtor's bank, or turning the account over to a collection agency or a lawyer. The number of reminders and collection letters sent to a delinquent debtor before action is taken varies according to circumstances.

In collecting outstanding accounts, extensive use is made of sets of printed notices or form letters. Such a set, which usually consists of three parts, is known as a *collection series* (or: *collection sequence*).

Humour and novelty can sometimes be employed to advantage in the collection process. Humorous letters, provided they display originality and skill, are often quite effective in the early stages of collection. It should be realized, however, that humorous letters have their limitations; they should therefore be used with discrimination.

2. Specimen Letters

a. Reminder

Dear Sir,

May we draw your attention to our invoice of 1st June for £68.31, which is now three weeks overdue.

Please let us have your remittance soon.

Yours faithfully,

---

b. Statement with Collection Sticker

					A/C. RENDERED	
					MONTH	
					Jan	113.44

TELEPHONES:
GRAYS THURROCK 5155 (5 LINES)

STATEMENT

G. Hunter (London) Ltd.

MATERIALS HANDLING SPECIALISTS

Hans Bauer KG,
Ingolstadt,
Germany.

ACCOUNTS DEPT.

GUMLEY ROAD,

GRAYS, ESSEX

April 28th 19..

TOTAL

DATE		REF. NO.	DETAILS	DEBITS	CREDITS	BALANCE
Jan			A/C. RENDERED			£113.44
Mar	24	22186	GO/4133	£144.34		£257.78

THIS ACCOUNT IS NOW SO MUCH OVERDUE THAT WE MUST REQUEST PAYMENT WITHOUT FURTHER DELAY.

PLEASE RETURN THIS STATEMENT WHEN REMITTING

THE LAST AMOUNT IN THE BALANCE COLUMN IS THE AMOUNT OWING

FOR USE WITH Kalamazoo "COPY-WRITER" REA-M0399-84cH

150

c. Hidden Reminder

Dear Sirs,

We have pleasure in sending you enclosed our price list and patterns of our new range of curtains. They are made from drip-dry cotton and come in a great variety of colours. Your customers will like them—and, as you will note, we offer them at very favourable prices. Please let us know your requirements soon.

May we take this opportunity to remind you that our invoice of the 26th January for £ 211.53 is still unpaid. We shall be glad to receive your cheque for this amount within the next few days.

Yours faithfully,

d. Collection Letter

Dear Sirs,

We wrote you on 5th March asking for payment of the overdue balance of £ 161.38, but so far we have not received any reply from you.

If there is an error or any other reason why payment has not been made, please let us know, and we shall look into the matter at once.

Otherwise we must ask you to send us your cheque without further delay.

Yours faithfully,

e. Collection Letter

Dear Mr. Trent: [1]

"How do they pay?"

That is the question we are called upon to answer many times. These inquiries come from the same sources through which we receive our information; therefore, we are obligated to answer—and answer truthfully.

When an account is past due and we know the reason, or if satisfactory arrangements have been made to take care of it, we are always glad to add an explanatory note. But—when we ourselves do not know—what can we add?

Won't you send your check promptly—please, so that in case we receive an inquiry about you tomorrow, we can report the account paid?

Very truly yours,
The P. F. Volland Co.

---

[1] By courtesy of Harper & Row, Publishers, *Business Letters*

f. Advice of Draft Drawn

Gentlemen:

As we are still without a reply to our various letters requesting payment of your overdue account in the amount of $376.20, we must inform you that we shall draw on you at sight for this amount through the First National Bank in your city.

Please arrange to honour the draft on presentation.

Very truly yours,

---

g. Collection Letter

Dear Sirs,

Although repeated requests have been made to you for settlement of the overdue balance of £ 638.61 on your account, we are still awaiting your remittance.

Unless we receive your cheque within seven days, we shall have no alternative but to place the matter in the hands of our solicitor.

Yours faithfully,

---

h. Collection Series

REFERENCE **R. D. BAXTER COMPANY** ACCOUNT NUMBER

1212 Pasadena Avenue
LOS ANGELES, CALIF. 90001 DATE_____19_____

If your remittance has already been sent, please disregard this notice. If not, we shall appreciate your prompt attention, and a remittance covering your past due account.

COURTESY NOTICE

AMOUNT DUE $_____

PLEASE ENCLOSE THIS NOTICE
WITH YOUR REMITTANCE.

REFERENCE **R. D. BAXTER COMPANY** ACCOUNT NUMBER

1212 Pasadena Avenue
LOS ANGELES, CALIF. 90001 DATE_____19_____

Just to remind you of your overdue account, which has doubtless been overlooked. Now that we have again reminded you, won't you please send us a remittance promptly? The amount past due is $_____ , and settlement will be confidently expected within the next week.

PAST DUE NOTICE

ENCLOSE THIS NOTICE WITH
YOUR REMITTANCE.

REFERENCE **R. D. BAXTER COMPANY** ACCOUNT NUMBER

1212 Pasadena Avenue
LOS ANGELES, CALIF. 90001 DATE_____19_____

Repeated requests for settlement of your past due account have, apparently, been ignored. Unless payment is received within ten days immediate action will be taken. Your past due balance amounts to $_____ .

FINAL NOTICE

THIS NOTICE IS TO BE ENCLOSED
WITH YOUR REMITTANCE.

i. Lawyer Makes Last Request for Payment

Gentlemen:

My clients, Smithson & Co., have informed me that their repeated requests for payment of your long overdue account for $638.50 have been ignored by you.

This is the final demand for settlement on an amicable basis. Unless payment of the above amount is made immediately, I shall be compelled to institute legal proceedings against you without further notice.

Yours truly,

---

k. Some Amusing Examples of Collection Correspondence:

Dear Mr. David: [1]

Back in the days of log cabins and wild Indians the firm foundations of our country were laid by the Early Settlers.

And the sound financial structure of our country is maintained by the early settlers of today.

Your account shows a past-due balance of $98.20, representing our invoices of February 16 and March 21.

As an early settler, you will, of course, remit by return mail.

Yours very truly,

(A paper clip was attached to the letter)

No, Mr. Davis— [2]

that little paper clip in the left-hand corner hasn't been left there by a careless stenographer.

That's Elmer, our pet paper clip.

His purpose in life is to hold two pieces of paper together. But Elmer has enlarged his scope of usefulness and has accepted two very definite tasks which we asked him to do.

ONE . . . to hold your check for $137.00 securely to this note—a check which is needed to clear up that little account we've talked about, and—

154

TWO ... by so doing, to bind the friendly relationship which has always existed between yourself and us.

Will you return Elmer with your answer, please?

Cordially,

Gentlemen: [3]

A friend of ours, passing through Hong Kong, saw a Chinaman carrying a lantern in broad daylight.

Being curious, he inquired about it. He was told that in China all debts must be paid with the closing of the year. The individual whose debts are unpaid with the beginning of the new year is obliged to carry a lighted lantern until the slate is clean.

No doubt there is some reason why you have allowed your account to become past due. But won't you put away the lantern and send your payment today?

A check in full or in part will help you to start your New Year off right.

Sincerely,

---

[1] From: *How to Make the Cash Register Register,* Johns-Manville Corporation
[2] By courtesy of Harper & Row, Publishers, *Business Letters*
[3] Parkhurst and Davis, Business Writing: Theory and Practice. Reprinted by permission of Prentice-Hall, Inc., Englewood Cliffs, N.J., U.S.A.

1. Customer Apologizes for Delay in Payment

Dear Sirs,

In response to your letter of the 28th December, we have today instructed our bank to transfer the amount of £ 51.50 to your account.

We are sorry that the due date of your invoice was overlooked in the pressure of business, and we offer our apologies for the delay.

Yours faithfully,

---

m. Customer Makes Payment on Account—Asks for Extension for the Balance

Dear Sirs,

We have received your letter of the 10th August and are sorry for the delay in settling our account.

Owing to the slackness of trade during the past few months, we have not yet been able to dispose of your last consignment. Besides, many of our customers have been slow in meeting their obligations.

We are sending you a cheque for £50 on account and should be grateful if you would grant us an extension for the balance until the 30th September. You can rely on receiving a remittance in full settlement by that date.

We should be greatly obliged to you for accommodating us in this matter.

Yours faithfully,

Encl.

n. Request for Prolongation of Draft

Dear Sirs,

We regret to inform you that we shall not be able to meet our acceptance for £450 on the 1st October.

The prolonged strike in our area has resulted in a general decline of business activity, leaving us temporarily short of ready cash. However, our financial position is sound and, as a settlement of the strike has just been negotiated, the business situation is expected to improve very soon.

Under these circumstances we should be grateful if you would renew the bill, on which we shall pay interest at 6 per cent., until the 1st November. This would give us time to meet our obligations without increasing our loan from the bank.

We hope that in view of our long and pleasant business relations you will see your way to granting us this favour.

Yours faithfully,

3. Terms and Phrases

a. Reminders

We wish to call your attention to our invoice of . . ., which is now . . . days overdue.

Wir möchten Sie auf unsere Rechnung vom . . . aufmerksam machen, die bereits vor . . . Tagen fällig war.

. . . which appears to have escaped your notice.

. . . die anscheinend Ihrer Aufmerksamkeit entgangen ist.

Evidently our statement for the month of June has been overlooked by you.

Anscheinend haben Sie unseren Kontoauszug für den Monat Juni übersehen.

May we remind you that the following invoices have not yet been paid: . . .

Dürfen wir Sie daran erinnern, daß die folgenden Rechnungen noch nicht beglichen sind: . . .

In looking through our books/In going over our accounts/On going through our ledgers/we note that a balance of . . . is still open on your account.

Bei Durchsicht unserer Bücher stellen wir fest, daß auf Ihrem Konto noch immer ein Saldo von . . . offensteht.

Please accept this as a friendly reminder that our invoice No. . . . is past due.

Dies ist lediglich eine freundliche Erinnerung daran, daß unsere Rechnung Nr. . . . noch nicht bezahlt ist.

If your cheque is already in the mail, please accept our best thanks and disregard this letter.

Wenn Sie Ihren Scheck bereits abgeschickt haben, danken wir Ihnen bestens und bitten Sie, dieses Schreiben als gegenstandslos zu betrachten.

b. Requests for Payment

We should appreciate an early settlement of our invoice.

Für baldigen Ausgleich unserer Rechnung wären wir dankbar.

We should be glad to receive your remittance within the next few days.

Wir würden uns freuen, Ihre Zahlung in den nächsten Tagen zu erhalten.

We must request you to let us have your payment without further delay.

Wir müssen Sie bitten, die Zahlung unverzüglich vorzunehmen.

We are still without reply to our letter of . . . and no remittance has yet been received.

Auf unser Schreiben vom . . . haben wir noch keine Antwort erhalten. Auch ist bisher keine Zahlung eingegangen.

We are at a loss to understand the reason for your failure to answer our letters of ...

Although we have several times urgently requested payment of your long overdue account in the amount of ..., we have not yet received a reply from you.

Evidently you are not interested in settling this matter amicably/out of court/, since you have ignored our previous letters.

You have not accorded us the courtesy of a reply to our repeated requests for payment.

This is our final notice/final request for payment.

We must insist on payment by ... Otherwise we shall draw on you at sight for the amount due.

We regret to inform you that we have no alternative but to hold up further shipments until your account has been balanced.

Unless payment is received by ..., we shall reluctantly be compelled to take immediate steps to recover the amount due.

... we shall have the amount collected through a collection agency.

... we shall be forced to take legal steps/to recover the debt at law.

Unless we receive your cheque within seven days, we shall have to place the

Wir können uns nicht erklären, warum Sie unsere Schreiben vom ... unbeantwortet ließen.

Obwohl wir mehrmals dringend um Zahlung der seit längerer Zeit fälligen Rechnung in Höhe von ... baten, haben wir noch keine Antwort von Ihnen erhalten.

Anscheinend sind Sie nicht daran interessiert, die Angelegenheit gütlich zu regeln, da Sie unsere bisherigen Schreiben unbeachtet ließen.

Sie haben es nicht für nötig gehalten, auf unsere wiederholten Zahlungsaufforderungen zu antworten.

Dies ist unsere letzte Mahnung.

Wir müssen auf Zahlung bis ... bestehen. Andernfalls werden wir über den fälligen Betrag einen Sichtwechsel auf Sie ziehen.

Wir bedauern, Ihnen mitteilen zu müssen, daß wir keine andere Wahl haben, als alle weiteren Lieferungen an Sie einzustellen, bis Ihr Konto ausgeglichen ist.

Falls die Zahlung nicht bis zum ... eingeht, sehen wir uns zu unserem Bedauern gezwungen, unverzüglich Schritte zur Einziehung des fälligen Betrages zu unternehmen.

... werden wir den Betrag durch eine Inkassofirma einziehen lassen.

... sind wir gezwungen, gerichtliche Schritte zu unternehmen/die Forderung auf gerichtlichem Wege einzutreiben.

Wenn wir Ihren Scheck nicht innerhalb von 7 Tagen erhalten, müssen wir die An-

matter in the hands of/to turn the matter over to/our solicitor (*US*: attorney).

... we shall instruct our solicitor to institute legal proceedings/to start suit/to bring action in court/to take legal action.

gelegenheit unserem Anwalt übergeben.

... werden wir unsern Anwalt beauftragen, Klage zu erheben.

c. Debtor's Reply—Requests for Extension

We have received your letter of ... and are sorry that it was necessary to remind us of the settlement of your invoice No. ...

Wir haben Ihr Schreiben vom ... erhalten und bedauern, daß es notwendig war, uns an die Erledigung Ihrer Rechnung Nr. ... zu erinnern.

Please accept our apologies for the delay, which is due to the fact that your invoice was misplaced.

Bitte entschuldigen Sie die Verzögerung, die darauf zurückzuführen ist, daß Ihre Rechnung verlegt worden war.

The sudden failure of a customer of ours has caused us considerable losses.

Der plötzliche Konkurs eines unserer Kunden hat uns beträchtliche Verluste verursacht.

We have great difficulties in collecting our outstanding accounts.

Wir haben große Schwierigkeiten beim Einzug unserer Außenstände.

Business has been slow/slack/dull/during the past few months.

Während der letzten Monate war ein schlechter Geschäftsgang zu verzeichnen.

The seasonal lull has caused us temporary financial embarrassment.

Die jahreszeitlich bedingte Flaute hat uns vorübergehend in finanzielle Verlegenheit gebracht.

We have every hope that we shall be able/We are confident of being able/to settle your invoice by 15th June.

Wir hoffen bestimmt, daß wir Ihre Rechnung bis zum 15. Juni begleichen können.

Will you please draw a second 60-day draft on us for ... plus interest at ... per cent.

Wir bitten Sie, einen zweiten 60-Tage-Wechsel über ... zuzüglich ... % Zinsen auf uns zu ziehen.

If you grant us this favour, you may rely on us to meet your draft at maturity.

Wenn Sie uns diesen Gefallen erweisen, können Sie sich darauf verlassen, daß wir Ihre Tratte bei Fälligkeit einlösen werden.

We hope that you will understand the difficulty of our present situation.

Wir hoffen, daß Sie für unsere augenblickliche schwierige Lage Verständnis haben werden.

d. Granting and Refusing Extension

As you have always paid your bills promptly, we are prepared to grant you the extension requested.

Da Sie Ihre Rechnungen stets prompt beglichen haben, sind wir bereit, Ihnen den erbetenen Zahlungsaufschub zu gewähren.

If you send us a cheque for half the amount of our invoice, we shall draw on you at 60 d/s (days' sight) for the balance.

Wenn Sie uns einen Scheck über die Hälfte des Rechnungsbetrages senden, ziehen wir auf Sie für den Restbetrag einen Wechsel per 60 Tage Sicht.

After careful consideration of your letter of . . . , we agree to a prolongation of the bill by one month.

Nach sorgfältiger Prüfung der in Ihrem Schreiben vom . . . gemachten Ausführungen sind wir mit einer Prolongation des Wechsels um 1 Monat einverstanden.

As we shall have to meet considerable engagements shortly, we are unable to comply with your request for a renewal of the bill due on . . .

Da wir in nächster Zeit beträchtliche Zahlungsverpflichtungen erfüllen müssen, ist es uns nicht möglich, Ihrer Bitte um Prolongation des am . . . fälligen Wechsels zu entsprechen.

Although we appreciate your difficulties, we cannot allow you to postpone payment of this account any longer.

Obwohl wir für Ihre schwierige Lage Verständnis haben, können wir Ihnen nicht gestatten, die Zahlung dieser Rechnung noch länger hinauszuschieben.

We think we have shown considerable patience and consideration, but we cannot wait any longer.

Wir glauben, erhebliche Geduld und Rücksicht gezeigt zu haben, können jetzt aber nicht länger zuwarten.

We regret that we cannot see our way to accommodating you any further.

Zu unserem Bedauern sehen wir keine Möglichkeit, Ihnen in dieser Angelegenheit noch weiter entgegenzukommen.

4. Exercises

Please translate the following letters into English:

a. Becker & Sohn, München, an Peter Ward, Glasgow

Haben Sie schon daran gedacht, sich für das Weihnachtsgeschäft einzudecken? Mit gleicher Post lassen wir Ihnen unseren neuesten Katalog für mechanische Spielwaren zugehen. Da mit einer großen Nachfrage nach unseren Neuheiten zu rechnen ist, können wir unseren Kunden rechtzeitige Lieferung nur dann garantieren, wenn sie ihre Bestellungen so frühzeitig wie möglich aufgeben.

Dürfen wir Sie bei dieser Gelegenheit daran erinnern, daß unsere Rechnung von 8. 7. bereits vor über einem Monat fällig war? Unsere Bank hat uns heute auf unsere Anfrage mitgeteilt, daß bisher noch keine Überweisung von Ihnen eingegangen ist.

Es kann natürlich vorkommen, daß einmal eine Rechnung übersehen wird. Nachdem wir Sie jedoch jetzt auf diese Angelegenheit aufmerksam gemacht haben, sind wir sicher, daß Sie die Zahlung umgehend vornehmen werden.

Wir würden uns freuen, bald von Ihnen zu hören.

b. Schultze & Co., Mannheim, an Garrett Industries Inc., Hoboken, N. J. (USA)

Wir haben Ihr Schreiben vom 6. 2. erhalten und bedauern sehr, daß es uns bisher nicht möglich war, Ihre Rechnung zu begleichen.

Der unerwartete Konkurs eines unserer Kunden hat uns große Unannehmlichkeiten bereitet. Außerdem war der Absatz in den letzten Wochen sehr gering, so daß es uns nicht leicht fiel, unsere laufenden Ausgaben zu bestreiten. Es bleibt uns deshalb nichts anderes übrig, als Sie um einen Monat Aufschub zu bitten. Das Geschäft ist gegenwärtig etwas besser und dürfte sich in Zukunft noch weiter beleben.

Wir wären für Ihr Entgegenkommen sehr dankbar und sind überzeugt, daß es uns gelingen wird, unsere Verpflichtungen innerhalb der nächsten 4 Wochen zu erfüllen.

Please draft letters in English from the following particulars:

c. Eisele & Breuer in Stuttgart haben am 5. 4. Büromaschinen an Carey & Co. Ltd., London, geliefert. Die Zahlung des Rechnungsbetrages (£ 3615.50) sollte vereinbarungsgemäß innerhalb von 30 Tagen nach Ausstellung der Rechnung erfolgen. Da am 5. 6. noch keine Überweisung eingegangen ist, erinnern Eisele & Breuer die Londoner Firma an die fällige Zahlung.

Diese Zahlungserinnerung bleibt unbeantwortet. Eisele & Breuer schreiben daher am 26. 6. nochmals an Carey & Co. Ltd. und fragen an, wann sie mit der Zahlung rechnen können. Wenn die englische Firma irgendwelche Schwierigkeiten hat, so soll sie dies mitteilen, damit eine für beide Teile zufriedenstellende Lösung gefunden werden kann.

Carey & Co. Ltd. reagiert auch auf das zweite Schreiben nicht. Am 17. 7. wenden sich Eisele & Breuer ein drittes Mal an diese Firma. Sie sind sehr enttäuscht darüber, daß sie bisher weder eine Überweisung noch eine Antwort auf ihre beiden Zahlungsaufforderungen erhalten haben, um so mehr, als sie sich in ihrem letzten Schreiben bereit erklärten, der englischen Firma entgegenzukommen, falls sie augenblicklich in Schwierigkeiten sein sollte. Eisele & Breuer müssen daher Carey & Co. Ltd. bitten, ihr Konto bis 31. 7. auszugleichen. Falls die Zahlung bis dahin nicht eingegangen ist, werden sie den ausstehenden Betrag zuzüglich Zinsen und Kosten über die Bankverbindung der Londoner Firma mittels Sichttratte einziehen lassen.

Da am 1. 8. immer noch keine Zahlung eingegangen ist, ziehen Eisele & Breuer einen Sichtwechsel auf Carey & Co. Ltd. und übergeben diesen zusammen mit den notwendigen Unterlagen der Stuttgarter Bank mit der Bitte um Weiterleitung an die Midland Bank in London. Gleichzeitig senden sie eine kurze Benachrichtigung an Carey & Co. Ltd. und fordern die Firma auf, den Wechsel, der ihr in ein paar Tagen vorgelegt wird, prompt einzulösen.

Nach etwa 14 Tagen teilt die Stuttgarter Bank Eisele & Breuer mit, daß Carey & Co. Ltd. die Einlösung des von der Midland Bank vorgelegten Sichtwechsels verweigert hat. Eisele & Breuer übergeben daher die Angelegenheit dem Londoner Anwaltsbüro Fuller & Fuller, Solicitors, das schon in mehreren Fällen ihre Interessen in England vertreten hat. Gleichzeitig teilen Eisele & Breuer der Firma Carey & Co. Ltd. mit, daß sie ihre Anwälte beauftragt haben, die Forderung auf dem Klageweg einzuziehen.

d. Krämer & Pasetti in Augsburg haben von Parson & Co. in London keine Antwort auf ihre wiederholten Zahlungsaufforderungen erhalten. Auf dem Konto der englischen Firma steht seit etwa 3 Monaten ein Betrag von £ 1866.48 offen.

In einem weiteren Schreiben machen Krämer & Pasetti die Firma Parsons & Co. darauf aufmerksam, daß sie bei ihren äußerst kalkulierten Exportpreisen auf prompten Eingang ihrer Außenstände bedacht sein müssen. Sie haben der englischen Firma nur unter der Voraussetzung offenes Ziel eingeräumt, daß die Zahlungen pünktlich erfolgen.

Da Parsons & Co. jetzt jedoch mit ihren Zahlungen beträchtlich im Rückstand sind, müssen Krämer & Pasetti — falls die englische Firma nicht umgehend für den Ausgleich ihres Kontos sorgt — bei allen weiteren Lieferungen auf Zahlung per Nachnahme bzw. Kasse gegen Dokumente bestehen.

e. Nagel & Söhne in München erhalten ein Schreiben der Fulton Engineering Company Ltd., Chichester, Sussex (England), in dem diese eine seit ca. 6 Wochen fällige Rechnung in Höhe von £ 683.53 anmahnt.

Mitte April wurden einige Abteilungen der Münchener Firma, darunter auch die Buchhaltung, in einen neu errichteten Erweiterungsbau verlegt. Als Folge der Umzugsarbeiten wurde die Rechnung der Fulton Engineering Company Ltd. übersehen. Sofort nach Eingang der Zahlungserinnerung beauftragen Nagel & Söhne ihre Bank, die Bayerische Hypotheken- und Wechselbank, den Betrag an die Lloyds Bank, Chichester Branch, zu überweisen, und bitten die Fulton Engineering Company Ltd. in einem höflichen Schreiben, die Verzögerung zu entschuldigen.

If I Were You

Dear Customer:

If I were you
And you were me,
A different story this would be.

If you were me
And I were you,
This bill would not be overdue.

Since I am I
And you are you,
Please send your check in
P.D.Q.[1]

A Gentleman Pays Promptly

"My good man," said Mr. Benningham to the grocery-store owner, "how is it you have not called on me for my account?"

"Oh, I never ask a gentleman for money."

"Indeed! But what do you do if he doesn't pay?"

"Why, after a certain time," said he, "I conclude he is not a gentleman, and then I ask him."

[1] pretty damn quick

XI. Letters of Application

1. Introduction

No business letter is of such direct and personal importance to the writer as the letter of application. It may have a decisive influence on a person's career and advancement and thus help to shape his future.

Letters of application fall into two categories: *solicited* and *unsolicited applications*. Solicited applications are written in response to advertisements ("Situations Offered," "Situations Vacant," "Jobs Offered") or at the request of a prospective employer; unsolicited applications are addressed to firms on the chance that there is or will be an opening. Frequently, unsolicited applications are sent at the suggestion of a third person.

Applicants usually enclose with their application a *curriculum vitae*, or a *personal data sheet*. A curriculum vitae (or: *résumé*) contains details about the applicant, his education, training and experience. In a personal data sheet (or: *personal record sheet*) the information about the applicant is tabulated.

Letters of application may also be accompanied by a recent photograph and copies of testimonials or letters of recommendation (sending the originals would be too risky). Many firms send *application forms* to candidates for positions, requesting them to complete the forms and return them.

2. Specimen Letters

a. Solicited Application

Dear Sirs,

I should be grateful if you would consider my application for the position of foreign-language correspondent as advertised in today's "Daily Telegraph."

My age is 22. For the past four years I have been employed by Messrs. Hamilton & Smith of Harton Street.

I hold the G.C.E. "A" Level Certificate in three subjects, including French and German. I obtained the Certificate in 19 . . . Since leaving school, I have continued to study these two languages at the Oxford Institute. I can speak, read and write both languages fluently.

In the firm where I am working, I am responsible for shipping and insurance, and for making out invoices and customs documents.

I should like to obtain a post which would provide opportunities for further experience and promotion in this field. I am prepared to take up the study of any subjects likely to be useful to me in my work.

For information about my character, I refer you to:

. . . . .

. . . . .

May I have an interview with you at your convenience?

Yours faithfully,

---

b. Solicited Application

Gentlemen:

I refer to your advertisement for a secretary in today's "Chicago Tribune" and would like to be considered an applicant for this position. Here are my reasons for believing that I meet your requirements.

In 19 . . I graduated from Madison Central High School, where I completed the course in secretarial studies. This course includes business English, shorthand, typing and bookkeeping. For the past three years I have been attending evening classes at Lincoln College. In one more year I will graduate with a B.S. degree in Business Administration.

My practical experience consists of one year as assistant to Dr. George R. Shelden, Principal, Madison Central High School, and four years as secretary for Miller & Brown, where I am still employed. The duties of my present position consist of taking and transcribing dictation, filing, interviewing visitors and answering telephone calls. I also handle routine correspondence, which is assigned to me for attention.

Conditions at my place of employment are pleasant, but there are no opportunities for promotion. It has been my wish for some time to obtain a position with a large company in order to increase my knowledge and assume greater responsibilities. My present employer knows of my application and has kindly offered to give you any desired information about my ability and character.

I enclose a personal data sheet with details on my education and experience.

If you feel my qualifications fit me for the position advertised, I would appreciate the opportunity of a personal interview. You may reach me by calling MO 6—1920 at any time after 6 p.m. or by writing to the address given above.

Yours very truly,

Enclosure

---

c. Unsolicited Application

116 Elsham Road,
London, W.14,
11th June, 19...

Messrs. Rogers & Longford Ltd.,
312 North End Road,
London, N.W.11.

Dear Sirs,

I have learned from Mr. Stone that there will soon be a vacancy for a bookkeeping clerk in your company and should like to apply for this position.

After obtaining the G.C.E. 'O' Level Certificate in seven subjects, I attended Pitman College for two years, taking courses in bookkeeping, shorthand and typing.

In 19.. I was employed as a junior clerk by Messrs. Jones & Co. Three years ago, when one of the bookkeepers was ill, I was asked to help out. My employers were so pleased with my work that they transferred me to the bookkeeping department, where I have been engaged in keeping accounts ever since. To supplement my practical knowledge of bookkeeping, I have taken evening courses in general accounting, cost accounting and auditing at the Brightlea Technical College for the past two years.

You will find enclosed a curriculum vitae and a copy of a testimonial from the Head Master of Ealing Grammar School. It is of course possible for you to obtain information from my present employers if you wish to make inquiries.

I should appreciate it if you would give me the opportunity to discuss my application with you personally.

Yours faithfully,

Harold Miller

Harold Miller.

Encl. 2

d. Headings of a Personal Data Sheet

Data Sheet

Name: . . . . .

Address: . . . . .

Age: . . . . .

Birthplace: . . . . .

Education: . . . . .

Practical Training and Experience: . . . . .

References: . . . . .

---

e. Letter of Recommendation

Miss Johanna Schuster has been employed as a secretary by the Farland International Corporation for the past three years. In addition to the regular functions of taking dictation, typing and normal office routine, her duties have included interviewing visitors, arranging travel itineraries, and translating German and English texts of a technical nature.

Miss Schuster has an excellent command of German and English and is thoroughly familiar with business and technical terminology in both languages. She is conscientious and ambitious and has always performed her work in a most commendable manner. Owing to her pleasant personality, she is well liked by her colleagues.

Miss Schuster is leaving our company at her own request. I regret her departure and wish her the best for her future career.

Farland International Corporation
E. D. McMartin
Manager, Overseas Operations

---

3. Terms and Phrases

a. Opening Phrases

In reply to/In answer to/With reference to/your advertisement in ... I wish to apply for/to submit my application for/the position of a shorthand typist.

Ich beziehe mich auf Ihre Anzeige in ... und möchte mich um die Stelle einer Stenotypistin bewerben.

I see from your advertisement in ... that you are looking for a secretary with a good command of French.

Ihrer Anzeige in ... entnehme ich, daß Sie eine Sekretärin mit soliden Französischkenntnissen suchen.

After three years of experience in the textile trade, I feel that I am qualified to fill the position of chief buyer advertised in today's "Times."

Nach dreijähriger praktischer Tätigkeit in der Textilbranche glaube ich mich für die in der heutigen Nummer der „Times" ausgeschriebene Stelle eines Chefeinkäufers zu eignen.

Mr. Brown has told me that some time in May there will be an opening/a vacancy/for a secretary in your office.

Von Mr. Brown habe ich erfahren, daß im Laufe des Monats Mai in Ihrem Büro die Stelle einer Sekretärin frei wird.

... that you are seeking an efficient salesman.

... daß Sie einen tüchtigen Vertreter suchen.

b. Education and Training

I attended ... Secondary School for three years.

Ich besuchte drei Jahre lang die ... Secondary School (*höhere Schule in England*).

In 19.. I graduated from ... High School.

Im Jahre 19.. schloß ich meine Ausbildung an der ... High School (*höhere Schule in den USA*) ab.

... I registered for a year's course at ... Commercial College.

... schrieb ich mich für einen Jahreskurs am ... Commercial College ein.

... I transferred to ... College, which is considered one of the best secretarial institutions in Kansas.

... wechselte ich in das ... College über, das als eine der besten Ausbildungsstätten für Sekretärinnen im Staate Kansas angesehen wird.

... I entered ... University, where I majored in business administration.

... immatrikulierte ich mich an der ... Universität, wo ich Betriebswirtschaft als Hauptfach studierte.

At ... Commercial High School I studied business correspondence, shorthand, typing and other business subjects for two years.

In der ... Commercial High School ließ ich mich 2 Jahre lang in Handelskorrespondenz, Kurzschrift, Maschinenschreiben und anderen kaufmännischen Fächern ausbilden.

I served my apprenticeship with one of the leading export-import houses of this city.

Ich legte meine Lehre bei einem der führenden Export-Import Häuser am Platze ab.

In winter I took a course to increase my knowledge of foreign trade.

Im Winter besuchte ich einen Kurs, um meine Kenntnisse auf dem Gebiet des Außenhandels zu erweitern.

c. Qualifications and Practical Experience

During my apprenticeship with ... I acquired a sound knowledge of bookkeeping.

Während meiner Lehrzeit bei ... eignete ich mir gute Buchhaltungskenntnisse an.

I hold diplomas for Pitman's shorthand at 100 w.p.m. (words per minute) and typewriting at 40 w.p.m.

Ich besitze Diplome in Pitman Kurzschrift für 100 Wörter pro Minute (*etwa 140 Silben*) und Maschinenschreiben für 40 Wörter pro Minute (*etwa 200 Anschläge*).

I am thoroughly familiar with export procedure.

Ich bin mit dem Exportverfahren bestens vertraut.

I speak French fluently and have a fair knowledge/a working knowledge/of Italian.

Ich spreche fließend Französisch und habe gute Italienischkenntnisse.

My proficiency in Spanish enables me to handle Spanish correspondence on my own.

Auf Grund meiner sehr guten Spanischkenntnisse bin ich in der Lage, spanische Korrespondenz selbständig zu erledigen.

I have had five years of experience in selling electrical appliances.

Ich habe eine fünfjährige Erfahrung im Verkauf von elektrischen Geräten.

In the firm where I am now engaged, my duties consist of taking and transcribing dictation, filing, cutting stencils, and compiling reports.

In der Firma, bei der ich z. Z. beschäftigt bin, bestehen meine Aufgaben in der Aufnahme von Diktaten und deren Übertragung in die Maschine, der Ablage, dem Schreiben von Matrizen und der Zusammenstellung von Berichten.

d. Reasons for Wanting a Change

My reason for seeking a change is the better opportunities offered in a large company like yours.

I intend to give up my present job, as I see no possibility here of assuming greater responsibility.

My present employer is closing down his business and dismissing all his staff.

As my parents are moving to New York, I am seeking employment there.

Ich suche mich zu verändern, weil mir eine Firma Ihrer Größe bessere Möglichkeiten bietet.

Ich gebe meine jetzige Stelle auf, da ich hier keine Möglichkeit habe, eine verantwortungsvollere Tätigkeit zu übernehmen.

Mein gegenwärtiger Arbeitgeber löst sein Geschäft auf und entläßt alle Angestellten.

Da meine Eltern nach New York ziehen, suche ich dort eine Anstellung.

4. Exercises

Please translate the following letter into English:

a. Unter Bezugnahme auf Ihre gestrige Anzeige in der „Frankfurter Allgemeinen Zeitung" möchte ich mich um die ausgeschriebene Stelle einer Fremdsprachensekretärin bewerben.

Ich bin 22 Jahre alt und ledig. Im Juni 19 .. habe ich in München das Abitur gemacht und anschließend in einem Jahreskurs der Handelsschule Maier kaufmännische Grundkenntnisse erworben. Nach einem einjährigen Aufenthalt in England als au-pair Hilfe begann ich mein Sprachstudium am Sprachen- und Dolmetscher-Institut München. Von August 19 .. bis Februar 19 .. unterbrach ich meine dortige Ausbildung, da ich die Möglichkeit hatte, im Londoner Anwaltsbüro Grey & White als Aushilfskraft zu arbeiten. Während dieser Zeit machte ich mich mit den üblichen Büroarbeiten vertraut und hatte zudem Gelegenheit, meine englischen Stenografie- und Schreibmaschinenkenntnisse anzuwenden. Nach meiner Rückkehr nach München setzte ich mein Studium am Sprachen- und Dolmetscher-Institut fort und legte im Februar 19 .. die Wirtschaftskorrespondentenprüfung für Englisch mit gutem Erfolg ab. Während meiner Ausbildungszeit habe ich meine französischen Schulkenntnisse in Abendkursen am Institut Français erweitert.

Von . . . bis . . . werde ich mich bei Freunden meiner Eltern in Paris aufhalten und könnte dann frühestens am . . . die Stelle antreten. Einen handgeschriebenen Lebenslauf, Zeugnisabschriften, Referenzen und Paßbild lege ich diesem Schreiben bei.

Ich suche eine sprachlich interessante und verantwortungsvolle Tätigkeit und würde mich freuen, wenn Sie mir Gelegenheit zu einer persönlichen Unterredung gäben.

Anlagen

Please draft letters in English from the following particulars:

b. Bewerben Sie sich auf eine der folgenden Anzeigen:

US COMPANY IN MUNICH

has opening for experienced

SECRETARY.

Fluency in English, French, and German typing and shorthand required. Excellent working conditions. Salary commensurate with ability and experience.

Résumé and references requested under AHS 66367.

Qualified Linguist

required by large English chemical company for its subsidiary in Frankfurt. Must be able to conduct correspondence in English and German, and act as interpreter at business conferences. Please write, stating details of qualifications, previous experience, and salary requirements, to

Personnel Manager, Hewitt GmbH, Bockenheimer Landstraße 366, Frankfurt/Main.

Industrieunternehmen in Stuttgart sucht

Fremdsprachenkorrespondentin,

die englische Korrespondenz nach deutschem Text oder Stichworten führen kann. Bewerbungen (deutsch *und* englisch) mit Lichtbild, tabellarischem Lebenslauf, Zeugnisabschriften, Gehaltswünschen und Angabe des frühest möglichen Eintrittsdatums unter

AKL 108763 an die Süddeutsche Zeitung.

c. In der heutigen Nummer der „Süddeutschen Zeitung" finden Sie eine Anzeige der Bayerischen Metallwerke AG. Die Firma sucht eine Korrespondentin für Englisch, die in der Lage ist, selbständig zu arbeiten. Bewerbungen sind in englischer Sprache einzureichen.

Sie bewerben sich auf diese Anzeige, da Sie glauben, den gestellten Anforderungen zu genügen. Nach Abschluß der Wirtschaftsoberschule gingen Sie 1 Jahr nach England, wo Sie u. a. aushilfsweise im Büro einer Exportfirma arbeiteten. Nach Ihrer Rückkehr nahmen Sie eine Stellung bei Hartmann & Co. an. Anfänglich bestand Ihre Aufgabe darin, englische Diktate aufzunehmen. Später wurde Ihnen ein Teil der englischen Korrespondenz zur Bearbeitung übertragen. Sie suchen sich zu verändern, da Sie glauben, daß Ihnen ein großer Betrieb die Möglichkeit bietet, umfassendere Kenntnisse auf dem Gebiet der Außenhandelstechnik zu erwerben. Sie legen einen Lebenslauf bei und hoffen, daß Ihnen die Firma Gelegenheit geben wird, sich persönlich vorzustellen.

Smart Girl

An office manager was asking a girl applicant if she had any unusual talents. She said she had won several prizes in crossword-puzzle contests. "Sounds good," the manager told her, "but we want somebody who will be smart during office hours." "Oh," said the girl, "this was during office hours."

Part Three

Glossary of Commercial Terms

agent. See **mercantile agents.**

arbitration. The settlement of disputes between parties to a contract by a person or persons chosen by the parties themselves or appointed by a *court of arbitration*. There are many courts of arbitration and arbitration associations; one of the best-known courts of arbitration is that of the **International Chamber of Commerce** in Paris.
Attempts to submit a dispute to arbitration often fail because the parties cannot agree on a particular form of arbitration, place of arbitration, etc. It is therefore advisable to include an arbitration clause in the contract. The arbitration clause of the International Chamber of Commerce reads as follows: "All disputes arising in connection with the present contract shall be finally settled under the Rules of Conciliation and Arbitration of the International Chamber of Commerce by one or more arbitrators appointed in accordance with the Rules."

bank draft (or: *banker's draft*). A **cheque** drawn by one bank on another.
A person who has to effect payment at a distant place (at home or abroad) may purchase from his bank a bank draft drawn on a bank at the creditor's place of residence and send it to the creditor, who will present it to the drawee bank for payment.

bankruptcy. An insolvent debtor, or his creditors, may apply to the proper court for the opening of bankruptcy proceedings. If the court finds sufficient proof of insolvency, the debtor is adjudged a bankrupt. The bankrupt's assets are placed under the control of the *official receiver,* a Department of Trade official, pending the appointment of a *trustee in bankruptcy* by the creditors. The trustee causes the bankrupt's property to be sold and distributes the proceeds of the sale among the creditors The *secured creditors* (those holding a mortgage or lien) can realize their security; the *unsecured creditors* receive their share after the *preferential debts* (court costs, wages, taxes, etc.) have been paid. After the bankrupt's property has been distributed, the court gives him a *discharge* from his unpaid debts, provided he has conducted himself honestly.

bank transfer (or: *banker's transfer*). A transfer of money from one bank account to another.
In the Anglo-Saxon countries, bank transfers are used chiefly in foreign trade. A debtor in country A asks his bank to arrange for the payment of a certain sum of money (in foreign currency) to his creditor in country B. The bank in country A debits its customer's account with the equivalent in domestic currency (plus bank charges) and

Bill of Lading

BILL OF LADING

OUTWARD

B/L No.

REFERENCE No.

BEN ⚓ LINE

THE BEN LINE STEAMERS LIMITED

Managers: Wm. Thomson & Co.   Edinburgh

Brokers: Killick Martin & Co. Ltd.   London

Agents: Menzell & Co., Schiffsmakler, Hamburg

CARRIAGE OF GOODS BY SEA ACT, 1924

SHIPPER

CONSIGNEE

NOTIFYING ADDRESS

LOCAL VESSEL   FROM

OCEAN VESSEL   PORT OF LOADING

PORT OF DISCHARGE   PORT OF DESTINATION (IF ON-CARRIAGE)   FREIGHT PAYABLE AT   NUMBER OF ORIGINAL Bs/L

MARKS AND NUMBERS	NUMBER AND KIND OF PACKAGES: DESCRIPTION OF GOODS	GROSS WEIGHT—KILOS	MEASUREMENT

SHIPPERS

PARTICULARS DECLARED B

NUMBER OF PACKAGES (in words)

SHIPPED in apparent good order and condition unless otherwise stated hereon, on board the above vessel lying in or off the port of loading named above and bound on a voyage as described and agreed by clause 5 on the reverse side of this Bill of Lading, the packages or pieces of merchandise described above (hereinafter called "the goods") being marked and numbered as above (weight, measurement, quality, contents and value (except for purposes of estimating freight) unknown) to be carried to and delivered, subject always to the exceptions and conditions stated in this Bill of Lading, in the like good order and condition from the vessel's tackles (where the vessel's responsibility shall in all circumstances finally cease), at the port of discharge named above or such other port or place as is provided in the clause hereinbefore referred to or so near thereunto as she may safely get always afloat, unto the abovementioned consignee or to his or their assigns.

IN WITNESS WHEREOF the number of original bills of lading stated above all of this tenor and date has been signed, one of which being accomplished the others to stand void.

PLACE AND DATE OF ISSUE :

FOR THE MASTER :

AS AGENTS

C/N

SUBJECT TO THE EXCEPTIONS AND CONDITIONS STATED OVERLEAF

instructs its branch or correspondent in country B (by mail or cable) to pay the amount, to the debit of its account, to the person in question.

A transfer made by mail is called *mail transfer* (M.T.), a transfer by telegraph or cable is called *telegraphic transfer* (T.T.) or *cable transfer* (C.T.). T.T. 's provide the quickest method of transferring funds from one country to another.

bill of exchange (B/E). Legally, a bill of exchange is defined as "an unconditional order in writing, addressed by one person to another, signed by the person giving it, requiring the person to whom it is addressed to pay on demand or at a fixed or determinable future time a certain sum of money to, or to the order of, a specified person, or to bearer."

This definition covers both **cheque** and *draft*, but in practice the word *bill of exchange* or *bill* is applied to drafts only. There are *inland* (or: *domestic*) *bills* and *foreign bills*. Inland bills are drawn and payable within the British Isles; all other bills are foreign bills. Foreign bills include the word *Exchange* and are usually issued in a set. The two or three bills making up the set are identical in all respects, except that each refers to the other. Issuing bills in a set is a precaution against loss in transit, as the parts of the set can be sent by different mails. When any of the bills forming the set has been paid, the others become void.

Bills of exchange have three parties: the *drawer* (the person who makes out the bill), the *drawee* (the person who is directed to pay) and the *payee* (the person who is to get the money). The payee may be the drawer himself or a third person.

With regard to maturity, we distinguish between *sight bills* (*sight drafts*) and *time bills* (*time drafts*). Sight bills are payable at sight, time bills are payable on a fixed future date, or a certain time after date or sight.

A bill is of no practical value unless the drawee accepts it by writing his name across its face. The drawee thus becomes the *acceptor*; his signature on the draft, and the accepted draft itself, are called *acceptance*. A *trade acceptance* is a draft accepted by a buyer of goods, a *bank acceptance* (or: *banker's acceptance*) is a draft accepted by a bank.

The holder of a bill of exchange can use it in any of the following ways: 1. keep it until it is due and present it for payment (or give it to his banker for collection), 2. sell it to a bank before maturity (see **discounting of bills**), 3. pass it on in payment of a debt. Before a bill of exchange can be transferred, it has to be endorsed (see **endorsement**).

In Great Britain, bills of exchange are subject to a stamp duty of 2d.

Also see **clean draft, documentary draft, prolongation of bills.**

bill of lading (B/L). A document issued when goods are entrusted to a shipping company for conveyance by sea. It gives the person to whom it is issued or transferred title (right of ownership) to the goods it represents (*document of title*).

Bills of lading are issued in sets, usually consisting of three originals signed by the master of the ship or another authorized person on behalf of the shipping company. In addition to the originals, copies may be prepared in any desired number. The master is instructed to deliver the goods on presentation of any of the originals. When the goods have been released on the strength of one of the originals, the other originals become void.

The set of signed bills of lading is given in exchange for a *wharfinger's receipt* (*dock receipt*) or *mate's receipt*. Both are temporary receipts. The wharfinger's receipt is signed by the man in charge of the wharf and certifies that the goods have been received for subsequent loading; the mate's receipt is signed by the ship's chief officer and certifies that the goods are on board the vessel. Before these receipts are issued, the outward condition of the packages is examined. If the packages are in good condition, a *clean receipt* is given for them, if there is any defect in the condition of the packages, a note to that effect is made on the receipt, which is then known as a *foul* (or: *dirty*) *receipt*. When a clean receipt is presented, the shipping company will issue a clean bill of lading. A note on the receipt is also put on the bill of lading; thus a bill issued on the basis of a foul receipt is also foul.

A bill of lading stating that the goods have been loaded on board the carrying vessel is known as a *shipped* or *on-board bill of lading*. A *received-for-shipment* (or: *received*) *bill of lading*, on the other hand, merely states that the goods have been received for subsequent loading. It does not provide evidence of the actual shipment and is therefore less valuable than a shipped bill of lading. (After the goods have been loaded, a received bill may be converted into an on-board bill by means of a notation dated and signed by the carrier or his agent.)

Bills of lading may be either *order bills* or *straight bills*. Most order bills of lading are issued to shipper's order, in which case they are simply consigned "to order," but there are also bills issued to the order of a named consignee or a bank. Bills of lading made out to shipper's order include a *notify clause* giving the name and address of the person to be notified on arrival of the shipment (usually the buyer or his agent). An order bill of lading (and title to the goods it represents) can be transferred by **endorsement**. A straight bill of lading is issued to a named consignee, but not to his order, and is therefore not transferable.

Bills of lading contain the terms and conditions of the contract of carriage concluded between the shipper and the shipping company. They clearly specify the risks for which the shipping company will not accept any responsibility.

Compare **consignment note**.

carriage paid to frontier. Under these terms, the seller pays carriage to the frontier and bears the risks of the goods until they have been delivered into the custody of the first carrier.

carrier. A person, firm, etc., engaged in transporting goods (or passengers) for hire. The most important carriers are railways, road hauliers, airlines and shipping companies.

cash discount. A **discount** granted to a customer for immediate payment or payment within a stated period of time (*discount period*).

certificate of origin. A document showing the origin of goods, signed by a chamber of commerce or customs officer in the exporting country. Certificates of origin are required by many countries and entitle the importer to claim the benefit of preferential tariffs granted by his country to the country of the exporter.

C. & F. (*cost and freight*). Under C. & F. terms, the seller's and the buyer's duties are the same as under **C.I.F.** terms, except that the seller does not arrange for insurance. Also see **Incoterms**.

chamber of commerce. A voluntary[1] association of merchants, manufacturers and others engaged in business, for the purpose of promoting the interests of its members and the trade of the country as a whole. Chambers of commerce, among other things, furnish information and advice to businessmen, assist them in establishing business contacts, appoint experts, certify documents, and issue **certificates of origin**.
In addition to the national chambers of commerce there are special chambers set up for the purpose of furthering trade between two countries, such as the *German-American Chamber of Commerce*. The national chambers of commerce of most countries are linked up with the **International Chamber of Commerce.**
[1] Membership in the German chambers of commerce and industry is compulsory.

cheque. A cheque (*US*: check) is a **bill of exchange** drawn on a bank and payable on demand. A person or firm having a current account at a bank can draw cheques up to the amount of the credit balance on his account.
The parties to a cheque are: the *drawer* (the person who makes out the cheque and signs it), the *drawee* (the bank on which it is drawn), and the *payee* (the person who is to get the money).
An *order cheque* is payable to a specified person or order and can be transferred by **endorsement**. A *bearer cheque* is payable to bearer; it can pass freely from person to person without endorsement.
An *open cheque* is paid in cash by the bank on which it is drawn. A *crossed cheque* is not paid over the counter but credited to a banking account. A person receiving a crossed cheque must hand it to his banker for collection. Cheques have to be presented for payment within a reasonable period of time. If the holder keeps the cheque too long, it becomes "stale." Stale cheques are not paid immediately on presentation, but the drawee bank will first ask the drawer whether he still wants the cheque to be honoured. A cheque is returned by the bank unpaid if there are insufficient funds or no funds, or if the cheque is not in order.
Also see **bank draft.**

C.I.F. (*cost, insurance, freight*). Under C.I.F. terms, the seller's and the buyer's duties are as follows:

The seller must contract for the carriage of the goods to the agreed port of destination and load the goods on board the vessel at his own expense. The seller must bear the risks of the goods until they have effectively passed the ship's rail at the port of shipment, pay the freight to the port of destination, and take out insurance, at his own cost, for the benefit of the buyer. The insurance has to cover the C.I.F. price plus 10 per cent (buyer's anticipated profit).

The buyer must bear the risks of the goods from the time when they have effectively passed the ship's rail and bear all costs incurred in transit, except freight and insurance, as well as unloading costs, including lighterage and wharfage, unless these costs are included in the freight. (When goods are sold *C.I.F. landed,* unloading costs, including lighterage and wharfage, are borne by the seller.)

Also see **Incoterms**.

clean draft. A foreign **bill of exchange** without documents.

C.O.D. (cash on delivery). When goods are delivered C.O.D., the post office, railway, or forwarding agent is entrusted with the collection of the invoice amount. When the buyer has paid this amount, the goods are released to him.

Compare **documents against payment**.

collection of documentary drafts. When goods are sold on **D/A** or **D/P** terms, the seller draws a **documentary draft** on the buyer. D/P drafts are (usually) sight drafts, D/A drafts are time drafts payable after sight. The task of presenting the draft to the buyer at his residence and delivering the **documents** to him when he pays or accepts the draft is usually entrusted to a bank. (Sometimes collections are handled by a forwarding agent or the exporter's subsidiary abroad.) The exporter's bank carries out the collection through its branch office or correspondent in the foreign country.

The exporter must give his bank detailed instructions with regard to the collection. The bank usually asks the exporter to complete a *documentary bill lodgment form* (or: *letter of transmittal*). The exporter has to inform the collecting bank whether the documents are to be surrendered on payment or acceptance of the draft, how the collection proceeds are to be remitted, what is to be done if the draft is dishonoured, etc. To avoid loss of documents in transit, drafts and documents are usually made out in duplicate, the originals being sent by first air mail, the duplicates by the following air mail.

Combined Certificate of Value and Origin. See **customs invoice**.

commercial invoice. See p. 85/86.

Air Consignment Note

Mitglied der / Member of
International Air Transport
Association (IATA)

nicht begebbar LUFTFRACHTBRIEF not negotiable
AIR WAYBILL – AIR CONSIGNMENT NOTE 220—
ausgestellt von / issued by

Deutsche Lufthansa
Aktiengesellschaft
5 Köln, Claudiusstraße 1

Bestimmungsflughafen
Destination (Airport of)

Adresse
Address

Außerdem zu benachrichtigen
Also Notify

Stückzahl No. of Packages	Art der Verpackung Method of Packing	Art und Menge der Güter Nature and Quantity of Goods	Markierung Marks and Numbers	Maße oder Rauminhalt Dimensions or Volume	Bruttogewicht / Gross Weight Angabe / Specify KGS. oder LBS.

Dem Luftfrachtbrief beigefügte Begleitpapiere
Documents to accompany Air Waybill

Wertangabe des Absenders (Währung angeben)
Shipper's declared Value (Specify Currency)

Für Zollzwecke
For Customs

Für d. Beförderung
For Carriage

LEITWEGE UND KOSTENBERECHNUNG - Vereinbarte Zwischenlandeplätze sind (mit Ausnahme des Abgangs und Bestimmungsflughafens) die in der Rubrik LUFTTRANSPORT und/oder die im Flugplan des Frachtführers für diese Strecke vorgesehenen regulären Landeplätze. Siehe umseitig aufgef. Vertragsbedingungen.

METHOD OF ROUTING AND CHARGES - Agreed stopping places are those places (other than the places of departure and destination) shown under AIR CARRIAGE, and/or those places shown in carrier's timetable or scheduled stopping places for...

Absender muß
die Nummer der
ihm zu belastenden
Kostenspalte an-
geben
Shipper must
Insert Item Number

Die stark umrandeten
Felder werden vom
Frachtführer ausge-
füllt/ausgenommen
Zeile 17
Portions Surrounded by
Bold Lines Reserved
for Carrier

Abgangs-flughafen Departure (Airport of)	(ANSCHRIFT DES ERSTEN FRACHTFÜHRERS) ADDRESS OF FIRST CARRIER		Chargeable Weight Angabe/Specify KGS. or LBS.	Tarifn Rate Classification	Tariffraten Rates	Vorausbezahlt Prepaid	Wäh-rung Cur-rency	Beträge in der berechneten Währung Amounts in Curren-cies as charged	Beträge in der Währung des Bestimmungslandes Amounts in Currency at Destination
1. Nach To	1. Frachtf. First Carrier								
2. Nach To	2. Frachtf. Carrier								
3. Nach To	3. Frachtf. Carrier								
3a. Nach To	3a. Frachtf. Carrier								
4. Wertzuschlag/Valuation Charge Von/From		Nach/To							
5. Wertzuschlag/Valuation Charge Von/From		Nach/To							
6. Versicherung/Insurance	Betrag in Worten/Amount In Words								
	7. Abgang/Origin								
VERSICHERUNG : Sofern der Absender gemäß umsatigen Bedin-gungen Transport-Versicherung ver-langt, ist die Versicherungssumme oben in Buchstaben einzutragen. Wenn keine Eintragung erfolgte, wird die Sendung nicht versichert. INSURANCE: If Shipper requests insurance in accordance with conditions stoted on reverse hereof, indicate amount of insurance in words in space provided above. If no insert is made, shipment will not be insured.	8.								
	9.								
	10.								
	11. Transit/Transit								
	12. Ankunft/Destination								
	13.								
	14.	Sonstige Kosten Other Charges (Specify)							
	15.								
	16. Nachnahme · Inkassoprovision / C.O.D. Fee								
	17. Nachnahme des Absenders/Shipper's C.O.D.								

ENDSUMMEN TOTALS

Nachnahme des Absenders in Worten
Shipper's C.O.D. In Words

Der Absender bestätigt die Richtigkeit obiger Angaben sowie sein Einverständnis mit den **umseitig aufgeführten Vertragsbedingungen.** The Shipper certifies that the particulars on the face hereof are correct and agrees to the **conditions on the reverse hereof**

NAME DES ABSENDERS   Telefon
NAME OF SHIPPER _____ Phone
ANSCHRIFT
ADDRESS _____

UNTERSCHRIFT DES ABSENDERS
SIGNATURE OF SHIPPER _____
DURCH MAKLER/AGENT
BY BROKER/AGENT

Ausfertigungen 1, 2 und 3 dieses Luftfrachtbriefes gelten als gleichwertige Originale
Copies 1, 2 and 3 of this Air Waybill are Originals and have the same validity

Form 2812-64 (CGN XA 2)

Die vorstehend beschriebenen Güter wurden in äußerlich gutem Zustand (sofern nichts anderes vermerkt) zur Be-förderung AUF GRUND DER UMSEITIG AUFGEFÜHRTEN BEDINGUNGEN übernommen. / Carrier certifies above-described goods were received for carriage SUBJECT TO THE CONDITIONS ON REVERSE HEREOF, the goods then being in apparent good order and condition except as noted hereon.

Ausgestellt am/Executed on _____ In/at _____
                              (Datum/Date)   (Ort/Place)
NAME UND ANSCHRIFT DES AGENTEN DES FRACHTFÜHRERS
NAME & ADDRESS OF ISSUING CARRIER'S AGENT

Unterschrift des ausstellenden Frachtführers oder seines Agenten
Signature of Issuing Carrier or its Agent

Printed in Germany

commercial traveller (US also: *traveling*[1] *salesman*). An employee who calls on customers and solicits orders.

[1] *US for* travelling.

consignment note (US: *waybill*). A document used when goods are sent by rail, by road, or by air.

The consignment note has to be completed by the consignor and delivered to the carrier together with the goods. A copy (*duplicate consignment note*) is given to the consignor as a receipt. Unlike the **bill of lading**, the consignment note or waybill is not a document of title. (The American railway companies issue a special *railroad bill of lading* which has all the legal characteristics of an ocean bill of lading. There is no comparable document in Great Britain and Continental Europe.)

consignment stock. A stock of goods which a manufacturer or trader (*consignor*) places at the disposal of his agent (*consignee*). The consignee sells these goods (*consignment goods*), which are consignor's property, for consignor's account.

Also see **mercantile agents**.

consular invoice. A special invoice for customs purposes which, like the **customs invoice**, has to be prepared by the exporter on a special form. Unlike the customs invoice, however, the consular invoice must be legalized by a consulate of the importing country. For legalization of consular invoices (and other documents) the consulate charges a *consular fee*. Consular invoices are required by many Latin-American countries.

credit association. Usually connected with a **trade association**. It compiles credit information on firms with which any of its members have had dealings and makes this information available to all members.

credit-inquiry agency (US: *commercial agency, mercantile agency*). An agency which collects information about business firms and furnishes it to its subscribers.

The subscribers pay a subscription fee; in return they receive the *rating books* published by the agency and *special reports* on any firm about which they inquire. The large credit-inquiry agencies have branches or correspondents abroad and can also furnish reports on foreign firms. The most famous agency is *Dun & Bradstreet* in the United States, which operates all over the world.

credit note. See p. 86.

customs invoice. A special invoice for customs purposes which importers in many countries have to present to the customs authorities when filing a *customs entry*, and which serves as the basis for the assessment of **import duty**. It has to be prepared by the

Order Cheque

20-80-06
29/42   19___   20-80-06

BARCLAYS BANK LIMITED
SOUTH HARROW.

Pay_____ _or Order_

£

JOHN ENGLAND

'SPECIMEN

711982   ⑈711982⑈ 22⑈8006⑈ 34 567 3⑈

Foreign Bill of Exchange

Exchange for...   ....19..........

.... of this FIRST OF EXCHANGE
(SECOND of same date and tenor unpaid) pay to the order of

....

....

Value received.

To...   ....

....

exporter on a special form which can be obtained from printers and stationers specializing in the sale of export forms. On this invoice the exporter must show, in addition to the usual invoice details and the export price, the domestic value of the goods in the exporting country, and the country of origin.

Customs invoices are required by the Commonwealth countries, the British colonies, and a number of other countries (but not Great Britain). In most of these countries the official designation of the customs invoice is *Combined Certificate of Value and Origin*. In the United States, a *Special Customs Invoice* has to be presented on all shipments valued at over $500 and subject to ad valorem duty.

Compare **consular invoice.**

D/A (*documents against acceptance*). Under D/A terms, the **documents** relating to a shipment of goods are released to the buyer on acceptance of a **documentary draft** (time draft) drawn on him by the seller.

Also see **collection of documentary drafts**. Compare **documents against bank acceptance.**

debit note. See p. 86.

discount. 1. A deduction from the invoice price or list price. See **cash discount, quantity discount, trade discount.** Compare **rebate.** 2. A deduction from the face amount of a **bill of exchange**. Also see **discounting of bills**.

discounting of bills. Buying bills of exchange before maturity for a sum less than their face value. (The term *to discount* may also mean *to have a bill discounted*, as, for example, in the following sentence: *The holder of a bill can obtain immediate cash by discounting it.*)

Bills are discounted by banks and other financial institutions. The bank deducts the discount, that is, interest for the time until maturity, from the face amount of the bill and pays the balance in cash or credits it to the customer's account.

A bank which has discounted a bill can *re-discount* it at the central bank, provided the bill is eligible for re-discounting.

documentary letter of credit (or: *documentary credit*). A documentary letter of credit is a promise by a bank to a seller of goods to pay a certain amount of money if the **documents** relating to the goods are presented on time and in strict compliance with the terms of the credit.

When the buyer and the seller have agreed on payment by documentary letter of credit, the buyer requests his bank to open (*or*: to issue) the credit in favour of the seller. The buyer's bank (*opening* or *issuing bank*) instructs its correspondent in the seller's country (by mail or by cable) to pay the seller the amount in question on presentation of the documents specified in the credit. Sometimes the letter of credit is addressed direct to the beneficiary by the opening bank.

184

The amount of the credit may be made available to the beneficiary in any of the following ways:
1. The beneficiary is authorized to draw a sight draft on the correspondent bank, which this bank pays on presentation of the documents.
2. The beneficiary is authorized to draw a time draft on the correspondent bank, which this bank accepts on presentation of the documents. The accepted draft (*bank acceptance*) is then discounted.
3. The beneficiary is authorized to draw a draft (in foreign currency) on the opening bank or the buyer, which the correspondent bank negotiates (that is, purchases) on presentation of the documents.
Documentary credits may be *irrevocable and confirmed, irrevocable and unconfirmed,* or *revocable and unconfirmed.*
An irrevocable credit cannot be revoked by the opening bank except with the beneficiary's consent. A revocable credit can be modified or cancelled at any time without notice to the beneficiary. When an irrevocable credit is to be confirmed, the opening bank instructs its correspondent to send the beneficiary a confirmation. Such a confirmation is a definite undertaking on the part of the correspondent to pay, accept, or negotiate the beneficiary's draft or drafts, provided the documents required are presented within the required time. In the case of irrevocable and unconfirmed credits or revocable credits (which are always unconfirmed), the opening bank merely instructs the correspondent bank to advise the beneficiary of the credit, such advice being without any obligation for the correspondent.
Irrevocable and confirmed credits constitute an engagement of both the opening bank and its correspondent and thus offer maximum security to the exporter. In many cases, however, irrevocable and unconfirmed credits are preferred because they are cheaper.
Also see **How Payment Is Made by Irrevocable and Confirmed Documentary Credit** p. 197.

documentary draft. A foreign **bill of exchange** with **documents** attached.
Also see **collection of documentary drafts.**

documents. The most important documents used in connection with export shipments are:
bill of lading, insurance policy, insurance certificate, commercial invoice, customs invoice, consular invoice and **certificate of origin.**

documents against bank acceptance. Under these terms, the **documents** relating to a shipment of goods are released to a bank on acceptance of a **documentary draft** (time draft) drawn on it by the seller. Bank acceptances are first-class bills and can be discounted at a favourable rate.
When the terms of "documents against bank acceptance" have been agreed upon, the buyer instructs his bank to accept the seller's draft or to arrange for its correspondent

in the seller's country to provide the acceptance. (The latter procedure is the usual one.) Upon acceptance, the documents are handed over to the bank. The seller can get funds immediately by discounting the banker's acceptance. The buyer, on the other hand, is required by his bank to provide cover before maturity of the bill.

Also see **bill of exchange, discounting of bills.** Compare **D/A.**

D/P (*documents against payment*). Under D/P terms, the **documents** relating to a shipment of goods are released to the buyer on payment of a **documentary draft** (usually a sight draft) drawn on him by the seller.

Also see **collection of documentary drafts.** Compare **C.O.D.**

draft. See **bill of exchange.**

duplicate consignment note. See **consignment note.**

endorsement. Instruments payable to order, for example, **bill of exchange,** order **cheque, promissory note** and order **bill of lading,** can be transferred by endorsement.

Endorsements are placed on the back of the instrument. The person who writes the endorsement is called the *endorser*, the person to whom the instrument is endorsed is the *endorsee*. The most important endorsements are *blank endorsement* and *special endorsement*.

A blank endorsement consists only of the endorser's signature; it turns an order paper into a bearer paper negotiable by delivery only.

John Smith

blank endorsement

A special endorsement includes endorser's signature, name of endorsee, and sometimes also the date. A blank endorsement can be converted into a special endorsement by writing *Pay to the order of* and the endorsee's name above the signature of the endorser.

Pay to the order of
William Brown.

17th June, 19..

John Smith

special endorsement

Documentary Credit (Advice of Credit Opened)

BARCLAYS BANK LIMITED

CHIEF FOREIGN BRANCH
168 FENCHURCH STREET, LONDON, E.C.3
TELEPHONE: MANSION HOUSE 0505
TELEGRAPHIC ADDRESS: *Inland:* BARCLABAN, LONDON, TELEX. *Overseas:* BARCLABAN, LONDON, E.C.3

To

COPY ONLY

Our Reference No.

Dear Sir(s),

We have received advice from

that they have opened/issued their
in favour of
for account of
  (amount)

available for

to be accompanied by the following documents:-

SPECIMEN COPY ONLY

Every draft drawn under this credit must be marked "Drawn under
credit of
No.   " and drawn and negotiated/presented to us

It is to be understood that this letter is solely an advice
of the credit opened or issued by the above mentioned bank and conveys
no engagement by us.

The credit is subject to Uniform Customs and Practice for
Documentary Credits (1962 revision), International Chamber of Commerce
Brochure No.222.

Yours faithfully,
for BARCLAYS BANK LIMITED,

FB 714

Customs Invoice

Combined Certificate of Value and of Origin of Goods for Exportation to the

Commonwealth of Australia

Intermediate and General Tariffs.

(1) Full name and position Manager, Chief Clerk or as the case may be

I, (1) ....

(2) Name of firm or company

of (2) ....

(3) Name of city or country

of (3) ....

manufacturer/supplier of the goods enumerated in this invoice amounting to ....
hereby declare that I ([4]) have the authority to make and sign this certificate on behalf of the aforesaid manufacturer/supplier and that I) have the means of knowing and I do further declare as follows:—

(4) These words should be omitted when the manufacturer or supplier himself signs the certificate

VALUE.

1 a.   That this invoice is in all respects correct and contains a true and full statement of the price actually paid or to be paid for the said goods, and the actual quantity and description thereof.

1 b.   That this invoice is in all respects correct and contains a true and full statement as to the quantity and description of the goods and of the price which would have had to be paid by a purchaser in Australia had the goods been sold to an Australian importer instead of being consigned for sale in Australia.

2.   That no different invoice of the goods mentioned in the said invoice has been or will be furnished to anyone; and that no arrangements or understanding affecting the purchase price of the said goods has been or will be made or entered into between the said exporter and the purchaser, or by anyone on behalf of either of them either by way of discount, rebate compensation or in any manner whatever other than as fully shown on this invoice or as follows.

(5) Particulars of any special arrangement

(5) ....

3.   That the domestic values shown in the column headed "Current Domestic Values in Currency of Exporting Country" are those at which the above-mentioned firm or company is supplying or would be

(6) 'Warehouse' 'factory' 'port of shipment'

(6) .... per cent, cash discount, ...
subject to ....
and that such values include/exclude the cost of outside packages, if any, in which the goods are sold in such country for domestic consumption.

4. That the said domestic values includes any duty leviable in respect of the goods before they are delivered for home consumption and that on exportation a drawback or remission of duty amounting to

.... has been/will be allowed by the revenue authorities in the country of exportation.

5. That each article on this invoice is bona fide the produce or manufacture of the country specified on this invoice as its country of origin.

ORIGIN.

Enumerate the following charges and state whether each amount has been included in or excluded from the current domestic value above : —	Amount in currency of exporting country	State if included or excluded
1. Cartage to rail, docks or airport		
2. Inland freight (rail or canal) and other charges to dock area or airport including inland insurance		
3. Labour in packing the goods into outside packages . . .		
4. Value of outside packages		
5. If the goods are subject to any charge by way of Royalties State full particulars of Royalties below:—		
....		
....		

Dated at .... this .... day of .... 19 ......

.... Signature ....

Witness ....

ex works (*ex factory, mill, plantation, warehouse,* etc.). Under ex works terms, the seller's and the buyer's duties are as follows:

The seller must place the goods at the buyer's disposal at his factory or warehouse and bear all costs and risks until the goods have been placed at the buyer's disposal.

The buyer must take delivery of the goods and bear all costs and risks from the time when the goods have been placed at his disposal.

Also see **Incoterms.**

F.A.S. (*free alongside ship*). Under F.A.S. terms, the seller's and the buyer's duties are as follows:

The seller must deliver the goods alongside the vessel named by the buyer and bear all costs and risks of the goods until they have been delivered alongside the vessel, either at the quay or by means of lighters.

The buyer must charter a vessel or reserve the necessary space on board a vessel and inform the seller of the name of the vessel, loading berth of and delivery dates to the vessel. The buyer must bear all costs and risks of the goods from the time when they have been delivered alongside the vessel.

Also see **Incoterms.**

F.O.B. (*free on board*). Under F.O.B. terms, the seller's and the buyer's duties are as follows:

The seller must deliver the goods on board the vessel named by the buyer and bear all costs and risks of the goods until they have effectively passed the ship's rail at the port of shipment.

The buyer must charter a vessel or reserve the necessary space on board a vessel and inform the seller of the name of the vessel, loading berth of and delivery dates to the vessel. The buyer must bear all costs and risks of the goods from the time they have effectively passed the ship's rail.

Also see **Incoterms.**

F.O.R./F.O.T. (*free on rail/free on truck*). Under F.O.R/F.O.T. terms, the seller's and the buyer's duties are as follows:

In the case of a wagonload, the seller must obtain a wagon, load it, and deliver it into the custody of the railway. In the case of a load less than a wagonload, the seller must deliver the goods into the custody of the railway, either at the dispatching station or into a vehicle provided by the railway. The seller must bear all costs and risks of the goods until the wagon on which they are loaded, or the goods themselves, have been delivered into the custody of the railway.

The buyer must bear all costs and risks from the time when the wagon on which the goods are loaded, or the goods themselves, have been delivered into the custody of the railway.

Also see **Incoterms.**

forwarding agent (US also: *forwarder, freight forwarder*). The main function of a forwarding agent is to arrange for the conveyance of goods to the agreed place of destination. He takes over the goods, delivers them to the **carrier** and—through his branch offices or correspondents—makes arrangements for transshipment, if necessary. Forwarding agents usually have their own lorries or vans and also transport goods themselves, for example, from consignor's warehouse to the railway station.

Other services which forwarding agents render to their customers are: making up grouped consignments (*US*: consolidated shipments) and thus helping to save transport charges, providing storage space, obtaining the necessary shipping documents, taking out insurance, attending to customs clearance of goods, handling collections, etc. Customs clearance and collections in foreign countries are arranged through the forwarding agent's foreign correspondents.

franco domicile (or: *free buyer's address*, US: *F.O.B. buyer's warehouse*). Under these terms, the seller bears costs and risks until the goods have been delivered at the buyer's address.

franco frontier. Under these terms, the seller bears all costs and risks until the goods reach the frontier or border.

freight or carriage paid to ... Under these terms, which are used only in rail, road and inland waterway transport, the seller's and the buyer's duties are as follows:
The seller must deliver the goods at his own expense to the agreed point and bear the risks of the goods until they have been delivered into the custody of the first carrier. The buyer must pay all costs from the time of arrival of the goods at the agreed point and bear the risks from the time the goods have been delivered into the custody of the first carrier.
Also see **Incoterms.**

import duty. A duty levied on dutiable goods on importation. It is usually assessed on the basis of the value of the goods (*ad valorem duty*) or their weight (*specific duty*).

import licence. A government permit for which an importer must apply if the goods he wants to import are *subject to quota*. (An *import quota* is the maximum quantity of a certain commodity which the government allows to be imported.)

Incoterms (*International Commercial Terms*). The Incoterms are uniform definitions of terms of delivery in foreign trade, which were drafted by the **International Chamber of Commerce.** They were first published in 1936; a revised edition appeared in 1953. The most important Incoterms are: **ex works, F.O.R./F.O.T., F.A.S., F.O.B., C.I.F., C. & F.** and **freight or carriage paid to** ...
The Incoterms indicate the seller's and the buyer's duties, and the costs and risks to be borne by each. They also serve as the basis of price quotations. When a supplier quotes

a price, for example, on a C.I.F. basis, his quotation includes all the costs he has to assume under the contract.

The application of the Incoterms is completely voluntary. However, when a contract is concluded on the basis of the Incoterms, the buyer and the seller know exactly what their duties are, a fact which helps to avoid misunderstandings and disputes in international trade.

It should be noted, however, that there are terms of delivery which have not been defined in the Incoterms and that the Americans generally prefer to use their own terms (*Revised American Foreign Trade Definitions of 1941*), which differ from the Incoterms in many respects.

inquiry agency. See **credit-inquiry agency.**

insurance certificate. See **insurance policy.**

insurance policy. In marine insurance the most important types of policies are *voyage policy, open policy* and *floating* (or: *declaration*) *policy.*

Under a voyage policy, the goods are insured for a particular voyage. Open policies are taken out for recurring shipments; they may give cover for a fixed period, or for an indefinite period (until notice has been given). The insured is required to declare the individual shipments effected under the policy and to pay the premium assessed by the insurance company. A floating policy is taken out for a lump sum on which the premium is assessed. The individual shipments are declared to the insurance company and deducted from this sum. When the policy is exhausted it has to be renewed.

An exporter who wants proof of insurance for an individual shipment under an open or floating policy must obtain an *insurance certificate*. The certificate takes the place of the policy in respect of the shipment to which it refers.

International Chamber of Commerce (I.C.C.). A world federation of chambers of commerce and similar organizations, with headquarters in Paris, founded in 1919.

The I.C.C. acts as a spokesman for the international business community and has an important advisory position with the U.N. It has done much to standardize international business practices by creating uniform rules, including the **Incoterms**, *Uniform Customs and Practice for Documentary Credits* (1974 Revision), supplemented by the *Standard Forms for the Opening of Documentary Credits* (1951), and the *Uniform Rules for the Collection of Commercial Paper* (1957). Furthermore, the I.C.C. has established a court of arbitration for the settlement of international commercial disputes (see **arbitration**).

letter of credit (L/C). See **documentary letter of credit.**

limited company. A company limited by shares in Great Britain. Its capital is divided up into shares; the liability of the shareholders is limited to the par value of the shares held by them. (The name of the company must end with the word *Limited* or the abbreviation *Ltd.*)

A limited company which offers its shares (and debentures) to the public is called *public limited company*. A *private limited company* restricts the right to transfer its shares and limits the number of its members (*shareholders*).

The shareholders elect *directors*, who are responsible for the management of the company. The actual management may be in the hands of a *managing director*. Limited companies are also required to have a *secretary*, who has special duties and responsibilities.

Compare **stock corporation.**

Lloyd's. The *Corporation of Lloyd's* in London is an association of underwriters. Insurance business is not transacted by Lloyd's itself, but only by its members, the underwriters.

Lloyd's agent. See **survey report.**

mercantile agents. In this classification there are *commission agents, factors* and *brokers*. A commission agent sells (or buys) goods for his principal. For his work he receives a *commission* calculated at a certain percentage of the amount of the transaction. An agent having the exclusive right to represent his principal in his territory (*sole agency*) is called *sole agent*. A *foreign agent* represents his principal in a foreign market.

A factor (consignee) is an agent to whom goods are consigned for the purpose of sale (see **consignment stock**). He has possession of the goods and sells them in his own name on a commission basis.

A broker is an agent who negotiates contracts for other parties for a compensation called *brokerage*. He acts as an intermediary in bringing the parties together. The services of brokers are employed in the following fields of business activity: purchase and sale of goods, security dealings, real estate, shipping and insurance.

money order. Money orders are issued for any amount up to £50. They may be crossed in the same way as **postal orders.** For urgent remittances, *telegraphic money orders* are used. Money orders purchased in the United Kingdom can be made payable overseas.

In the United States, money orders are issued by post offices, banks, or express companies. They are transmitted through the post, by telegraph or cable, and may be payable within the United States (*domestic money orders*) or abroad (*international money orders*).

one-man business (US: *sole proprietorship*). A business owned and operated by one person (*sole trader*).

partnership. An association of two or more persons (*partners*), who carry on business together for the purpose of making a profit. The partners of an *ordinary partnership* (US: *general partnership*) have unlimited liability. A *limited partnership* consists of at least one *general partner*, who has unlimited liability, and one or more partners with limited liability, called *limited partners*.

postal order. Postal orders are issued for sums ranging between 1s. and 21s. The sender of the order enters on it the name of the payee and the name of the post office where payment is to be made. Postal orders may be crossed, in which case payment will be made only through a bank. Compare **money order.**

pro-forma invoice. See p. 86.

prolongation of bills. The acceptor of a **bill of exchange,** who is faced with financial difficulties, may approach the drawer before maturity and ask for a prolongation of the bill. The drawer will agree to a prolongation only if the acceptor is a reliable businessman and his difficulties are of a temporary nature.
Prolongation may be effected in either of the following ways: If the drawer is the holder of the bill, a new bill, payable at a later date, is made out and accepted by the debtor. (The old bill is destroyed.) For the time of extension interest is charged. If the bill is not in the hands of the drawer, the drawer must advance the amount of the bill to enable the acceptor to meet it when it is presented for payment. The debtor, in turn, is required to accept a new bill and to pay interest for the additional time allowed.

promissory note. Legally, a promissory note is defined as "an unconditional promise in writing, made by one person to another, signed by the maker, engaging to pay on demand or at a fixed or determinable future time a certain sum of money to, or to the order of, a specified person, or to bearer."
Promissory notes have only two parties: the *maker*, who makes the promise, and the *payee*, to whom the promise is made.
Compare **bill of exchange.**

Pty. Ltd. Abbreviation of *proprietary limited*. Proprietary companies are private limited companies in Australia and South Africa. See **limited company.**

quantity discount. A **discount** granted to a customer who buys a large quantity of goods.

railroad bill of lading (*US*). See **consignment note.**

rebate. An amount returned out of a sum already paid. A rebate is, for example, the

Postal Order

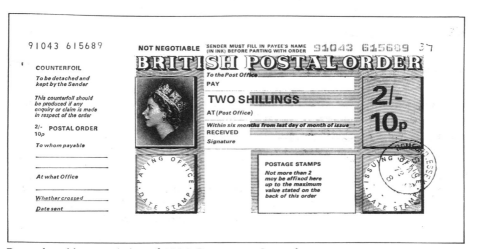

Reproduced by permission of H.M. Postmaster General

Money Order

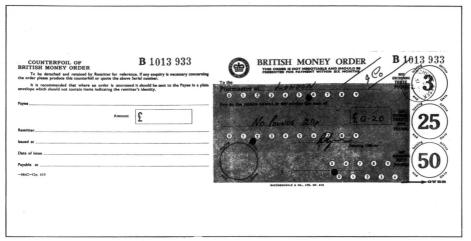

Reproduced by permission of H.M. Postmaster General

refund granted by a manufacturer to a dealer who achieves a specified volume of trade within a fixed period of time. Compare **discount**.

salesman (*US*). See **commercial traveller**.

sole agency. See **mercantile agents**.

stock corporation. A type of business organization in the United States, which corresponds to the **limited company** in Great Britain.

The shares of *open corporations* are bought and sold on the open market. *Closed corporations* do not offer their shares to the public.

As in a British limited company, the *shareholders* of a corporation elect *directors*. The directors select (from among themselves) the *officers* or *executives*, who are entrusted with the actual management. These officers are: a *president*, a *vice-president* (or several vice-presidents), a *secretary* and a *treasurer* (or a secretary-treasurer). (If there are only a few directors, these are also the officers.)

survey report. When a shipment arrives in damaged condition, the consignee has to notify the *surveyor* named in the **insurance policy** or certificate, who will examine the damage and issue a survey report. Surveyors are representatives of the insurance company; a surveyor representing **Lloyd's** in London is known as a *Lloyd's agent*.

tender. The tender system, utilized by government agencies and other organizations, is a method of placing contracts for supplies or work. Under this system, the fact that supplies have to be bought or work has to be performed is made publicly known, and all companies interested in the contract are invited to submit offers (*tenders*, US: *bids*) by a certain date. On the appointed day the tenders are opened and compared, and the tenderer offering the best terms is awarded the contract.

trade association. An association of firms engaged in a particular trade. Its purpose is the protection and advancement of the interests of its members.

trade discount. A **discount** on the list price granted to a middleman (wholesaler or retailer) who buys goods for resale.

warehouse-to-warehouse insurance. Insurance covering a consignment of goods from the time it leaves the seller's warehouse until it is delivered into the buyer's warehouse, or until the expiry of a certain time after discharge at the port of destination.

How Payment Is Made by Irrevocable and Confirmed Documentary Credit

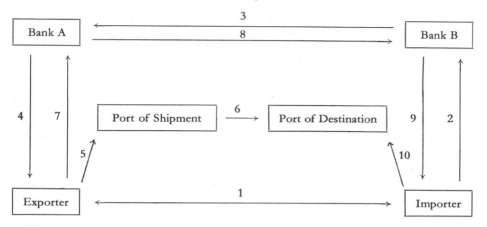

1. The exporter and the importer agree on payment by irrevocable and confirmed documentary credit.
2. The importer instructs his bank (Bank B) to open an irrevocable and confirmed documentary credit in the exporter's favour.
3. The importer's bank (opening or issuing bank) opens the credit and instructs its correspondent (Bank A) by air mail or cable to confirm the credit to the exporter (beneficiary).
4. Bank A (confirming bank) sends its confirmation of the credit to the beneficiary.
5. The exporter arranges for the shipment of the goods and obtains the necessary documents.
6. The goods are on board the carrying vessel en route to the port of destination.
7. The exporter draws a draft as provided for in the credit and presents it to Bank A together with the bill of lading and the other documents (commercial invoice, insurance policy or certificate, customs invoice, etc.). Bank A examines the documents carefully and, if it finds that they are in strict conformity with the terms of the credit, pays the exporter's draft (or, as the case may be, accepts or negotiates it).
8. Bank A debits Bank B's account with the amount of the credit, its expenses and commission, and sends the documents to Bank B. (To avoid loss in transit, the documents are forwarded in two sets, one set by the first air mail and the other set by the following air mail.)
9. On receipt of the documents Bank B debits the importer's account with the amount of the credit plus Bank A's and its own expenses and commission, and releases the documents to the importer.
10. On the strength of the documents the importer secures the release of the goods from the shipping company and the customs.

Partnership

A story of the mid-nineteenth century tells of the man who, upon meeting a friend, told him he was going into business.

"What sort of business?" the friend asked.

"A partnership," the other replied.

"Are you putting in much capital?"

"No. I put in no capital. I put in the experience."

"And he puts in the capital, is that it?"

"Yes. We go into business for three years. He puts in the capital and I put in the experience. At the end of three years I'll have the capital, and he'll have the experience."

Expert's Advice

A small businessman was in trouble with his sales. He decided to call in an expert to give him an outsider's viewpoint. After he had gone over his plans and problems, the businessman took the sales expert to a map on the wall and showed him brightly colored pins stuck wherever he had a salesman.

"Now," he asked the expert, "for a starter, what is the first thing we should do?"

"Well," replied the expert, "the first thing is to take those pins out of the map and stick them in the salesmen."

Part Four
Vocabulary Lists

Der Wortschatzteil besteht aus einem fortlaufenden und einem alphabetischen Verzeichnis der in diesem Buch verwendeten englischen Fachterminologie mit deutschen Übersetzungen und Erklärungen.

Das fortlaufende Wörterverzeichnis umfaßt die in den englischen Einführungstexten und Musterbriefen vorkommenden kaufmännischen und technischen Fachausdrücke. (Wörter, die in den *Terms and Phrases* enthalten und dort übersetzt sind, werden in der Folge nicht mehr aufgeführt.)

Die im fortlaufenden Wörterverzeichnis angegebenen kaufmännischen Ausdrücke sind auch im alphabetischen Wörterverzeichnis enthalten, das darüber hinaus die im Glossar und in den Anekdoten vorkommende kaufmännische Fachterminologie umfaßt.

I. Progressive Vocabulary

Part One
The Form of the Business Letter

I. Essential Parts

heading	Briefkopf
inside address	Anschrift des Empfängers (*auf dem Briefbogen*)
salutation	Anrede
body (*of the letter*)	Brieftext
complimentary close	Grußformel, Schlußformel
signature	Unterschrift
reference initials	Diktatzeichen
1. letterhead	(*gedruckter*) Briefkopf; Briefbogen mit gedrucktem Briefkopf, Briefblattvordruck
telegraphic address, cable address (*for cablegrams*)	Telegrammadresse, Kabeladresse (*für Überseetelegramme*)
code	Code, Telegrammschlüssel
telex number	Telex-Nummer (*Nummer des Fernschreiberanschlusses*)
partner	Gesellschafter (*einer Personengesellschaft*)
director	Direktor, Mitglied des Verwaltungsrats (*einer englischen oder amerikanischen Kapitalgesellschaft*)
partnership	Personengesellschaft
to carry on a partnership	eine Personengesellschaft betreiben
circular	(Werbe-)Rundschreiben
limited company	Kapitalgesellschaft (*Großbritannien*)
branch office	Zweigstelle, Filiale
bank(ing) account	Bankkonto
letterhead stationery	Briefpapier mit gedrucktem Briefkopf
trade-mark	Warenzeichen
advertising matter	*hier*: Werbeaufdrucke
2. memorandum, *pl.* memoranda *or* memorandums	interne Mitteilung, Aktennotiz
3. inside address	Anschrift des Empfängers (*auf dem Briefbogen*)

addressee	Empfänger, Adressat
firm name	Firmenname, Firma
one-man business, sole proprietorship (*US*)	Einzelunternehmung
impersonal name (*of a firm*)	Sachfirma
stock corporation	Kapitalgesellschaft (*USA*)
personal name (*of a firm*)	Personenfirma
place of destination	Bestimmungsort
post-office box (P.O.B.)	Postfach
P.O.B. number	Postfachnummer
Postcode	englische Postleitzahl
ZIP Code Number	amerikanische Postleitzahl
c/o	bei, i. Fa. (*in Firma*)
postal instructions	Beförderungsvermerke
special directions pertaining to the addressee	besondere Hinweise für den Empfänger
4. salutation	Anrede
5. body (*of the letter*)	Brieftext
paragraphing	Gliederung in Absätze
second sheet	Zweitbogen
6. complimentary close	Grußformel, Schlußformel
7. signature	Unterschrift
undersigned	Unterzeichneter
the power to sign is vested in ...	Zeichnungsvollmacht hat ...
active partner	geschäftsführender Gesellschafter
officer (*of a company*)	Vorstandsmitglied
to delegate a power	eine Vollmacht übertragen
power of attorney	(*schriftlich erteilte*) Vollmacht
per proc., per pro., p. p. (= *per procurationem*)	*etwa*: ppa., pp.
8. shorthand typist	Stenotypistin
reference initials, identification initials (*US*)	Diktatzeichen
dictator	*hier*: Diktierender
transcriber	die Sekretärin oder Schreibkraft, die den Brief in die Maschine überträgt

II. Miscellaneous Details

1. attention line	der Vermerk „zu Händen"
department	(Betriebs-)Abteilung
2. reference	Bezugszeichen
to handle the mail	die Post bearbeiten
file number	Aktenzeichen
subject	*hier*: der Betreff
Your reference/Our reference	Ihre Zeichen/Unsere Zeichen
3. subject line	Betreffzeile
subject-matter (*of the letter*)	Gegenstand (*des Briefes*)
"Subject", "Re"	„Betreff", „Betrifft"
4. enclosure (*also: in*closure)	Anlage
carbon copy	Durchschlag
representative	Vertreter (*allg.*); Reisender; Handelsvertreter

notations regarding enclosures and carbon copies	Anlage- und Verteilervermerke
5. postscript (P.S.)	Postskriptum (P.S.)

III. Envelope

envelope	Briefumschlag, Briefhülle
envelope address	Anschrift des Empfängers (*auf dem Brief-umschlag*)
return address	Anschrift des Absenders (*auf dem Briefumschlag*)
window envelope	Fensterbriefumschlag, Fensterbriefhülle

IV. Layout and Punctuation

1. layout	Layout, äußere Form
punctuation	Zeichensetzung, Interpunktion
flush (*adj.*)	in einer Fluchtlinie
to block	in Blockform schreiben
2. punctuation mark	Satzzeichen

Part Two
Types of Business Letters

I. Inquiries

1. inquiry (*also*: enquiry)	Anfrage
supplier	Lieferant, Lieferer
prospective customer, prospect	(Kauf-)Interessent
inquiry form	Anfrageformular
inquirer	der Anfragende
terms	Bedingungen
delivery date	Liefertermin, Lieferfrist
(sales) literature	Verkaufsliteratur, Prospektmaterial
general inquiry, routine inquiry	allgemeine Anfrage
offer	Angebot, Offerte
special inquiry, specific inquiry	bestimmte Anfrage
pattern	Muster (*vor allem Stoffmuster*); Modell
2a. Scotch tweed	schottischer Tweed
trade reference	Handelsreferenz
2b. film strip	Filmstreifen, Standbildstreifen
(electromagnetic) tape	Tonband
record	Schallplatte
2c. construction kit	Baukasten
sample	Muster, Probe
quotation	Preis, Preisangabe; Angebot
packing	Verpackung
shipping weight	Versandgewicht
to grant s.b. the sole agency	jm. die Alleinvertretung übertragen
demand	Nachfrage
2d. mechanical toys	mechanische Spielwaren
catalogue	Katalog
terms of payment	Zahlungsbedingungen
financial standing	finanzielle Lage, Vermögenslage
keenest price	äußerst kalkulierter Preis

2e. activated bleaching earth	aktivierte Bleicherde
associates	*hier*: befreundete Firma
refinery	Raffinerie
cottonseed oil	Baumwollsamenöl, Cottonöl
date of shipment	Versanddatum, Verschiffungsdatum
2f. proprietor	Eigentümer
department store	Warenhaus
sales	Verkäufe, Absatz, Umsatz
merchandise	Ware(n), Handelsware
manufacturer	Hersteller, Fabrikant
2g. to participate in a tender	sich an einer Ausschreibung beteiligen
government purchasing organization	staatliche Einkaufsorganisation
two-wheel trailer unit air compressor	auf Einachsanhänger montierter Kompressor
bhp (= *brake horsepower*)	Brems-PS
pneumatic speed governor	Druckluft-Drehzahlregler
tilting drum concrete mixer	Schwenktrommel-Betonmischer
capacity	Fassungsvermögen
to quote	*hier*: ein Angebot unterbreiten
to credit	gutschreiben
2h. filing cabinet	Aktenschrank
advertisement	Anzeige, Annonce
2i. ship stores	Schiffsbedarf
resale terms	Wiederverkaufsbedingungen
carriage	Fracht(-gebühr)
battery-operated	mit Batteriebetrieb
lift-truck	Hubstapler
solid rubber tyre	Vollgummireifen
specifications	(technische) Angaben, Daten
inter-shop transport of material	innerbetrieblicher Materialtransport
platform	(Lade-)Plattform
ground clearance	Bodenfreiheit
to be able to negotiate turns of a minimum radius of ...	einen Wenderadius von nicht mehr als ... haben
to be able to scale ramps of 1-in-10 gradient	eine Steigfähigkeit von 10 % haben
tool box	Werkzeugkasten
spares (*or*: spare parts)	Ersatzteile
maintenance	Wartung
electrical equipment	elektrische Ausrüstung
ambient temperature	Umgebungstemperatur

II. Offers

1. offer	Angebot, Offerte
acknowledgment (of receipt)	(Empfangs-)Bestätigung
agent	(Handels-)Vertreter
distributor	(Groß-)Händler
source of supply	Bezugsquelle
quotation	Preis, Preisangabe; Angebot
pro-forma invoice	Proforma-Rechnung
tender	(Submissions-)Angebot; Ausschreibung

bid (*US*)	(Submissions-)Angebot
to award a contract	einen Auftrag vergeben
to confirm	bestätigen
quotation form	Angebotsformular
covering letter	Begleitschreiben
solicited offer	verlangtes Angebot
unsolicited offer, voluntary offer	unverlangtes Angebot
inactive account	umsatzloses Konto
potential customer	potentieller Abnehmer
mailing list	Anschriftenverzeichnis
firm offer	festes Angebot, bindendes Angebot
time limit for acceptance	Annahmefrist
to withdraw an offer	ein Angebot zurückziehen
to revoke an offer	ein Angebot widerrufen
without engagement, subject to confirmation	freibleibend, unverbindlich
the prices are subject to change without notice	Preisänderungen vorbehalten
the goods are subject to being unsold	Zwischenverkauf vorbehalten
discount	Preisabzug (*Skonto oder Rabatt*)
order form	Bestellformular, Bestellschein
follow-up letter	Nachfaßbrief
to build goodwill	Kontakt zu den Kunden herstellen oder pflegen, das Wohlwollen oder Vertrauen der Kunden gewinnen, sich bei den Kunden einen guten Ruf schaffen
circular	(Werbe-)Rundschreiben
to mimeograph	vervielfältigen
automatic typewriter	automatische Schreibmaschine
printing typeface	Schriftart
sales series	Werbebriefreihe
2b. car washing plant	Autowaschanlage
to complete a form	ein Formular ausfüllen
2d. piece (*of cloth*)	Stück (*normale Länge eines Gewebes*)
2e. belt conveyor	Förderband
range (*of products*)	(Fertigungs-, Produktions-)Programm, Typenreihe
boom (*of a conveyor*)	Traggerüst (*eines Förderbands*)
rigid, rectangular, hollow section	starrer, kastenförmiger Hohlträger (Kastenträger)
self-lubricating ball bearing	selbstschmierendes Kugellager
grocer	Lebensmittelhändler
warehouse	Lager (*Lagerhaus bzw. Lagerraum*)
retailer	Einzelhändler
stationary version	ortsfeste Ausführung
adjustable	verstellbar
castors	(Schwenk-)Rollen
2f. to submit a quotation	ein Angebot unterbreiten
to guarantee	die Garantie übernehmen
dispatch (*or*: despatch)	Versand
leaflet	(Kurz-)Prospekt

2g. caravan	*hier*: Camping-Bus
road-holding and manoeuvring qualities	Straßenlage und Wendigkeit
to step up performance	die Leistung steigern
acceleration	Beschleunigung
cruising speed	Reisegeschwindigkeit
hill climbing	Steigfähigkeit
special discount	Sonderrabatt
without obligation	unverbindlich
cash against documents	Kasse gegen Dokumente
2h. charge posting cash register	Registrierkasse mit Vorrichtung zur Verbuchung von Kreditverkäufen
charge account	Kundenkreditkonto
cash sale	Barverkauf
2i. broker's commission	Maklerprovision
to add an item to a line (*of goods*)	einen Artikel in ein Sortiment aufnehmen
subject to licence [1]	vorbehaltlich der Erteilung einer Einfuhrgenehmigung
freight	*hier*: Fracht(-gebühr)
2k. power tools	Elektrowerkzeuge
electric drill	elektrische Bohrmaschine
export agent	Exportagent (*Mittelsperson im Lande des Herstellers, die für den Hersteller den Export durchführt*) [2]
sander	Schleifmaschine, Schleifgerät
polisher	Poliermaschine, Poliergerät
irrevocable letter of credit	unwiderrufliches Akkreditiv
under separate cover	mit gleicher Post, gesondert
2l. electronic device	Elektronengerät
intercom(munication)	(Wechsel-)Sprechanlage
to plug into an electric line	an die elektrische Leitung anschließen
electric wiring	elektrisches Leitungsnetz
to transmit and receive sound	Sprechfrequenzen senden und empfangen
design	Konstruktion
production	Herstellung, Produktion
competitive product	Konkurrenzerzeugnis
introductory offer	Einführungsangebot
authorization-to-ship card	Antwortkarte (*durch die sich der Interessent mit der Zusendung auf Probe einverstanden erklärt*)
purchase order [3]	Bestellung
2m. brochure	(Werbe-)Broschüre
complimentary copy	Freiexemplar
2n. kitchen utensils and appliances	Küchenartikel und -geräte
output	Produktion (= *produzierte Menge*)
2o. laboratory equipment	Laborgeräte
2p. line (*of products*)	Fertigungs-, Produktionsprogramm

---

[1] BE: licence n., to license v.; US: license n. and v.
[2] darf nicht mit dem deutschen *Exportvertreter* verwechselt werden, der zwischen Hersteller und Ausfuhrhändler vermittelt
[3] *purchase orders* sind die eigenen Bestellungen der Firma, *orders* die von den Kunden erteilten Aufträge

III. Orders

1. order	Bestellung, Auftrag
unqualified acceptance	Annahme ohne Änderungen, Annahme ohne Erweiterungen oder Einschränkungen
refusal (*of an offer*)	Ablehnung (*eines Angebots*)
counter-offer	Gegenangebot
first order, initial order	Erstauftrag
repeat order, re-order	Nachbestellung
trial order	Probeauftrag, Probebestellung
advance order	Vorausbestellung
standing order	Dauerauftrag
confirmation	Bestätigung
order letter	Bestellschreiben
order form, order blank, purchase order form	Bestellformular, Bestellschein, Auftragsformular
regular supplier	regelmäßiger Lieferant
to acknowledge an order	den Eingang einer Bestellung bestätigen
to revoke an order	eine Bestellung widerrufen
cancellation of an order	Widerruf einer Bestellung
to perform one's contractual duties	seine vertraglichen Pflichten erfüllen
2a. glue for plastics	Kleber für Kunststoffe
2b. competition	Wettbewerb
2c. refusal of quotation	Ablehnung eines Angebots
tinplate	Weißblech
2d. office supplies	Büromaterial
by parcel post	als Postpaket
spiral-bound note book	Spiral(-Steno-)block
coloured pencil	Farbstift
coloured crayon	bunter Kreidestift
stapler	Heftmaschine
pencil sharpener	Bleistiftspitzer
shipment	Sendung
to invoice	in Rechnung stellen
2e. package	Packstück, Kollo (*Pl.* Kolli)
label	Etikett, Aufklebeadresse
conditions of purchase	Einkaufsbedingungen
free from defect	einwandfrei
advice note	Versandanzeige
invoice	(Waren-)Rechnung, Faktura
to reject goods	Waren zurückweisen
to cancel an order	eine Bestellung widerrufen
to comply with conditions	Bedingungen einhalten
to effect delivery	Lieferung durchführen
in duplicate	zweifach, in zweifacher Ausfertigung
2f. unit price	Preis pro Einheit
to back-order	zur späteren Auslieferung vormerken
vendor	Verkäufer, Lieferant, Lieferer
2g. to fill an order (*US*)	eine Bestellung ausführen
2h. marking instructions	Markierungsanweisungen
gross weight	Bruttogewicht

to mark (*packages*)	(*Kolli*) beschriften, markieren
consignment	Sendung

IV. Acknowledgments

1. acknowledgment (*of an order*)	Bestätigung des Eingangs einer Bestellung, Bestätigung der Bestellungsannahme, Auftragsbestätigung
without qualifications	ohne Änderungen, ohne Erweiterungen oder Einschränkungen
qualified acceptance	Annahme mit Änderungen, Annahme unter Erweiterungen oder Einschränkungen
to carry in stock	(*Waren*) führen, auf Lager haben
to be financially embarrassed	in finanzieller Verlegenheit sein
dealer	Händler
substitute	Ersatz (*ähnliche Waren*)
the goods are out of stock	die Waren sind ausgegangen, sind nicht mehr vorrätig
to place on file	(*zur späteren Erledigung*) vormerken
to execute an order	einen Auftrag ausführen
acknowledgment copy or counterfoil	Durchschlag oder Abschnitt (*des Bestellformulars*) für die Bestellungsannahme
advice of dispatch	Versandanzeige
credit information	Kreditauskunft
sales note, contract note	Auftragsbestätigung, schriftliche Bestätigung des Vertragsabschlusses
2a. salesman (= traveling salesman *US*)	Vertreter, Reisender
railroad bill of lading	Frachtpapier im amerikanischen Bahnverkehr (*ein Traditionspapier wie das Konnossement im Seeverkehr*)
order	*hier*: die bestellten Waren
quantity discount	Mengenrabatt
2b. service	Kundendienst, Service
factory-trained mechanic	im Werk ausgebildeter Mechaniker
2d. knitting mill	Strickwarenfabrik
fashion shop	Modegeschäft
to enter an order	einen Auftrag buchen, vormerken
cardigan	Strickjacke, Strickweste
conditions of sale	Verkaufsbedingungen
force majeure	höhere Gewalt
strike	Streik
lock-out	Aussperrung
circumstances beyond s.b.'s control	unabwendbare Ereignisse
settlement of account	Rechnungsausgleich, Begleichung einer Rechnung
$2^{1}/_{2}$ % discount (= *cash discount*)	$2^{1}/_{2}$ % Skonto
bill of exchange	Wechsel
charges	Kosten, Spesen, Gebühren
expenses	Spesen, Auslagen
2e. high-capacity air cleaner	Hochleistungs-Luftreinigungsanlage
in quintuplicate	fünffach, in fünffacher Ausfertigung
print (*photographic copy*)	Fotografie, fotografischer Abzug
2f. safe	Safe, Geldschrank

finish	*hier*: Lackierung
3-number combination lock	Kombinationsschloß mit dreistelliger Zahlen-kombination
transaction	Geschäft, Geschäftsabschluß
credit department	(Waren-)Kreditabteilung
2g. to supersede	ersetzen, an die Stelle treten von
(synthetic) resin	Kunstharz
2h. frostless freezer	Gefriertruhe mit Abtau-Automatik
appliance	Gerät
sealed refrigeration system	versiegeltes Kühlsystem
guarantee	Garantie
2i. to hold an order in the pending file	eine Bestellung zur späteren Erledigung zurück-stellen (*pending file = Akte für Unerledigtes*)
2k. wall paper	Tapete
2l. to discontinue production	die Produktion einstellen
Tsingtao pongee	Tsingtau Pongé (*Seidenstoff*)
sample cutting	Stoffmuster

V. Delivery

1. packing container	Versandbehälter
import duty	Einfuhrzoll
marks (*on packages*)	(Kolli-)Markierungen
caution marks	Vorsichtsmarkierungen
to collect goods	Waren abholen
forwarding agent	Spediteur
carrier	Frachtführer; Verfrachter
loss or damage in transit	Verlust oder Beschädigung während des Transports
to take out insurance, to effect insurance	Versicherung abschließen
marine insurance	Seeversicherung
warehouse-to-warehouse insurance	Versicherung von Haus zu Haus
dispatch advice	Versandanzeige
shipping advice	Versandanzeige, Verschiffungsanzeige
packing list	Packliste
progress report	Zwischenbericht
invoice	(Waren-)Rechnung, Faktura
bill	Rechnung (*für Waren und Leistungen*)
to render an invoice	eine Rechnung (aus-)stellen
invoice form, billhead (*US*)	Rechnungsvordruck, Rechnungsformular
extension	*hier*: Gesamtpreis (*Preis pro Einheit × Menge*)
to extend	*hier*: den Gesamtpreis errechnen
deduction	(Preis-)Abzug, Nachlaß
total invoice amount	Gesamtrechnungsbetrag
method of transport	Beförderungsart
commercial invoice	Handelsrechnung
customs invoice	Zollfaktura
consular invoice	Konsulatsfaktura
to conform to the regulations	den Vorschriften entsprechen
to certify	beglaubigen
chamber of commerce	Handelskammer

pro-forma invoice	Proforma-Rechnung
on approval	auf Probe, zur Ansicht
to consign (*goods*) for sale	(*Waren*) in Konsignation geben
import licence	Einfuhrgenehmigung, Importlizenz
statement (of account)	Kontoauszug
current account	laufendes Konto, Kontokorrentkonto
to balance	saldieren
balance	Saldo
entry	Buchung, Eintragung
debit note, debit memorandum (*US*), debit memo (*US*)	Belastungsanzeige
credit note, credit memorandum (*US*), credit memo (*US*)	Gutschriftsanzeige
2a. to draw on s.b. at one month	auf jm. (*einen Wechsel*) per 1 Monat ziehen
draft	Tratte
acceptance	Annahmevermerk, Akzept
2b. non-negotiable	nicht begebbar, nicht übertragbar
in triplicate	in dreifacher Ausfertigung, dreifach
full set of clean on-board bills of lading	voller Satz reiner Bordkonnossemente
certificate of insurance, insurance certificate	Versicherungszertifikat
collection	*hier*: Inkasso
sight draft	Sichttratte
2c. to the order of ...	an die Order von ...
consigned to ...	adressiert an ... (*to consign = senden*)
d/d = dated	datiert
new wool	Schurwolle
worsted	Kammgarn(-stoff)
canvas	(Pack-)Leinwand, Sackleinwand
net weight	Nettogewicht
net net weight	Reinnettogewicht
remittance	Zahlung, Überweisung
2d. S.S. (*or*: S/S) = steamship	D. = Dampfer
by order of ...	im Auftrage von ...
for account and risk of ...	für Rechnung und Gefahr von ...
on first presentation	bei der ersten Vorlage
2e. to bill	eine Rechnung ausstellen; in Rechnung stellen, berechnen
2g. to charge an account with an amount	ein Konto mit einem Betrag belasten
to credit an account with an amount	einem Konto einen Betrag gutschreiben
2h. wire-drawing machine	Drahtziehmaschine
measurements	Abmessungen
to stencil	mittels Schablone anbringen
collection	*hier*: Abholung
2i. after verification	nach Richtigbefund

VI. Payment

1. records (*pl.*)	*hier*: (Geschäfts-)Bücher
indebtedness	Schulden
means of payment	Zahlungsmittel

postal order, money order	Postanweisung
cheque	Scheck
bank draft (*or:* banker's draft)	Bankscheck
bank transfer (*or:* banker's transfer)	Banküberweisung
promissory note	Solawechsel
conversion	Umtausch
currency	Währung
foreign exchange	Devisen
remittance advice	Zahlungsanzeige
receipt	Quittung
to solicit further business	um weitere Aufträge bitten
to take a discount	Skonto abziehen
discount period	Frist für Skontogewährung, Kassafrist
to take unearned discounts	unberechtigterweise Skonto abziehen
discount piracy	„Skontoschinderei"
2c. to mature	fällig werden (*Wechsel*)
to honour	honorieren (*d. h. prompt akzeptieren bzw. einlösen*)
to present for payment	zur Zahlung vorlegen
2d. bucket	*hier*: Schaufel (*eines Schaufelladers*)
loading shovel	Schaufellader
replacement	Ersatz (*gleiche Waren*)
(price) reduction	(Preis-)Ermäßigung, Nachlaß
2e. to debit	belasten
2i. overcharge	der zuviel berechnete Betrag
to cancel a charge	eine Belastung stornieren
2k. discount	*hier*: Rabatt
to cancel an invoice	eine Rechnung stornieren
to re-bill	eine neue Rechnung ausstellen

VII. Credit Letters

1. credit inquiry, status inquiry	Anfrage (*wegen der Kreditwürdigkeit einer Firma*), Bitte um Kreditauskunft
creditworthy	kreditwürdig
credit information sources, sources of credit information	(Kredit-)Auskunftsstellen
credit information	Kreditauskunft
credit application form	Kreditantragsformular
balance sheet	Bilanz
trade reference	Handelsreferenz
bank reference	Bankreferenz
(credit-)inquiry agency, commercial agency (*US*), mercantile agency (*US*)	Handelsauskunftei
stamped and self-addressed envelope	adressierter Freiumschlag
International Reply Coupon	Internationaler Antwortschein
defamation	Beleidigung (*Oberbegriff*)
slander	Beleidigung, Verleumdung (*mündlich*)
libel	Beleidigung, Verleumdung (*schriftlich*)

action for libel	Beleidigungsklage (*wegen schriftlicher Verleumdung*)
2a. financial status	finanzielle Lage, Vermögenslage
2b. to establish credit with s.b.	sich von jm. Kredit bzw. eine Kreditlinie einräumen lassen
credit on open account	offener Buchkredit
general management	allgemeine Geschäftsführung
2d. financial responsibility	finanzielle Zuverlässigkeit
credit standing	Kreditwürdigkeit
accommodation	*hier*: Kredit
security	Sicherheit
2f. to collect bills	Rechnungen einziehen
2g. subsidiary	Tochtergesellschaft
rating	Krediturteil
rating book	Sammelauskunftsbuch
to incorporate	gründen (*Kapitalgesellschaft*); in eine Kapitalgesellschaft umwandeln
authorized capital	autorisiertes Kapital
to operate a partnership business	eine Personengesellschaft (offene Handelsgesellschaft) betreiben
export merchant	Exporthändler
finance department	Finanzabteilung
wholly-owned subsidiary	100%ige Tochter(-gesellschaft) [1]
importers of general merchandise	Importeure von Waren aller Art
office manager	Büroleiter
the subject company	die genannte Gesellschaft
import agent	Importvertreter, Importagent
commitment	Verpflichtung
deposit .	*hier*: Anzahlung
parent company	Muttergesellschaft
net worth (*US*)	Eigenkapital
current assets	Umlaufvermögen
current liabilities	kurzfristige Verbindlichkeiten
to maintain a liquid condition	über ausreichende Liquidität verfügen
depository	*hier*: Bank
to make an advance	ein (*kurzfristiges*) Darlehen gewähren

VIII. Delay in Delivery

1. delay in delivery	Lieferungsverzögerung, Lieferungsverzug
non-delivery	Nicht(aus)lieferung, Lieferungsverzug
to follow up orders	die Einhaltung der Liefertermine überwachen
reminder	Mahnung
to rescind a contract	von einem Vertrag zurücktreten
to perform a contract	einen Vertrag erfüllen
action for damages	Schadenersatzklage
to enter into a contract	einen Vertrag schließen
damages (*pl.*)	Schadenersatz
breach of contract	Vertragsbruch

---

[1] Tochtergesellschaft, deren Kapital zu 100 % im Besitz der Muttergesellschaft ist

liquidated damages	im voraus vertraglich festgesetzter Schadenersatz, Vertragsstrafe, Konventionalstrafe
performance of a contract	Vertragserfüllung
act of God	Naturereignis
to sustain a loss	einen Verlust erleiden
liability	Haftung
balance (*of the order*)	Rest (*der bestellten Waren*), Restmenge
to release s.b. from a contract	jm. von einem Vertrag entbinden
legal action	gerichtliches Verfahren, Prozeß
missing consignment	abgängige Sendung
to misdirect	fehlleiten
in transit	auf dem Transport, unterwegs
2a. photographic equipment	fotografische Geräte
2d. central heating radiators	Heizkörper für Zentralheizung
to claim damages	Schadenersatz verlangen
to meet a deadline	einen Termin einhalten
2e. in the pressure of business	im Drange der Geschäfte
M/V (*or*: M. V.) = motor vessel	M/S = Motorschiff
2f. to call a strike	einen Streik ausrufen
metal worker s'union	Metallarbeitergewerkschaft
production schedule	Produktionsplan
2g. to sail	auslaufen (*Schiff*)
2h. heavy-duty compressor	Hochleistungskompressor
2i. postal authorities	Postverwaltung

IX. Complaints and Adjustments

1. complaint	Beschwerde, Beanstandung, Reklamation
letter of complaint, claim letter	schriftliche Beschwerde
defect	Mangel
adjustment	Regelung, Regulierung
unsalable	unverkäuflich
allowance	Preisnachlaß (*bei mangelhaften Waren*)
to remedy defects	Mängel beheben
warranty	Garantie
free of charge	kostenlos
guarantee period	Garantiezeit
faulty material or workmanship	Materialfehler oder Fehler in der Verarbeitung
to grant a claim	einer Beschwerde stattgeben
to refuse a claim	eine Beschwerde ablehnen
adjustment policy	Verfahren(-sweise) bei der Erledigung von Beschwerden
unfounded complaint	unbegründete Beschwerde
insurance company	Versicherungsgesellschaft
to enter a claim with the carrier	einen Schadenersatzanspruch beim Frachtführer bzw. Verfrachter anmelden
compensation	Entschädigung
to assign a claim to s.b.	einen Anspruch an jm. abtreten
settlement of a claim	Erledigung eines Schadenersatzanspruchs
dispute	Streit, Streitigkeit
to settle a dispute	einen Streit beilegen
court of arbitration	Schiedsgericht

court of law	ordentliches Gericht
litigation	Rechtsstreit, Prozeß
arbitrator	Schiedsrichter
2a. industrial sewing machine	Industrie-Nähmaschine
drive belt	Antriebsriemen
2b. shutter	Verschluß
advertising	Werbung
workmanship	Verarbeitung
2c. catalyst	Katalysator
2d. brand	(Handels-)Marke
2e. cutting	(Stoff-)Muster
2f. clock-radio	Radiowecker
repair department	Reparaturabteilung
tube (*US*), *BE*: valve	(Radio-)Röhre
loudspeaker	Lautsprecher
perfect working condition	einwandfreier Betriebszustand
2g. flashlight (*US*), *BE*: electric torch	Taschenlampe
a leaky battery	eine undichte Batterie
armour-clad battery	Batterie mit Metallmantel
paper-clad battery	Batterie mit Pappmantel
moisture-resistant paper case	feuchtigkeitsbeständige Papierhülse
leakproof	leakproof (*nicht auslaufend*)
2h. proof	Probeabzug
to run	*hier*: drucken
grade of paper	Papierqualität
2i. (glass) jar	(Marmelade-)Glas
clean bill of lading	reines Konnossement
shipping company	Reederei
survey report	Havariezertifikat
Lloyd's Agent	Lloyd's-Kommissar (*der für Lloyd's tätige Hava-*
2k. check-up	Inspektion *riekommissar*)
to service	den Kunden- und Wartungsdienst durchführen
estimate	Kostenvoranschlag
2l. to warrant	Garantie übernehmen

X. Collection Letters

1. reminder	Zahlungserinnerung
collection letter, dunning letter	Mahnschreiben
to collect an account	eine Rechnung einziehen
collection agency	Inkassobüro
collection	Inkasso, Einziehung (*fälliger Forderungen*)
debtor	Schuldner
creditor	Gläubiger
presentation for payment	Vorlage zur Zahlung
refusal to pay	Zahlungsverweigerung
outstanding loan	noch nicht zurückbezahltes Darlehen
outstanding accounts	Außenstände, Forderungen
amicable settlement	gütliche Regelung
to institute legal proceedings	Klage erheben
extension	*hier*: Stundung, Zahlungsaufschub
payment on account	Abschlagszahlung, Akontozahlung

acceptance	Akzept (*hier*: der akzeptierte Wechsel)
drawer	Aussteller, Trassant
prolongation	(Wechsel-)Prolongation
to charge interest	Zinsen berechnen
overdue, past due	überfällig, noch offenstehend, noch nicht bezahlt
collection sticker	Aufklebezettel mit Zahlungsaufforderung
form letter	Formbrief
hidden reminder	versteckte Mahnung
trade association	Wirtschaftsverband, Fachverband
credit association	Kreditschutzorganisation
delinquent debtor	säumiger Schuldner
collection series, collection sequence	Mahnbriefreihe
2b. accounts department	Buchhaltungsabteilung
2c. drip-dry cotton	bügelfreier Baumwollstoff
2g. solicitor [1]	Rechtsanwalt
2i. client	*hier*: Klient
2m. slackness of trade	stockender Geschäftsgang, Flaute
on account	als Abschlagszahlung, a conto
2n. to meet an acceptance	ein Akzept einlösen
decline of business activity	Rückgang der Geschäftstätigkeit, Konjunkturrückgang, Konjunkturabschwächung
ready cash	flüssige Mittel, Bargeld
to renew (*or*: to prolong) a bill of exchange	einen Wechsel prolongieren
loan	Darlehen, Kredit

XI. Letters of Application

1. letter of application	Bewerbungsschreiben
solicited application	verlangte Bewerbung
unsolicited application	unverlangte Bewerbung
"Situations Offered", "Situations Vacant", "Jobs Offered"	„Stellenangebote" (*Rubrik im Anzeigenteil der Zeitung*)
applicant	Bewerber
curriculum vitae, résumé	Lebenslauf
personal data sheet, personal record sheet	tabellarischer Lebenslauf
testimonial	(Dienst-)Zeugnis
letter of recommendation	Empfehlungsschreiben
application form	Bewerbungsbogen
2a. foreign-language correspondent	Fremdsprachenkorrespondent(-in)
G.C.E. 'A' Level (General Certificate of Education, Advanced Level)	*etwa*: Abitur
certificate	Zeugnis
customs documents	Zolldokumente
post	Stelle (*besonders*: „gehobene Stelle")

---

[1] In England gibt es zwei Arten von Rechtsanwälten: *solicitors* und *barristers*. Die *solicitors* vertreten ihre Klienten in streitigen und nichtstreitigen Angelegenheiten, können aber nur vor niederen Gerichten plädieren. Vor höheren Gerichten darf nur ein *barrister* plädieren, der sein Mandat von einem solicitor und nicht vom Klienten direkt entgegennimmt.

2b. to graduate	die Ausbildung an einer Lehranstalt abschließen, das Abschlußexamen ablegen
course in secretarial studies	Ausbildungskurs für Sekretärinnen
bookkeeping	Buchführung
business administration	Betriebswirtschaft
to take dictation	Diktat aufnehmen
to transcribe dictation	Diktat in die Maschine übertragen
to file	(*Schriftgut*) ablegen
to handle routine correspondence	Routinekorrespondenz erledigen
to assign (*correspondence, etc.*) to s.b. for attention	jm. (*Korrespondenz usw.*) zur Bearbeitung übertragen
2c. vacancy	offene Stelle
bookkeeping clerk	Buchhaltungskraft
G.C.E. 'O' Level (General Certificate of Education, Ordinary Level)	*etwa:* mittlere Reife
junior clerk	Anfangskraft, Anfangskontorist(-in)
bookkeeper	Buchhalter
general accounting	allgemeine Buchführung
cost accounting	Kostenrechnung, Kalkulation
auditing	Rechnungsprüfung, Revision
2e. office routine	täglich anfallende Büroarbeiten, Routinearbeiten
to arrange travel itineraries	Reisevorbereitungen treffen (*itinerary = Reiseroute, -plan*)

II. Alphabetical Vocabulary

A

to accept	annehmen, akzeptieren
acceptance	Annahme, Annahmevermerk, Akzept
acceptor	Akzeptant
account	Konto; Rechnung
accounts department	Buchhaltung(-sabteilung)
acknowledgment of an order	Bestätigung des Eingangs einer Bestellung, Bestätigung der Bestellungsannahme, Auftragsbestätigung
act of God	Naturereignis
action for damages	Schadenersatzklage
action for libel	Beleidigungsklage (*wegen schriftlicher Verleumdung*)
active partner	geschäftsführender Gesellschafter
to adjudge s.b. a bankrupt	Konkursverfahren über jds. Vermögen eröffnen
adjustment	Erledigung (*einer Reklamation*), Regulierung (*eines Schadenersatzanspruchs*), Beilegung (*eines Streitfalls*)
~ manager (*department store*)	Leiter des Büros für Kundenreklamationen
ad valorem duty	Wertzoll
advance (by a bank)	(*kurzfristiges*) Darlehen
~ order	Vorausbestellung
advertisement	Anzeige, Annonce
advertising	Werbung
advice note	Benachrichtigung, Versandanzeige
advice of dispatch	Versandanzeige
agent	(Handels-)Vertreter, Agent
allowance	Preisnachlaß (*bei mangelhaften Waren*)
amicable settlement	gütliche Regelung, außergerichtliche Einigung
applicant	Bewerber
application	Antrag, Bewerbung
~ form	Bewerbungsbogen
arbitration	Schiedswesen, Schiedsgerichtsverfahren, Arbitrage
~ association	Arbitrageverband
~ clause	Schiedsklausel, Arbitrageklausel
arbitrator	Schiedsrichter
to assess import duty	den Einfuhrzoll festsetzen
to assign a claim	einen Anspruch abtreten
at sight	bei Sicht
attention line	der Vermerk „zu Händen"
auditing	Rechnungsprüfung, Revision
authorized capital	autorisiertes Kapital
to award a contract	einen Auftrag vergeben, den Zuschlag erteilen (*Ausschreibung*)

B

to back-order	zur späteren Auslieferung vormerken
balance	Saldo, Differenzbetrag, Restbetrag oder -menge

to ~	saldieren; (*Konto*) ausgleichen
~ sheet	Bilanz
bank	Bank
~ (*or:* banker's) acceptance	Bankakzept
~ (*or:* banking) account	Bankkonto
~ (*or:* banker's) draft	Bankscheck
~ reference	Bankreferenz
~ (*or:* banker's) transfer	Banküberweisung
bankrupt	Gemeinschuldner
bankruptcy	Konkurs
~ proceedings	Konkursverfahren
basis of quotation	Preisbasis
bearer	Inhaber, Überbringer
~ cheque	Inhaberscheck
~ paper	Inhaberpapier
beneficiary (*letter of credit*)	Begünstigter
bid (*US*)	(Submissions-)Angebot
bill	Rechnung (*für Waren und Leistungen*); Wechsel (*bill of exchange*)
to ~	eine Rechnung ausstellen; in Rechnung stellen, berechnen
~ of exchange	Wechsel
~ of lading	Konnossement
billhead (*US*)	Rechnungsformular
blank endorsement	Blankoindossament
to book an order	einen Auftrag buchen, vormerken
bookkeeper	Buchhalter
bookkeeping	Buchführung
~ clerk	Buchhaltungskraft
~ department	Buchhaltung(-sabteilung)
branch	(*rechtlich unselbständige*) Niederlassung, Zweigstelle, Filiale
brand	(Handels-)Marke
breach of contract	Vertragsbruch
brochure	(Werbe-)Broschüre
broker	Makler
brokerage	Maklerlohn, Courtage
business administration	Betriebswirtschaft(-slehre)

C

cable address	Kabeladresse (*für Überseetelegramme*)
cable transfer	telegrafische Auszahlung
to cancel	widerrufen, rückgängig machen, stornieren
cancellation	Widerruf, Stornierung
carriage	Beförderung; Fracht(-gebühr)
~ paid to frontier	frachtfrei Grenze
carrier	Frachtführer; Verfrachter
to carry in stock	(*Waren*) führen, auf Lager haben
cash	Bargeld, Bar ...
~ against documents	Kasse gegen Dokumente

216

~ discount	Skonto
~ sale	Barverkauf
catalogue, catalog (*US*)	Katalog
caution marks	Vorsichtsmarkierungen
central bank	Zentralbank, Notenbank
certificate	Bestätigung, Bescheinigung, Zeugnis
~ of insurance	Versicherungszertifikat
~ of origin	Ursprungszeugnis
to certify	bestätigen, beglaubigen
C.&F. (*cost and freight*)	c & f (*Kosten und Fracht*)
chamber of commerce	Handelskammer
charge	Belastung; Gebühr; *meist Pl.*: Kosten, Spesen
to ~	berechnen, belasten
~ account	Kundenkreditkonto (*Einzelhandel*)
to charter a vessel	ein Schiff chartern
cheque, check (*US*)	Scheck
C.I.F. (*cost, insurance, freight*)	cif (*Kosten, Versicherung, Fracht*)
circular	(Werbe-)Rundschreiben
claim .	Anspruch; Beschwerde, Reklamation
to ~ damages (*pl.*)	Schadenersatz verlangen
clean bill of lading	reines Konnossement
clean draft	nichtdokumentäre Tratte
clean receipt	reiner Empfangsschein
client	Kunde; Klient
closed corporation (*US*)	*entspricht der englischen* private limited company
C.O.D. (*cash on delivery*)	per Nachnahme
code (telegraph ~)	Code, Telegrammschlüssel
collecting bank	Inkassobank
collection	Abholung; Inkasso, Einziehung
	(*von fälligen Forderungen*)
~ agency	Inkassobüro
~ letter	Mahnschreiben
~ of a documentary draft	Einziehung einer Dokumententratte,
	Dokumenteninkasso
~ proceeds (*pl.*)	Inkassoerlös
~ sequence	Mahnbriefreihe
~ series	Mahnbriefreihe
~ sticker	Aufklebezettel mit Zahlungsaufforderung
Combined Certificate of Value and Origin	Kombiniertes Wert- und Ursprungszeugnis
commercial agency (*US*)	Handelsauskuntei
commercial invoice	Handelsrechnung
commercial traveller	(Handlungs-)Reisender, Vertreter
commission	Provision
~ agent	*etwa*: Handelsvertreter
compensation	Entschädigung, Schadenersatz, Vergütung, Entgelt
competition	Wettbewerb
competitive	konkurrenzfähig; Konkurrenz . . .
complaint	Beschwerde, Beanstandung, Reklamation
complimentary close	Grußformel, Schlußformel
confirmation of an order	Bestätigung einer (*mündlich oder telegrafisch erteilten*) Bestellung (*durch den Besteller*)

confirmed irrevocable (letter of) credit	bestätigtes, unwiderrufliches Akkreditiv
confirming bank (*letter of credit*)	bestätigende Bank
to conform to the regulations	den Vorschriften entsprechen
to consign	(*Waren*) zusenden, übersenden, (*Sendung*) an jm. adressieren; in Kommission oder Konsignation geben
consignee	Empfänger; Kommissionär, Konsignatar
consignment	Sendung; Konsignation
~ goods	Kommissionswaren, Konsignationswaren
~ note	Frachtbrief
~ stock	Kommissionslager, Konsignationslager
consignor	Versender; Kommittent, Konsignant
consolidated shipment (*US*)	Sammelladung
consular fee	Konsulatsgebühr
consular invoice	Konsulatsfaktura
contract	Vertrag
to ~ for the carriage of goods	einen Vertrag über die Beförderung von Waren schließen
~ note	Auftragsbestätigung, Bestätigung des Vertragsabschlusses; Schlußnote (*des Maklers*)
~ of carriage	Frachtvertrag, Beförderungsvertrag
conversion	Umrechnung; Umtausch (*Währung*)
corporation (stock ~)	Kapitalgesellschaft (*USA*)
cost accounting	Kostenrechnung, Kalkulation
counter-offer	Gegenangebot
country of origin	Ursprungsland
court of arbitration	Schiedsgericht
court (of law)	(ordentliches) Gericht
covering letter	Begleitschreiben
credit	Kredit, (Zahlungs-)Ziel; Gutschrift; Akkreditiv (*letter of credit*)
to ~	gutschreiben
~ application form	Kreditantragsformular
~ association	Kreditschutzorganisation
~ balance	Habensaldo, Guthaben
~ department	(Waren-)Kreditabteilung
~ information	Kreditinformation(-en), Kreditauskunft
~ inquiry	Anfrage (*wegen der Kreditwürdigkeit einer Firma*), Bitte um Kreditauskunft
~-inquiry agency	Handelsauskunftei
~ memo(randum) (*US*)	Gutschriftsanzeige
~ note	Gutschriftsanzeige
~ on open account	offener Buchkredit, offenes Ziel
~ standing	Kreditwürdigkeit
creditor	Gläubiger
creditworthy	kreditwürdig
crossed cheque	gekreuzter Scheck (*entspricht dem deutschen Verrechnungsscheck*)
currency	Währung
current account	laufendes Konto, Kontokorrentkonto
current assets	Umlaufvermögen

current liabilities	kurzfristige Verbindlichkeiten
curriculum vitae	Lebenslauf
customs authorities	Zollbehörden
customs clearance	Zollabfertigung
customs entry	Zollanmeldung, Zollantrag
customs invoice	Zollfaktura
customs officer	Zollbeamter
cutting	Stoffmuster

D

D/A (*documents against acceptance*)	Dokumente gegen Akzept
damages (*pl.*)	Schadenersatz
dealer	Händler
debenture	Schuldverschreibung, Obligation
to debit	belasten
debit memo(randum) (*US*)	Belastungsanzeige
debit note	Belastungsanzeige
debtor	Schuldner
debts (*pl.*)	Schulden
declaration policy	Abschreibepolice
decline of business activity	Rückgang der Geschäftstätigkeit, Konjunkturrückgang, Konjunkturabschwächung
deduction	(Preis-)Abzug, Nachlaß
defect	Mangel
delay in delivery	Lieferungsverzögerung, Lieferungsverzug
delinquent debtor	säumiger Schuldner
to deliver	liefern, ausliefern, übergeben, zustellen
to ～ from stock	ab Lager (*d. h. sofort*) liefern
to ～ into the custody of the railway	der Bahn aushändigen
delivery	Lieferung, Auslieferung, Übergabe, Zustellung
～ date	Liefertermin; Lieferfrist
～ date to the vessel	Zeitpunkt der Lieferung zum Schiff
demand	Nachfrage
Department of Trade	Handelsministerium (*Großbritannien*)
department store	Warenhaus
director	Direktor, Mitglied des Verwaltungsrats (*einer englischen oder amerikanischen Kapitalgesellschaft*)
discharge (*bankruptcy*)	Befreiung des Gemeinschuldners von der Haftung für die nicht befriedigten Forderungen
discharge (*of a ship or cargo*)	Löschung, Entladung
discount	Skonto; Rabatt; Diskont
to ～ a bill (of exchange)	einen Wechsel diskontieren (bzw. diskontieren lassen)
～ period	Frist für Skontogewährung, Kassafrist
～ piracy	Skontoschinderei
to dishonour	nicht honorieren (*d. h. nicht rechtzeitig akzeptieren bzw. einlösen*)
dispatch	Versand
～ advice	Versandanzeige
dispatching station	Versandbahnhof
dispute	Streitigkeit, Streitfall

distributor	(Groß-)Händler
dock receipt	Kai-Empfangsschein
document of title	Traditionspapier
documentary bill lodgment form	Inkassoauftrag (*Dokumenteninkasso*)
documentary draft	Dokumententratte, dokumentäre Tratte
documentary (letter of) credit	Dokumentenakkreditiv, dokumentäres Akkreditiv
documents against bank acceptance	Dokumente gegen Bankakzept (*Remboursgeschäft*)
domestic bill	Inlandswechsel
domestic money order	Inlandspostanweisung
domestic value	Inlandswert
D/P (*documents against payment*)	Kasse gegen Dokumente
draft	Tratte
to draw (a bill of exchange)	einen Wechsel ziehen, einen Wechsel ausstellen
to draw on s.b. at sight	auf jm. einen Sichtwechsel ziehen
drawee	Bezogener, Trassat
~ bank	bezogene Bank
drawer	Aussteller, Trassant
dunning letter	Mahnschreiben
duplicate, in ~	zweifach, doppelt, in zweifacher Ausfertigung
~ consignment note	Frachtbriefdoppel
dutiable goods	zollpflichtige Waren

E

to effect insurance	Versicherung abschließen
to effect payment	Zahlung leisten
eligible for re-discounting (*bill of exchange*)	rediskontfähig, zentralbankfähig
enclosure	Anlage
to endorse	indossieren, girieren
endorsee	Indossatar, Giratar
endorsement	Indossament, Giro
endorser	Indossant, Girant
to enter a claim	einen Schadenersatzanspruch anmelden
to enter an order	einen Auftrag buchen, vormerken
to enter into a contract	einen Vertrag schließen
entry	Eintragung, Buchung; Zollanmeldung (*customs entry*)
to establish credit with s.b.	sich von jm. Kredit bzw. eine Kreditlinie einräumen lassen
to execute an order	einen Auftrag ausführen
executive (*corporation*)	Vorstandsmitglied
expenses (*pl.*)	Spesen, Auslagen, Kosten
export agent	Exportagent (*Mittelsperson im Lande des Herstellers, die für den Hersteller den Export durchführt*)
export merchant	Exporthändler
express company	Expreßgesellschaft (*die express companies in den USA befassen sich mit der Beförderung von Expreßgut und führen auch Bankgeschäfte durch*)

to extend	ausdehnen, erweitern; (*Frist*) verlängern, prolongieren; den Gesamtpreis errechnen
extension	Erweiterung, Vergrößerung; Fristverlängerung, Zahlungsaufschub, Stundung, Prolongation; Gesamtpreis (*Preis pro Einheit* × *Menge*)
ex works	ab Werk

F

factor	*etwa*: Kommissionär
F.A.S. (*free alongside ship*)	fas (*frei Längsseite Schiff*)
to file	(*Schriftgut*) ablegen
file number	Aktenzeichen
to fill an order (*US*)	einen Auftrag ausführen
financial standing, financial status	finanzielle Lage, Vermögenslage
firm name	Firmenname, Firma
firm offer	festes Angebot, bindendes Angebot
first order	Erstauftrag
floating policy	Abschreibepolice
F.O.B. (*free on board*)	fob (*frei an Bord*)
F.O.B. buyer's warehouse (*US*)	frei Haus
follow-up letter	Nachfaßbrief
F.O.R./F.O.T. (*free on rail/free on truck*)	frei Waggon
force majeure	höhere Gewalt
foreign agent	Auslandsvertreter
foreign bill	Auslandswechsel
foreign exchange (*sing.*)	Devisen
foreign-language correspondent	Fremdsprachenkorrespondent(-in)
form letter	Formbrief
forwarding agent, forwarder (*US*)	Spediteur
foul bill of lading	unreines Konnossement
foul receipt	unreiner Empfangsschein
franco domicile	frei Haus
franco frontier	frei Grenze
free buyer's address	frei Haus
free of charge	kostenlos
freight	Fracht
~ forwarder (*US*)	Spediteur
~ or carriage paid to ...	frachtfrei ...

G

general accounting	allgemeine Buchführung
general partner	Vollhafter, Komplementär
general partnership (*US*)	*etwa*: Offene Handelsgesellschaft (OHG)
general inquiry	allgemeine Anfrage
goodwill	Kundentreue, Wohlwollen oder Vertrauen der Kunden; Firmenwert, Goodwill
to grant s.b. the sole agency	jm. die Alleinvertretung übertragen
grocer	Lebensmittelhändler
grocery store (*US*)	Lebensmittelgeschäft
gross weight	Bruttogewicht
grouped consignment	Sammelladung

government agency	Behörde, staatliche Stelle
guarantee	Garantie
~ period	Garantiezeit

H

heading (*of a letter*)	Briefkopf
hidden reminder	versteckte Mahnung
holder (*of a bill, etc.*)	Inhaber
to honour	honorieren (*d. h. prompt akzeptieren bzw. einlösen*)

I

identification initials (*US*)	Diktatzeichen
import agent	Importvertreter, Importagent
import duty	Einfuhrzoll
import licence	Einfuhrgenehmigung, Importlizenz
import quota	Einfuhrkontingent
inactive account	umsatzloses Konto
to incorporate	gründen (*Kapitalgesellschaft*); in eine Kapital-gesellschaft umwandeln
indebtedness	Verschuldung, Schulden
initial order	Erstauftrag
inland bill	Inlandswechsel
inland waterway transport	Binnenschiffahrtsverkehr
inquirer	Anfragender
inquiry	Anfrage
~ agency	Auskunftei
~ form	Anfrageformular
inside address	Anschrift des Empfängers (*auf dem Briefbogen*)
insolvency	Zahlungsunfähigkeit, Insolvenz
insolvent	zahlungsunfähig, insolvent
to institute legal proceedings	Klage erheben
insurance	Versicherung
~ certificate	Versicherungszertifikat
~ company	Versicherungsgesellschaft
~ policy	Versicherungspolice
interest (*always sing.*)	Zinsen
International Chamber of Commerce	Internationale Handelskammer
international money order	Auslandspostanweisung
International Reply Coupon	Internationaler Antwortschein
in transit	auf dem Transport, während des Transports
introductory offer	Einführungsangebot
invoice	(Waren-)Rechnung, Faktura
to ~	in Rechnung stellen
~ form	Rechnungsvordruck, Rechnungsformular
irrevocable (letter of) credit	unwiderrufliches Akkreditiv
to issue a documentary (letter of) credit	ein Dokumentenakkreditiv eröffnen
issuing bank (*letter of credit*)	eröffnende Bank

J

junior clerk	Anfangskraft, Anfangskontorist(-in)

L

leaflet	(Kurz-)Prospekt
legal action	gerichtliches Verfahren, Prozeß
legalization	Beglaubigung, Legalisierung
to legalize	beglaubigen, legalisieren
letter of credit	Akkreditiv; Kreditbrief
letter of recommendation	Empfehlungsschreiben
letter of transmittal	Inkassoauftrag (*Dokumenteninkasso*)
letterhead	(gedruckter) Briefkopf; Briefbogen mit gedrucktem Briefkopf, Briefblattvordruck
to levy duty	Zoll erheben
liability	Haftung
libel	Beleidigung, Verleumdung (*schriftlich*)
lien	Pfandrecht
lighter	Leichter (*Hafenfahrzeug, das dazu dient, Ladung an und von Bord der Seeschiffe zu bringen*)
lighterage	Leichterung (*Beförderung durch Leichter*); Leichtergebühr
limited company	Kapitalgesellschaft (*Großbritannien*)
limited liability	beschränkte Haftung
limited partner	Teilhafter, Kommanditist
limited partnership	*etwa*: Kommanditgesellschaft (KG)
line of goods	Sortiment, Verkaufs-, Lieferprogramm (*des Händlers*)
line of products	Fertigungs-, Fabrikations-, Lieferprogramm (*des Herstellers*)
liquid assets	flüssige Mittel, Umlaufvermögen
liquidated damages	im voraus vertraglich festgesetzter Schadenersatz, Vertragsstrafe, Konventionalstrafe
list price	Listenpreis
litigation	Rechtsstreit, Prozeß
Lloyd's agent	Lloyd's-Kommissar (*der für Lloyd's tätige Havariekommissar*)
load less than a wagonload	Stückgut
loading berth	Ladeplatz
loan	Darlehen, Kredit
lock-out	Aussperrung
lump sum	Pauschalsumme; Abschreibesumme (*Abschreibepolice*)

M

mail-order house	Versandgeschäft
mail transfer	briefliche Auszahlung
mailing list	Anschriftenverzeichnis
maker	Aussteller (einer *promissory note*)
management	Geschäftsführung
manufacturer	Hersteller, Fabrikant
marine insurance	Seeversicherung
to mark (*shipping packages*)	(*Kolli*) beschriften, markieren
marking	Beschriftung, Markierung
~ instructions	Markierungsanweisungen

master (*of a ship*)	Kapitän
mate's receipt	Steuermannsquittung, Mate's Receipt
maturity	Fälligkeit
means of payment	Zahlungsmittel
memorandum, *pl.* memoranda *or* memorandums	interne Mitteilung, Aktennotiz
mercantile agency	Handelsauskunftei
mercantile agent	Handelsmittler
merchandise	(Handels-)Ware(n)
merchant	Kaufmann
method of transport	Beförderungsart
middleman	(Zwischen-)Händler, Wiederverkäufer
money order	Postanweisung
mortgage	Hypothek

N

negotiable	begebbar, übertragbar
to negotiate	verhandeln; abschließen, vermitteln (*Vertrag, Geschäft*); weitergeben (*Order- und Inhaberpapiere*); negoziieren (*Währungstratten ankaufen*)
net weight	Nettogewicht
net net weight	Reinnettogewicht
net worth (*US*)	Eigenkapital
no funds	keine Deckung (*Bankvermerk auf nicht eingelösten Schecks*)
non-delivery	Nicht(aus)lieferung, Lieferungsverzug
non-negotiable	nicht begebbar, nicht übertragbar
notify clause	Notadresse (*Konnossement*), Notify-Adresse

O

offer	Angebot, Offerte
office manager	Büroleiter, Bürochef
officer (*company, corporation*)	Vorstandsmitglied
official receiver	amtlicher Konkursverwalter
on account	als Abschlagszahlung, a conto
on approval	auf Probe
on-board bill of lading	Bordkonnossement
on demand	bei Sicht
one-man business	Einzelunternehmung
open cheque	Barscheck
open corporation (*US*)	*entspricht der englischen* public limited company
open policy	Generalpolice
to open a documentary (letter of) credit	ein Dokumentenakkreditiv eröffnen
opening bank (*letter of credit*)	eröffnende Bank
order	Bestellung, Auftrag, Order; die bestellten Waren
~ bill of lading	Orderkonnossement
~ cheque	Orderscheck
~ form	Bestellformular, Bestellschein
~ paper	Orderpapier

ordinary partnership	*etwa*: Offene Handelsgesellschaft (OHG)
output	Produktion (= *produzierte Menge*)
outstanding accounts	Außenstände, Forderungen
outstanding loan	noch nicht zurückbezahltes Darlehen
overcharge	der zuviel berechnete Betrag
overdue	überfällig, noch offenstehend, noch nicht bezahlt

P

package	Paket; Packung; Packstück, Kollo (*Pl.* Kolli)
packing container	Versandbehälter
packing list	Packliste
parent company	Muttergesellschaft
par value	Nennwert
partner	Gesellschafter (*einer Personengesellschaft*)
partnership	Personengesellschaft
to pass the ship's rail	die Reling des Schiffes überschreiten
to pass on in payment of a debt (*bill of exchange*)	als Zahlungsmittel weitergeben
past due	überfällig, noch offenstehend, noch nicht bezahlt
pattern	(Waren-)Muster (*vor allem Stoffmuster*); Muster (*auf Stoffen, Tapeten u. dgl.*); Muster, Vorlage, Modell
payee	Zahlungsempfänger; Wechselnehmer, Remittent
payment on account	Abschlagszahlung, Akontozahlung
pending file	Akte für Unerledigtes
to perform a contract	einen Vertrag erfüllen
performance of a contract	Vertragserfüllung
personal data sheet	tabellarischer Lebenslauf
personal record sheet	tabellarischer Lebenslauf
place of destination	Bestimmungsort
to place a contract	einen Auftrag vergeben
port of destination	Bestimmungshafen
port of shipment	Verschiffungshafen
post-office box	Postfach
postal order	Postanweisung
Postcode	englische Postleitzahl
power of attorney	(*schriftlich erteilte*) Vollmacht
power to sign	Zeichnungsvollmacht
preferential debt (*bankruptcy*)	bevorrechtigte Forderung
preferential tariff	Vorzugszoll
premium (*insurance*)	Versicherungsbeitrag, Prämie
presentation for payment	Vorlage zur Zahlung
principal	Chef, Prinzipal; Unternehmer, Auftraggeber (*eines Handelsvertreters, Kommissionärs usw.*)
private limited company	Kapitalgesellschaft in Großbritannien, deren Aktien nicht öffentlich gehandelt werden (*entspricht etwa der deutschen GmbH bzw. Familien-AG*)
proceeds (*pl.*)	Erlös
production	Herstellung, Produktion

~ schedule	Produktionsplan
pro-forma invoice	Proforma-Rechnung
to prolong a bill of exchange	einen Wechsel prolongieren
prolongation	Verlängerung, Prolongation
promissory note	Solawechsel
proprietor	Eigentümer
prospect(ive customer)	(Kauf-)Interessent
public limited company	Kapitalgesellschaft in Großbritannien, deren Aktien öffentlich gehandelt werden
purchase order	Bestellung

Q

quadruplicate, in ~	vierfach, in vierfacher Ausfertigung
quantity discount	Mengenrabatt
quintuplicate, in ~	fünffach, in fünffacher Ausfertigung
to quote	(Preise) angeben; ein Angebot unterbreiten
quotation	Preis, Preisangabe; Angebot
~ form	Angebotsformular

R

rail (of a ship)	Reling
railroad bill of lading	Frachtpapier im amerikanischen Bahnverkehr
range of goods	Sortiment, Verkaufs-, Lieferprogramm (des Händlers)
range of products	Fertigungs-, Fabrikations-, Lieferprogramm (des Herstellers), Typenreihe
rating	Krediturteil
~ book	Sammelauskunftsbuch
ready cash	flüssige Mittel, Bargeld
real estate	Immobilien
to realize a security	sich aus einem verpfändeten Gegenstand befriedigen
rebate	Rabatt, Rückvergütung, Bonus
to re-bill	eine neue Rechnung ausstellen
receipt	Empfang, Erhalt; Empfangsbestätigung, Quittung
received-for-shipment bill of lading	Empfangskonnossement, Übernahmekonnossement
to re-discount	rediskontieren
reduction (price)	(Preis-)Ermäßigung, Nachlaß
reference	Referenz; Bezugszeichen
~ initials	Diktatzeichen
refusal to pay	Zahlungsverweigerung
to release s.b. from a contract	jm. von einem Vertrag entbinden
reminder	Mahnung, Zahlungserinnerung
remittance	Zahlung, Überweisung
~ advice	Zahlungsanzeige
to render an invoice	eine Rechnung (aus-)stellen
to renew a bill of exchange	einen Wechsel prolongieren
re-order, repeat order	Nachbestellung
representative	Vertreter (allg.); Reisender; Handelsvertreter

resale terms	Wiederverkaufsbedingungen
to rescind a contract	von einem Vertrag zurücktreten
to reserve space on board a vessel	Schiffsraum beschaffen
résumé	Zusammenfassung, Resümee; Lebenslauf
retailer	Einzelhändler
revocable (letter of) credit	widerrufliches Akkreditiv
road haulier	Kraftwagenunternehmer
routine inquiry	allgemeine Anfrage
Rules of Conciliation and Arbitration of the International Chamber of Commerce	Vergleichs- und Schiedsordnung der Internationalen Handelskammer

S

sales	Verkäufe, Absatz, Umsatz
~ literature	Verkaufsliteratur, Prospektmaterial
~ note	Auftragsbestätigung, Bestätigung des Vertragsabschlusses
~ series	Werbebriefreihe
salesman	Verkäufer; US: Reisender (traveling salesman)
sample	Muster, Probe
second sheet	Zweitbogen
secured creditor (bankruptcy)	absonderungsberechtigter Gläubiger
security	Sicherheit
~ dealings	Wertpapiergeschäfte
settlement of account	Rechnungsausgleich, Begleichung einer Rechnung
settlement of a claim	Erledigung eines Schadenersatzanspruches oder einer Beschwerde
share	Aktie
shareholder	Aktionär
shipment	Verschiffung; Versand; Beförderung; Sendung
shipped bill of lading	Verschiffungskonnossement
shipper	Versender; Befrachter
shipping advice	Versandanzeige, Verschiffungsanzeige
shipping company	Reederei
shipping documents	Versandpapiere, Versanddokumente, Verschiffungsdokumente
shipping weight	Versandgewicht
sight bill (of exchange)	Sichtwechsel
sight draft	Sichttratte
slackness of trade	stockender Geschäftsgang, Flaute
slander	Beleidigung, Verleumdung (mündlich)
sole agency	Alleinvertretung
sole agent	Alleinvertreter
sole proprietorship (US)	Einzelunternehmung
sole trader	Einzelunternehmer
solicited application	verlangte Bewerbung
solicited offer	verlangtes Angebot
solicitor	Rechtsanwalt
source of supply	Bezugsquelle
special discount	Sonderrabatt
special endorsement	Vollindossament
special inquiry	bestimmte Anfrage

special report (*by credit-inquiry agency*)	Einzelauskunft
specific duty	spezifischer Zoll
specific inquiry	bestimmte Anfrage
stale cheque	nicht rechtzeitig zur Zahlung vorgelegter Scheck
stamp duty	Stempelsteuer
Standard Forms for the Opening of Documentary Credits	Standardformeln für die Eröffnung von Dokumentenakkreditiven
standing order	Dauerauftrag
statement of account	Kontoauszug
status inquiry	Anfrage (*wegen der Kreditwürdigkeit einer Firma*), Bitte um Kreditauskunft
stock corporation	Kapitalgesellschaft (*USA*)
straight bill of lading	Namenskonnossement
strike	Streik
subject line	Betreffzeile
subject to quota	kontingentiert
to submit a dispute to arbitration	einen Streitfall von einem Schiedsgericht entscheiden lassen
subscriber	Abonnent
subscription fee	Abonnementsgebühr
subsidiary	(*rechtlich selbständige*) Niederlassung, Tochtergesellschaft
supply	Lieferung, Belieferung, Versorgung; Vorrat, Lager; Angebot (*im Gegensatz zur Nachfrage*)
to ~	liefern, beliefern
supplier	Lieferant, Lieferer
to surrender documents	Dokumente übergeben
survey report	Havariezertifikat
surveyor	Havariekommissar
to sustain a loss	einen Verlust erleiden

T

to take a discount	Skonto abziehen
to take dictation	Diktat aufnehmen
to take out insurance	Versicherung abschließen
telegraphic address	Telegrammadresse
telegraphic money order	telegrafische Postanweisung
telegraphic transfer	telegrafische Auszahlung
telex number	Telex-Nummer (*Nummer des Fernschreiberanschlusses*)
tender	(Submissions-)Angebot; Ausschreibung
terms of delivery	Lieferungsbedingungen, Lieferklauseln
terms of payment	Zahlungsbedingungen
testimonial	(Dienst-)Zeugnis
time bill (of exchange)	Zielwechsel
time draft	Zieltratte
title	Titel; Eigentum
trade acceptance	Handelsakzept, Warenwechsel
trade association	Wirtschaftsverband, Fachverband
trade discount	Händlerrabatt, Wiederverkäuferrabatt
trade-mark	Warenzeichen

trade reference	Handelsreferenz
trader	Kaufmann, Händler
transaction	Geschäft
to transfer an amount to an account	einen Betrag auf ein Konto überweisen
to transcribe dictation	Diktat in die Maschine übertragen
transshipment	Umladung
traveling salesman (*US*)	(Handlungs-)Reisender, Vertreter
trial order	Probeauftrag, Probebestellung
triplicate, in ~	dreifach, in dreifacher Ausfertigung
trustee in bankruptcy	(*von den Gläubigern bestimmter*) Konkursverwalter

U

unconfirmed irrevocable (letter of) credit	unbestätigtes, unwiderrufliches Akkreditiv
under separate cover	mit gleicher Post, gesondert
underwriter	(Einzel-)Versicherer
unearned discount	unberechtigter Skontoabzug
Uniform Customs and Practice for Documentary Credits	Einheitliche Richtlinien und Gebräuche für Dokumenten-Akkreditive
Uniform Rules for the Collection of Commercial Paper	Einheitliche Richtlinien für das Inkasso von Handelspapieren
unit price	Preis pro Einheit
unlimited liability	unbeschränkte Haftung
unloading costs	Ausladekosten, Löschkosten
unsalable	unverkäuflich
unsecured creditor (*bankruptcy*)	nicht absonderungsberechtigter Gläubiger
unsolicited application	unverlangte Bewerbung
unsolicited offer	unverlangtes Angebot

V

vacancy	offene Stelle
vendor	Verkäufer, Lieferant, Lieferer
verification	(Nach-)Prüfung; Richtigbefund
voluntary offer	unverlangtes Angebot
voyage policy	Einzelpolice

W

wagonload	Wagenladung
warehouse	Lager (*Lagerhaus bzw. Lagerraum*)
warehouse-to-warehouse insurance	Versicherung von Haus zu Haus
warranty	Gewährleistung, Garantie
waybill (*US*)	Frachtbrief
wharf	Kai
wharfage	Kaigebühr, Hafengeld
wharfinger's receipt	Kai-Empfangsschein
wholesaler	Großhändler
wholly-owned subsidiary	100 %ige Tochter(-gesellschaft)
workmanship	(Qualität der) Verarbeitung

Z

ZIP Code Number	amerikanische Postleitzahl

List of Abbreviations

Diese Liste enthält alle Abkürzungen, die nicht bereits an anderer Stelle erklärt sind.

abbr.	abbreviation
adj.	adjective
BE	British English
C.	Celsius, centigrade
cu.ft.	cubic foot (feet)
F.	Fahrenheit
ft.	foot (feet)
in.	inch(es)
lb.	pound (weight)
lbs.	pounds
n.	noun
oz.	ounce(s)
ozs.	ounces
pl.	plural
s.b.	somebody
sing.	singular
sq.yd.	square yard(s)
s.th.	something
US	American English
v.	verb
yd.	yard(s)
yds.	yards

Conversion Table

1 inch	= 2,54 cm	
1 foot	= 12 inches	= 0,305 m
1 yard	= 3 feet	= 0,914 m
1 mile	= 1760 yards	= 1,609 km

1 square inch	= 6,451 cm^2	
1 square foot	= 144 square inches	= 0,093 m^2
1 square yard	= 9 square feet	= 0,836 m^2

1 cubic inch	= 16,387 cm^3	
1 cubic foot	= 1728 cubic inches	= 0,028 m^3
1 cubic yard	= 27 cubic feet	= 0,765 m^3

1 ounce	= 28,35 g	
1 pound	= 16 ounces	= 453,59 g

$$\frac{(°F. - 32) \times 5}{9} = °C. \qquad \frac{°C. \times 9}{5} + 32 = °F.$$